THE UNRULY

VOICE

THE UNRULY VOICE

Rediscovering
Pauline Elizabeth
Hopkins

EDITED BY

John Cullen Gruesser

INTRODUCTION BY

Nellie Y. McKay

AFTERWORD BY

Elizabeth Ammons

University of Illinois Press
Urbana and Chicago

© 1996 by the Board of Trustees of the University of Illinois
Manufactured in the United States of America
1 2 3 4 5 C P 5 4 3 2 1

This book is printed on acid-free paper.

Library of Congress Cataloging-in-Publication Data
The unruly voice: rediscovering Pauline Elizabeth Hopkins / edited by
John Cullen Gruesser ; introduction by Nellie Y. McKay ; afterword
by Elizabeth Ammons.
     p.   cm.
Includes bibliographical references and index.
ISBN 0-252-02230-0 (cloth : alk. paper). —
     ISBN 0-252-06554-9 (pbk. : alk. paper)
     1. Hopkins, Pauline E. (Pauline Elizabeth)—Political and social
views. 2. Politics and literature—United States—History.
3. Literature and society—United States—History. 4. Women and
literature—United States—History. 5. Afro-American women in
literature. 6. Afro-Americans in literature. 7. Race in
literature. I. Gruesser, John Cullen, 1959–   .
     PS1999.H4226Z65   1996
     813'.4—dc20   95-32543
               CIP

For Humanity

CONTENTS

PREFACE

JOHN CULLEN GRUESSER

The first book devoted exclusively to the African American performer, playwright, orator, novelist, journalist, short story writer, biographer, and editor Pauline Elizabeth Hopkins (1859–1930), *The Unruly Voice: Rediscovering Pauline Elizabeth Hopkins* addresses itself to two questions: who was Hopkins and what significance does this versatile, iconoclastic, and politically committed—in a word, unruly—black woman writer whose life began before the Civil War and ended during the Great Depression have for us as late twentieth-century scholars and students of American and African American literature and culture?

The previously unpublished essays in this collection reveal different facets of Hopkins's career, including her short fiction, novels, and nonfiction. The authors of these essays pay careful attention to the specific social, political, and historical conditions that inform her literary works. Most of Hopkins's short stories and nonfiction as well as three of her novels appeared in the Boston-based *Colored American Magazine* (*CAM*), which has been described as the country's first black magazine, and her only other novel, *Contending Forces,* was brought out by the same company that published the periodical. Although rarely acknowledged as such, Hopkins acted as editor-in-chief of *CAM* in addition to contributing a remarkable number of stories, articles, biographical sketches, and editorials to the journal. She believed that fiction could serve a pedagogic function for her middle-class black readers, who were often unacquainted with history or biography. Her tenure at the magazine ended in 1904 when Fred R. Moore, an ally of Booker T. Washington, bought the periodical and fired Hopkins, apparently because of her editorial policies and unconciliatory politics.

Little is known about Hopkins's life between 1905 when several of her articles appeared in the *Voice of the Negro* and her death in 1930 other than that she served as the editor of a new journal entitled the *New Era Magazine* in 1916. Like *CAM* under Hopkins's direction, the *New Era* was based in Boston, contained articles on topics as diverse as music and career planning, and paid particular attention to literature in various forms; but where the earlier journal had sought to address the concerns of African Americans throughout the United States, this new magazine aspired to be international in scope. Hopkins's ambitious, long-range plans for the *New Era* were never realized, however, because the journal ceased publication after just two issues.

Since the mid-1980s, a small but impressive group of scholars, including Claudia Tate, Hazel Carby, Jane Campbell, Elizabeth Ammons, and Richard Yarborough, have focused critical attention on the once forgotten but increasingly significant Pauline Hopkins. In addition, Oxford University Press has recently reprinted all of Hopkins's novels and most of her short stories in its Schomburg Library of Nineteenth-Century Black Women Writers series, edited by Henry Louis Gates, Jr. In 1988 Oxford published two volumes of Hopkins's works: *Contending Forces,* her first novel, and *The Magazine Novels of Pauline Hopkins,* comprised of her three serialized novels, which had never previously appeared in book form. Three years later Oxford published seven of Hopkins's *CAM* short stories in *Short Fiction by Black Women, 1900–1920,* edited by Elizabeth Ammons. As a result, over 1,100 pages of Hopkins's fiction are available in hardcover as well as in reasonably priced paperback editions perfectly suited to classroom use. In addition, Hopkins's *Peculiar Sam; or, The Underground Railroad* (1879), the earliest extant play written by an African American woman, was published for the first time in 1991 in *The Roots of African American Drama: An Anthology of Early Plays, 1858–1938,* edited by Leo Hamalian and James V. Hatch. The critical rediscovery of Hopkins coupled with the ready availability of many of her works has generated not only considerable scholarly interest in the author, particularly among younger scholars (many of whom are writing or have recently completed books or dissertations that discuss Hopkins's work) but also the need on the part of professors assigning any one of the three Schomburg series volumes for complementary scholarship on Hopkins. For these reasons, this seems an extremely opportune time for a collection of essays that offers a comprehensive look at Hopkins's career.

Although this collection is intended primarily for scholars and teachers of African American and American literature, undergraduates studying Hopkins's works and turn-of-the-century American literature and culture will also find the book valuable. In addition to the biographical and historical approach to Hopkins and her era, which informs each of the essays in the collection, most of the contributors also use some form of contemporary critical theory, ranging from African American cultural studies to new historicism, to explore the larger implications of their subject. From a purely practical standpoint, the collection has been organized chronologically to enable readers to locate quickly the essays that most interest them.

Nellie Y. McKay's introduction provides biographical information about Hopkins, compares her career to that of other early black woman editors, and previews the seven essays that follow. The essays by Kate McCullough and Lois Lamphere Brown concern Hopkins's first novel *Contending Forces* (1900). These are followed by C. K. Doreski's essay on the author's *Colored American Magazine* biographical series "Famous Men of the Negro Race" (1900–1901) and "Famous Women of the Negro Race" (1901–2), my essay on her *CAM* short story "A Dash for Liberty" (1901), Kristina Brooks's essay on Hopkins's first serial novel *Hagar's Daughter* (1901–2), and essays on her final *Colored American Magazine* novel *Of One Blood* (1902–3) by Jennie A. Kassanoff and Cynthia D. Schrager. In her afterword, Elizabeth Ammons makes the case for Hopkins as a major writer, using her often overlooked third novel *Winona* (1902) to illustrate Hopkins's radical experimentation and the complex issues she engages in her writing. Malin LaVon Walther's list of works by and about Pauline Hopkins—the most comprehensive bibliography ever compiled on the author, which will surely prove an invaluable resource for scholars working on Hopkins—rounds out the collection.

This book grew out of "Pauline Elizabeth Hopkins: *Colored American Magazine* Editor and Contributor, Prolific Fiction Writer, Literary Missing Person," a special session I organized for the Modern Language Association conference in December 1992. Proposals for or first drafts of many of the essays in the collection came in response to my call for papers for this session. Shorter versions of the essays in this book by Lois Brown, C. K. Doreski, and Jennie Kassanoff were presented at that time, and Claudia Tate served as the respondent.

I want to thank all the contributors for their hard work, patience, and advice on what has truly been a collaborative project. In addition, I am indebted to Eric Sundquist and the other participants in his 1990 NEH summer seminar, "The Problem of Race in American and Afro-American Literature, 1860–1930," at the University of California, Berkeley. I would also like to express my gratitude to Augusta Rohrbach, Stephen Soitos, Ernest Wiggins, Charles Baker, William Doreski, and Jim Hatch. Ronald Johnson and the librarians at the Moorland-Spingarn Library of Howard University kindly assisted me in locating the *New Era Magazine*. Craig Werner, Dean Casale, Kelly Anspaugh, Sandra Adell, Rita Disroe, and Richard Katz offered helpful suggestions. Ann Lowry, Theresa Sears, and Margie Towery at the University of Illinois Press assisted me greatly. Finally, I must acknowledge the support of my parents John and Eileen Gruesser, my sister Jennifer, my son Jack (who lent me his erasers), and, last but always first, my wife Susan.

INTRODUCTION

Nellie Y. McKay

In 1892, the black feminist Anna Julia Cooper wrote that to be "a woman of the Negro race in America . . . [was] to have a heritage . . . unique in the ages" (144). Cooper, who, by accident of her birth date, barely missed the shackles of physical enslavement, knew of what she spoke.[1] Her early years were spent in the company of former slaves who carried with them forever the horrors of their experiences and the knowledge of their hard-won victories. Much more than a generation removed from a large number of this group, Cooper, by then a professional black woman, never took for granted the good that came to her, nor did she ever forget how devastating were the wounds of Reconstruction on the majority of the recently liberated slaves. She was especially aware of black women's lives: of their pain and suffering and how difficult it was to scale the walls of race and gender oppression but also of their will to live that never died. And she knew and took seriously that each successive generation of black women, heir to the combination of sorrow and triumph in that history, was responsible, through words and deeds, for preserving its honor. Cooper's life, defined by rebelliousness toward injustices against the human spirit, helped countless others to understand and respond with courage and determination to the demands of the black woman's unique heritage.

In the late nineteenth and early twentieth centuries there were dozens of African American women who, like Anna Julia Cooper, were extraordinary people. Largely ignored by the world outside of their immediate spheres and in spite of many obstacles, these women broke through significant barriers to achieve impressive records of successes, many in professional fields previously closed to them: education, belles lettres, medicine, the arts, music, journalism, science, and mission work, for example. In the 1894 volume, *The Work of the Afro-American Woman,* Mrs. N. F. Mossell, carefully documented the earliest history of the lives of professional black women in America. A celebratory feminist appraisal, the *Work* reminds us that the warrior spirit of Harriet Tubman, Sojourner Truth, and Harriet Jacobs did not die at the end of the Civil War, nor had the struggle for full black self-hood been won in that conflict. Black women moved onto and made remarkable gains on a new and unfamiliar battleground.

Pauline Elizabeth Hopkins (1859–1930), the subject of this collection, was one of those later warriors whose life fulfilled the spirit of Mossell's history. Both a great-granddaughter and honored foremother in the long line of women of remarkable achievements, she gave much of her life and talents toward the advancement of African Americans and enhancement of their lives in America. For her, the commitment to responsibility to her race did not develop by accident or chance, it preceded her in her family. On her mother's side, she was a great-grand-niece of the New Hampshire black poet and political activist James Whitfield (1822–71), and familial ties joined her to Nathaniel and Thomas Paul, nineteenth-century black activist abolitionists, church-men, and educators. Following in the tradition of these precursors, her life and work demonstrate her conviction that "the true romance of American life and customs is to be found in the history of the Negro [women included] upon this continent" (Campbell 577). As a woman bearer of that standard, a century ago Hopkins joined her name to those black women and men whose lives and work defined their unique American identity with dignity and honor.

Hopkins, the daughter of Northrup Hopkins, a migrant from Virginia, and the former Sarah Allen, a native of Exeter, New Hampshire, was born in Portland, Maine, but grew up in Boston, Massachusetts. She attended public schools and graduated from Girls High School. Her literary ambitions surfaced early—first in 1874, when she was fifteen years old. At that time she entered an essay contest sponsored by the Congregational Publishing Society of Boston and financially supported by former slave novelist and dramatist, William Wells Brown. Hopkins's essay, "Evils of Intemperance and Their Remedy," which won the first prize, ten dollars in gold, gained favor (the judges said) on the merits of the writer's skill. She identified intemperance (a topic then widely discussed especially by black and white women reformers) as a social and moral problem and called upon parents to take responsibility for their children's behavior by living clean and industrious lives. Later in her life Hopkins was a novelist, short story writer, essayist, orator, and journalist, but it was as a dramatist, actress, and singer that she first commanded public attention.

In 1879, at the age of twenty, Hopkins completed her first play: *Slaves' Escape; or, The Underground Railroad.* A year later, the drama, renamed *Peculiar Sam; or, The Underground Railroad,* had a run at Boston's Oakland Garden. It was produced and performed by the Hopkins Colored Troubadours, a group that included Pauline Hopkins, who sang the lead and played the central role. Also included were her mother; a man, probably her stepfather; the famous Hyers Sisters, who accompanied them; and a chorus of more than sixty people.[2] *Peculiar Sam* had five performances and received good notices. For the next twelve years, Hopkins, sometimes called "Boston's Favorite Soprano," also gave recitals and concerts in Boston and lectured on black history while she and her family toured as a performing group. These activities made her a minor celebrity. During these years she wrote a second play, a dramatization of Daniel in the lion's den called *One Scene from the Drama of Early Days.* It is not known if it was ever produced.

By the early 1890s, when Hopkins was past her thirtieth birthday and in search of greater financial stability, she left the entertainment world. For a practical skill, she studied stenography and gained the expertise to pass the civil service exam. This trade served her well until her death in 1930 at age seventy-one. But the security of such a livelihood did not put an end to Hopkins's ambitions to engage in more creative expression. She never gave up the idea of becoming a writer; through the 1890s she continued to nurture that dream and also lectured successfully on black history in the Boston area.

Then in 1900, a new journal, the *Colored American Magazine* (*CAM*), offered Hopkins an unusual opportunity to break into the literary world. *CAM*, brainchild of a black man in Boston, joined by three of his friends, was the first significant twentieth-century African American journal owned and published by blacks (Johnson and Johnson 4). An illustrated monthly, the founders envisioned it as *"Of the Race, by the Race, for the Race"* (*CAM*, Oct. 1900). To finance their idea, they formed the Colored Co-operative Publishing Company by advertising certificates of deposit, thus turning the project into a cooperative venture. Readers and contributors (the latter were offered certificates of deposit based on a cash valuation of their work) were encouraged to become members of the cooperative. In that respect, *CAM* was radically different from the white journals of that era (Carby xxxiii).

Pauline Hopkins, attracted by the prospects of a strong new public black voice, promptly became a member of the board of directors, shareholder, and creditor of *CAM*. Over the next four years her writings made up a substantial portion of the literary and historical materials the magazine promoted. The founders wanted a popular periodical that would appeal not only to a northern black elite but that "would encourage the flowering of any black talent that had been suppressed by a lack of encouragement and opportunity to be published" (Carby xxxiii). They planned to nurture talent wherever they found it. In May of that year, in its first issue, Hopkins's short story, "The Mystery within Us," appeared in the pages of *CAM*.[3] In the following October and December, two of Hopkins's stories, "Talma Gordon," and "George Washington, A Christmas Story," were published. Hopkins did not always attach her name to her work in *CAM*, and several of her pieces were attributed to Sarah A. Allen, her mother's maiden name. Richard Yarborough speculates she might well have done this to keep her name from appearing in the magazine too often. *Contending Forces,* her first novel, was published in 1900 by the Colored Co-operative Publishing Company.

Over the next four years Hopkins published four additional stories and serialized three novels, *Hagar's Daughter: A Story of Southern Caste Prejudice, Winona: A Tale of Negro Life in the South and Southwest,* and *Of One Blood; or, The Hidden Self,* in CAM. Looking at her publications between 1900 and 1905, Richard Yarborough compares her work favorably to such well-known African American writers of her time as Charles Chesnutt, Paul Laurence Dunbar, and Sutton Griggs. In relation to women's publications, he calls her "the single most productive black woman writer at the turn of the century" (Yarborough xxviii).

As important as her writings were as a model of literary excellence for *CAM*'s contributors, her other work for the magazine played as crucial a role in whatever successes that publication achieved in the first years of its existence. Although the what and when of her duties for *CAM* remain somewhat unclear, it appears that she was appointed editor of the Women's Department from 1901 to 1903 and literary editor in 1903. One thing is certain: in those years she had confidence in the magazine's future and publicly claimed that *CAM* was "the strongest Negro organ put upon the market since the days of Frederick Douglass."

As editor of the magazine, Hopkins was in a position only a few black women have ever held: she had the power to influence the magazine's editorial policies. Hers was an enviable place in the world of African American journalism (Shockley 291). But Hopkins was less interested in personal power and more in advancing a publication that she felt would make a difference in the lives of African Americans. One of her primary goals for *CAM* was that it should inspire the creation of an African American art and literature that would demonstrate the talents and skills of the group and prove to the rest of the world that black people, only recently released from slavery, were already as culturally advanced as other groups. Today's readers may find the expressed ends of that goal emblematic of the effects of racism and white paternalism on some black intellectuals of Hopkins's era, but she employed it subversively by grounding the literature in a radical black nationalism that promoted the superiority of people of African descent. She called for black protest literature, unconciliatory to all forms of white oppression, and opposed other kinds of literature that did not denounce all oppression of blacks.

Hazel Carby observes that two decades before the Harlem Renaissance, Hopkins's vision of the cultural function of *CAM* was that it would create a climate for "a black renaissance in Boston" (Carby xxxi). With such high hopes for *CAM*, Hopkins compares well with other turn-of-the-century black intellectuals, such as W. E. B. Du Bois. Both belonged to a new generation of educated radical freedom fighters whose distance from slavery (and perhaps their special New England upbringing) made them impatient and unwilling to accommodate to white racism. Unfortunately, by 1920 Hopkins had dropped out of sight while Du Bois's leadership in the black community had risen so steadily that he became one of the "godfathers" of the Harlem Renaissance of that later decade. She was forgotten; he was revered.

Before that, however, from her position on the magazine, Hopkins was able to influence the amount and nature of the fiction and poetry that *CAM* published among its other offerings. Through 1903 its focus was literary, a policy that changed when Hopkins left (or was forced from) the staff in 1904. Black history was always a priority for Hopkins, and her writings addressed its significance. Essays about people and events and news items (including some that appeared in other publications) of interest to the community were sizeable portions of the fare *CAM* offered.

C. K. Doreski's essay explores Hopkins's outspoken political and philosophical position on the crucial importance of African American history and her *CAM* contributions in the creation of a black revisionist history. Decades before the black revolution in the twentieth century, Hopkins was an adamant voice for the need to revise traditional American history, which had so far excluded evidence of a black intellectual perspective. She was adamant that African Americans themselves had to take responsibility for the making of new histories that included the lives and deeds of black people told by black people. For, she claimed, history was less about great events than the actions of individuals, an idea that makes biography an important element of history. She supported her claims in two series of biographical sketches, twelve in each group, profiles of "Famous Women of the Negro Race" and "Famous Men of the Negro Race" for *CAM*. The two series ran from November 1900 to October 1902 and were what Doreski calls "experiments in historiography and biography as they harness this once sacred impulse for secular service" (74 in this volume). Celebratory rather than critical in nature, the profiles introduced readers to African Americans whose accomplishments made them models to others of their group.

In the years of her association with the magazine, Hopkins devoted a great deal of energy to building a substantial readership and nurturing faithful contributors. She worked hard to make each issue as interesting and varied as possible. Although her main interests were in literature and history, she encouraged essays and articles from many disciplines to bring the thoughts and ideas of different kinds of writers to the magazine's readers. In editorials, she admired the creative work she received, and under her leadership the quality of these pieces was higher than at any other time in *CAM*'s history. Poetry by William Braithwaite, Benjamin Brawley, and James D. Corrothers, and fiction by Angelina Grimké appeared in the magazine in its early life. That Hopkins perceived the works of the imagination of vital significance to the ongoing progress of black people is evident in her response to her own question, "Of what use is fiction for the colored race at the present crisis in its history?" In *Contending Forces,* her first novel, echoing Anna Julia Cooper, she states unequivocally that literature preserves "manners and customs" as well as "the growth and development [of the group] from one generation to another" (13–14).

On still another front, she traveled and lectured across the country, spreading the word about the magazine. A founding member of the Colored American League in 1904, she was again in the forefront of a group of black women and men who raised funds for *CAM* by soliciting business and subscriptions for the journal. Under her editorship, the *Colored American Magazine*'s circulation grew to fifteen thousand. Unexplained, however, is the strange phenomenon of Hopkins's name appearing on the masthead as editor-in-chief of the magazine only once, in March 1904.

For all her efforts, at no time in its early years was the magazine adequately financially grounded. Then, in 1904 it experienced such severe financial stresses that Booker T. Washington surreptitiously gained control over it.[4] Although he stoutly disclaimed rumors of his part in the takeover, most scholars believe otherwise. There is no question that in 1904, one of his supporters, Fred R. Moore, bought *CAM* and moved the operation to New York City, where T. Thomas Fortune, a long-time supporter of Washington, took over its editorial duties. Although the sale of the journal and the change in its location stripped Hopkins of her power, she was retained briefly as assistant editor. However, to no one's surprise, in November of that year, *CAM* carried a notice that Pauline Hopkins was resigning from the magazine for reasons of ill health. There is evidence that by 1904 Hopkins's health may have already begun to deteriorate, but it is doubtful that the problems were then sufficiently severe to precipitate her departure from *CAM*. More critics believe, as Du Bois explicitly stated a few years later, that she was forced out in a clash of political ideologies between herself and the new owners. There can be little doubt that her outspoken radical ideas on race were not in alignment with the accommodationist philosophy of the supporters of Washington. Interestingly, Hopkins's departure did not improve the financial fortunes of *CAM;* it never became fiscally viable although it altered its focus. In the years that followed, *CAM* distanced itself from criticism of race matters, becoming a mouthpiece for the ideologies of Washington. It concentrated on the material successes of black people rather than on the problems of racism. The last issue of *CAM* appeared in November 1909.

Yet Hopkins did not immediately disappear from the world of print media in 1904. In 1905, a six-month sociocultural survey, "The Dark Races of the Twentieth Century," and an essay, "The New York Subway," appeared in the *Voice of the Negro* (the South's first black magazine), as well as a self-published thirty-one-page booklet, *A Primer of Facts Pertaining to the Early Greatness of the African Race and the Possibility of Restoration by Its Descendants—with Epilogue.* After that, however, she was silent until 1916, when she published a novella, "Topsy Templeton," in the *New Era Magazine,* a Boston publication that she founded (or helped to found) at that time. The masthead listed Hopkins as editor. Notably, at least one other staff member was a former colleague of hers at *CAM.* The goals of this new venture bore the Hopkins imprimatur: the magazine would follow the protest tradition and develop literature, science, music, and other areas of study related to black cultural life in America. Biography, fiction, and poetry were prominently featured and sought for, and sculptor Meta Warrick-Fuller, the art editor, wrote in support of black groups of artists engaging in discussions of common concerns. In the *New Era, CAM's* "Famous Men of the Race" reappeared as "Men of Vision," and "Famous Women" became "Sacrificing Women," which included entries on Frances E. W. Harper, Harriet Tubman, and Sojourner Truth. Unfortunately, for reasons not clear, the *New Era Magazine* had a life span of only two months, and its death went unremarked by other journals of the time. Perhaps discouraged by how little recognition she received in spite of her achievements and/or failing health, following the collapse of the *New Era Magazine,* Hopkins, then in her late fifties, appears to have withdrawn from the literary world. There is little information on her over the following fourteen years, but records show she was employed as a stenographer at the Massachusetts Institute of Technology at the time of her accidental death, which resulted from a fire in her home in Cambridge, Massachusetts, in 1930.

As a black woman in white America, Pauline Hopkins was laudably creative and talented, but until recently she received very little recognition for these attributes. Yet her writings made significant contributions to black literary culture, and her editorship of *CAM* did a great deal for black journalism. In this latter, many find her daunting. For although a number of black women, as early as in the 1830s, wrote in a variety of genres for black and white newspapers and journals, she was one of the very few who held a powerful position on a periodical in the nineteenth and early twentieth centuries.[5] Two of the most notable women in that small group were Mary Ann Shadd Cary and Ida B. Wells-Barnett; both aspired to similar goals and, for periods in their lives, also held such positions. The circumstances of these three lives differ significantly, but it is instructive to take a brief look at the rise and fall of their three careers to enable us to see more clearly the difficulties they encountered, and why Hopkins, without influential family or political connections, working almost entirely in the black community, met with such an unfortunate fate.

Mary Ann Shadd Cary (1823–93), the first North American black female editor, investigative reporter, and publisher, came from a prosperous Wilmington, Delaware, abolitionist family that moved to Canada after the Dred Scott decision became law. There, in 1853, Shadd Cary cofounded a newspaper, the *Provincial Freeman,* and used its pages to support black migration to Canada and to campaign against white antiabolitionists as well as all abolitionists who supported segregated facilities for blacks. She emphasized the same ideological position on her extensive lecture tours. The result was that serious conflicts and bitter opposition developed between her and several prominent black abolitionists and white abolitionist institutions. By 1859 her newspaper folded because those who disagreed with her outspoken and unpopular views no longer supported her, financially or otherwise. After Shadd Cary returned to the United States at the end of the Civil War, she pursued an enviable career as an activist, which included writing on sociopolitical issues for such publications as the *New National Era* and the *Advocate.* Yet she seems never to have revisited her early ambitions to be in editorial control of an important black periodical.

In recent times, the name of Ida B. Wells-Barnett (1862–1931) has become synonymous with the antilynching movement of the late nineteenth and early twentieth centuries. Born a slave, by 1889 she held a one-third ownership in the *Free Speech,* a black newspaper in Memphis, Tennessee, where she began her campaign against lynching. Forced to leave Memphis because of the deliberate destruction of her press and death threats made against her by white racists, in 1892 Wells-Barnett joined the staff of the *New York Age* and acquired a one-fourth interest in this influential black newspaper. From 1895 to 1897, she edited the *Chicago Conservator,* a newspaper founded by her husband before their marriage. Like Shadd Cary, Wells-Barnett was an outspoken critic of racial injustice who wrote fiery editorials against all oppression but especially against lynching and in favor of women's rights. She lectured widely in the United States and England and remained an activist until her death. But like Shadd Cary, she did not return to periodical editorship after 1897.

Although Shadd Cary and Wells-Barnett led exciting, productive, and fulfilling lives after the periods in which they were newspaper and magazine editors, they share with Hopkins the powerlessness common to women in their lack of full control to make decisions in their lives, especially in matters beyond the boundaries of female-prescribed roles. While Hopkins was forced to leave *CAM* because her political views were unacceptable to the new owners, given how few women held similar positions, she was undoubtedly also pushed out because she was a woman and controlling an important journal was not her place. Even William Braithwaite, whose work she published in *CAM,* in addition to printing a highly laudatory biographical sketch of him, deeply resented her editorial power (see Kassanoff 159 in this volume). Moreover, those who supported her were unable to maintain fiscal control of the magazine. It is reasonable to suspect that her 1916 attempt to return to a similar position at a new journal was also a financial failure.

In the absence of a great deal of supporting biographical information, Pauline Hopkins appears to have spent all of her life in the Boston area; she was never able to make the financial or political connections that might have served her interests better. Her early ambitions to be a writer were only partially fulfilled, and her editorial attempts to influence black literary and social trends were short-lived. In contrast to Wells-Barnett, Hopkins did not capture wide public interest because she lacked the kind of project, like the antilynching campaign, that attracted broad national and international support. Nor did she marry and have the support of an influential husband with interests and work compatible to hers that would have helped her as well. These are important elements in considerations of the fate of Pauline Hopkins, whose genius, for a long time, was lost to the world.

Like Hopkins, Shadd Cary lost the newspaper she founded because others, primarily men with whose opinions she disagreed, withdrew their financial support. Few if any black women in her time controlled the independent resources or had the political clout to keep such a venture afloat. But more fortunate than Hopkins, after the Civil War Shadd Cary was able, perhaps with the help of her family, to recover some of her early ambitions and to invest her energies in self-development and other activist causes. Still, the forced abandonment of her newspaper represented one aspect of the reality of women's lack of control over their life choices, as well as their dependence on a public image that conformed to the larger social views of woman. Shadd Cary lost it completely on that one. Often described as abrasive and unfeminine by her detractors, she was openly disparaged by men for qualities that they most admired in other men.

Although Wells-Barnett's life as an activist flourished after her first newspaper was destroyed, she too, as a woman with a clear, forceful agenda of her own and a talent for leadership, did not have full choice over deciding her life work. The time spent with the *New York Age* and the *Chicago Conservator* were unambiguous signals of her desire to continue as an editor. But in 1897, domestic obligations forced her to relinquish the reins of the *Chicago Conservator,* although not all her other political activities. Wells-Barnett also faced other difficulties common to women of her time. Even among those who most supported her, her outspokenness and tenacity made her a controversial figure who was often punished both by black men and white women who excluded her from debates or activities to which she would have made important contributions.

Shadd Cary and Wells-Barnett were fortunate in having family resources and political connections that served to open doors to satisfying lives for them after their first disappointments. Hopkins was much less fortunate. She faded into obscurity fourteen years before her death. Seen as a group, however, these were extraordinary women whose lives, through no fault of their own, fell short of what they might have been. Each was an uncommon person who, in the words of historian John Hope Franklin on Wells-Barnett, had the strength and moral fiber to be "uncompromising and unequivocal on every cause she espoused" (x).

Hopkins, Shadd Cary, and Wells-Barnett attacked racism and other forms of human oppression wherever they saw it and were as condemnatory of blacks whom they thought were not acting in the best interests of their race as they were of white liberals or southern racists. They were ostracized because they were not gentlewomen, especially in their use of language, a quality not admirable in women. Each, on the other hand, was driven by the search for justice for all black people in America, and Shadd Cary and Wells-Barnett made all women a priority in their agenda as well. They hated pretentiousness, regardless of the race or sex of the pretender; and they lived by and upheld the highest standards of morality at all costs to themselves. Each saw in periodical editorship a promise of access to a multidimensional public voice in the interests of the groups to which they were committed. Because they were black and women, more often than for others, their good

intentions were given less credit and often used against them. The world
is poorer for what they were not permitted to do.

Brief commentaries in histories of "Negro" fiction on the writings
of Pauline Hopkins appeared as early as the 1940s, but serious efforts
to recover her life and work did not begin until the late 1970s, part of
a conscious excavation project on nineteenth- and early twentieth-century black women writers, which since then has recovered dozens of
these women from a previously lost past. This project, spearheaded by
contemporary black feminist critics and others with interests in these
works, is one of the most exciting developments in American literary
history in the last quarter of this century. Credit for igniting early interest in Hopkins goes to the poet Gwendolyn Brooks who wrote the
afterword to the first contemporary reprint of *Contending Forces* (1978
ed.), to the curator, historian, and librarian Dorothy B. Porter for her
biographical essay on Hopkins in the *Dictionary of American Negro
Biography* (1982), to the bibliographer and librarian Ann Allen Shockley for her biographical essay in *Afro-American Women Writers, 1746–
1933* (1988), to the literary critic Mary Helen Washington for her essay on Frances E. W. Harper and Pauline Hopkins in *Invented Lives*
(1987), and to Jane Campbell for her entry on Hopkins in the *Dictionary of Literary Biography* (1986). Hazel Carby's analysis of Hopkins's
writings in *Reconstructing Womanhood* (1987) and her introduction
to *The Magazine Novels of Pauline Hopkins* in the Schomburg Library
of Nineteenth-Century Black Women Writers series (1988), Claudia
Tate's essays, "Pauline Hopkins: Our Literary Foremother" (1985),
"Allegories of Black Female Desire" (1989), and her discussions of
Hopkins in *Domestic Allegories of Political Desire* (1992), and Richard Yarborough's introduction to the Schomburg Library series edition
of *Contending Forces* have all been invaluable in prompting further investigations of this long neglected writer.

The present collection of seven new essays on Hopkins, with an introduction and afterword (which is also a new essay on one novel), is
a welcome addition to the kind of rigorous critical evaluations that have
been appearing on Hopkins since the mid-eighties. Except for the Introduction (McKay) and Afterword (Ammons), this volume is entirely
the work of a new generation of critics, none of whom published before the 1990s, who bring to this anthology their own postmodern
visions and inquisitiveness in pursuit of studies in history and literature. Criticism of Hopkins's writing over the past decade created the

first audience for her writings that can be called a critical mass, in works that offer insights into what Elizabeth Ammons describes as Hopkins's radical experimentation that broke from prevailing trends. She was an early modernist when most black writers were still engaged with fictional realism. The "outrageousness" and "disruliness" (to again quote Ammons) of Hopkins's style have in fact inhibited readers who find it difficult to characterize her with broad generalizations. These new essays present Hopkins as a complex writer and from their different perspectives they will help newcomers to her fiction to recognize, and earlier admirers confirm, that Hopkins was a major writer of her time.

The first and second essays in this collection, Kate McCullough's "Slavery, Sexuality, and Genre: Pauline Hopkins and the Representation of Female Desire," and Lois Lamphere Brown's "'To Allow No Tragic End': Defensive Postures in Pauline Hopkins's *Contending Forces*," express different opinions on Hopkins's relationship to the sentimental novel. McCullough positions herself between two sets of earlier critics of the narrative: those who chastise the writer for using this popular tradition, and those who suggest that she uses it to promote a political agenda. The third view holds that Hopkins revises the tradition to recode the black female body and reclaim a space for the woman of African descent in reworked notions "of erotic and maternal desire." Hopkins dismantles the image of true womanhood for a new kind of heroine in a new version of African American womanhood. For example, McCullough argues that in *Contending Forces*, the mulatto figure, often linked negatively to the sexuality of black women and the sign of rape, embodies a different kind of "sexual configuration" of relations between the races. In this novel, Hopkins foregrounds white male rape as the source of miscegenation and redefines the black female's identity in maternity and moral erotic desire, not black female lust nor the passionless virtue associated with the cult of true womanhood. Thus Hopkins's true woman refutes both the passionlessness of the white true woman and the lasciviousness of the stereotype of the African American woman. In addition, McCullough argues, Hopkins substitutes the conventional wisdom of the way in which white male rape deprives black women of the right to motherhood for a reading of the domestic sphere as liberatory and radical for this group. In her reworking of old stereotypes, Hopkins transforms the well-known trope of redemptive maternity into the answer for the disruption that white male rape causes in the black family. In her heroine's reclamation of

an illegitimate child conceived in rape, she converts unchosen maternity into an assertion of self and kin. Thus, while participating in "racial uplift," the novel keeps its focus on refiguring the African American woman, redefining passion and virtue, and affirming the status of
the African American woman.

In "'To Allow No Tragic End': Defensive Postures in Pauline Hopkins's *Contending Forces*," which also concentrates on Hopkins's first
novel, Lois Brown examines two postslavery issues: "the repercussions
of racially motivated sexual violence against women of African descent
and the attempts of African Americans to build and defend a cohesive
family" in her alterations to the sentimental tradition. Brown argues
that, in separate male and female narratives, these alterations create two
separate new paradigms of female empowerment and male self-realization in her mixed-blood female and male characters, even as they
are restrained by racial and sexual politics. A reorientation of African
American matriarchy, a critique of uplift programs, and a reconfiguration of female agency and empowerment, she points out, are at the
heart of Hopkins's work. Fluidity, metamorphoses, spontaneity, and
malleability in race and gender definitions are essential to each character's agency. Both main characters must change if she is to overcome
her past history of sexual abuse and he is to achieve self-actualized
success. Yet Hopkins does not produce a story with a happy ending.
Her male hero does not develop his potential within either his community or the nation at large: he is ultimately overwhelmed by whiteness. Nor does her heroine become an individual who can genuinely
assimilate into African American culture. In addition to an attempt to
revise the Anglo American sentimental novel, Brown reads Hopkins's
treatment of mixed-blood characters in this novel in opposition to
African American cultural politics, and her conclusion points to an
irresolution of the internal anxieties that mixed-bloods experience as
they negotiate identity and full membership within the African American community.

In "Inherited Rhetoric and Authentic History: Pauline Hopkins at
the *Colored American Magazine*," C. K. Doreski examines Hopkins's
efforts to create a revisionist black history that would not only be at-
tractive to an audience of intellectuals and those who usually read history or biography, but one that would be just as enticing for those who
never read such works. She attempted to do this through the biographical sketches she wrote for *CAM* from November 1900 to October

1902. In these she conflated discourses of history, biography, fictional narrative, and race and gender to shape a rhetorical self to take the place of the absence of a reliable race history. As Doreski sees it, this aspect of Hopkins's writings, which so far has received little attention, transformed the writer from an "author of individual significance" to one of "community force." Her creation of black history through the exemplary lives of some of its members (in the New England tradition of Cotton Mather, Ralph Waldo Emerson, and others) was less imitation than simply one way to elevate her race. Doreski argues that in her appropriation of the particular white rhetorical traditions that she brings to bear on her sketches, Hopkins found a dignified and accessible way to render homage to the African American past.

The subject of John Cullen Gruesser's essay, "Taking Liberties: Pauline Hopkins's Recasting of the *Creole* Rebellion," is one of Hopkins's short stories, a rewriting of the 1841 revolt on the slave ship *Creole*. Versions of the narrative, authored by William Wells Brown, Frederick Douglass, and Lydia Maria Child predate hers. Hopkins, Gruesser notes, commemorates the historical event by recoding it to speak more directly (than former versions) to challenges that faced African Americans at the turn of the century. Gruesser focuses on differences between Hopkins's and earlier versions of the account, including her revision of the hero's name, her possible reasons for her chosen name for the hero, and her emphasis on the serious implications of black women's vulnerability to rape. He argues that Hopkins wanted to emphasize that what black Americans needed to be most keenly aware of was the importance of the whole group's engagement in unified action to combat the various oppressions they suffered and that the achievement of true freedom for all black people was dependent on the removal of the threat of white male sexual violation of black women.

"Mammies, Bucks, and Wenches: Minstrelsy, Racial Pornography, and Racial Politics in Pauline Hopkins's *Hagar's Daughter*" is Kristina Brooks's interrogation of Hopkins's use of stereotypes in her second novel. In problematizing racial objectification through Hopkins's representation of certain kinds of characters, Brooks explores the reactions to the novel by Hopkins's contemporary readers against the author's stated fictional intentions. Brooks locates the narrative in a historical ideological context, particularly in its relations to race and evolution, then considers two of its overlapping interpretive frame-

works: the minstrel tradition and racial pornography. Brooks describes
Hopkins's characters as multivalent: as humorous minstrels and troubling examples of racial pornography, foregrounding cultural ambivalence to racial difference. As Brooks sees it, by drawing upon minstrelsy, Hopkins makes use of a form of popular culture that appealed to
both races—a double-edged force: the minstrel was a figure of ridicule
or irony depending upon the race of the reader. Brooks posits that
pornography shares representational qualities with minstrelsy: the
objectification of women as sexual objects and the relationship between
the viewer and the object. For a useful understanding of *Hagar's Daughter,* Brooks presses for readings of the novel in relation to its historical
context (minstrelsy) and in relation to its cultural context (racial pornography). Questions of good and bad should be bracketed while issues of pleasure between subject and object are foregrounded. Accurate perceptions of Hopkins's racial objectifications, she tells us, require
readers to engage in a continuous process of repositioning self in relation to race, class, and gender identifications, as well as considerations
of one's place in history.

Jennie A. Kassanoff's "'Fate Has Linked Us Together': Blood, Gender, and the Politics of Representation in Pauline Hopkins's *Of One
Blood*" uses this serialized novel as a springboard to probe the issue
of the identity of the representative Negro, which was a topic of many
discussions at the turn of this century as the black intelligentsia sought
answers to the question of who was the "New Negro." This debate was
so serious, Kassanoff points out, that in editorial pronouncements,
CAM assumed a representative role as "mouthpiece and inspiration of
the Negro race," not only in America, but in the world. At the same
time, the "problem" surfaced in many venues from the U.S. Supreme
Court's racist *Plessy v. Ferguson* decision (1896) to the pronouncements
of W. E. B. Du Bois, Booker T. Washington, and feminists like Anna
Julia Cooper, creating a whirlpool of discourse on blood, body, and
blackness.

Addressing the semiotics of blood played out in Hopkins's novel,
Kassanoff suggests several competing discourses to consider in the context of blood and the "New Negro" debate: the ideology of a common
human ancestry; the pure African heritage to be protected from dilution;
the signification of bonds of kinship and the possibilities of incest; and
the markers of gender difference. She believes Hopkins's position leaned
toward a monogenist creationism at the same time that the novel blurs

the color line and seems to argue against blood mixing and for the protection of African American blood. One rationale for this line of argument is the danger of incest in monogenist kinship: of siblings not being able to recognize each other. While the brotherhood of humanity appears to be one thread in Hopkins's argument, the novel's subtexts of incestuous blood and black eugenics dispute such a claim. Finally, Kassanoff sees Hopkins proposing woman as the locus of blood in this discourse. Among Hopkins's arguments in the novel Kassanoff identifies a revived Ethiopian royalty connected to the blood of a woman. Through a series of complex textual manipulations Kassanoff posits the maternal body as the site of intervention in this debate.

Cynthia D. Schrager's essay, "Pauline Hopkins and William James: The New Psychology and the Politics of Race," explores Hopkins's *Of One Blood* against the background of William James's essay, "The Hidden Self," and the emerging discipline of the "new psychology." Like Du Bois, Hopkins was greatly influenced by James's work, and both saw that the "new psychology" offered a rich new discourse for the discussion of race. Schrager begins by noting that the neurasthenic despair in Hopkins's first story, "The Mystery within Us" (1900), foreshadows *Of One Blood*. She then charts two movements in the novel, one in the United States, the other in Africa. In the first, she shows how Hopkins, through her black and white characters, uses the trope of the "hidden self" to demonstrate the fiction of the color line and the truth of miscegenation. This enables her to make of the "hidden self" a metaphor for the collective history of abusive social and familial relations under slavery.

In the African segment of the novel, Hopkins returns to the discourse on blood in relation to identity. For a positive representation of American race relations, she refigures the unconscious as a sociopolitical space: the Ethiopian source of Western civilization. Utilizing James's belief in the transpersonal or occult dimensions of the unconscious, Hopkins links concepts from turn-of-the-century psychical research to a Pan-Africanist political agenda as part of the work for "self-recovery" in African American cultural and political reconstruction. Schrager sees Hopkins's novel as a precursor for the art of later writers, such as Toni Cade Bambara and Toni Morrison, who also traverse the boundaries between the "scientific-academic" and the "feminine-mystical" minds.

In her fine "Afterword" to this pathbreaking collection, Elizabeth

Ammons, whose previous work on black and white women's writings makes her an undisputed authority in the field, adds a coda to the foregoing that reinforces the significance of this volume. First, she makes a convincing argument for the link between Hopkins and Mikhail Bakhtin that makes them partners in a practice and theory project on the workings of the modern novel. Then she proves her point by illustrating Hopkins's experimental virtuosity in *Winona: A Tale of Negro Life in the South and Southwest,* a novel that combines the "western, fugitive slave narrative, romance, potboiler/soap opera, political novel, and traditional allegory" into a story of a mixed-race family. In a refutation of colonialism and racism, Hopkins suggests that her white, black, and red family represents the human family in its "multicultural, multiracial, anti-imperialist, unnational, antimaterialistic, [and] environmentally attuned" configuration. But the idealization dissolves into contradictions in the face of its flawed construction, which includes a "dead black mother, fake Indian father, and silenced 'real' Indian housekeeper," and a heavy dependence on the western, a form apparently unreconcilable with the slave narrative. For all of that, Ammons sees *Winona,* which she calls revolutionary for its vision of a successful alliance between Native American and African American cultures and for its revision of the romantic American myth of the "great (white) 'founding fathers,'" as very worthy of readers' attention. This volume, she says, does not unproblematize the complexity of Hopkins's writings, but it will help readers to realize their value for literary history.

Although by no means an exhaustive evaluation of Pauline Hopkins's writings, *The Unruly Voice* takes a major step in establishing this long-neglected author in the place that she justly belongs in the literature of the turn of the century. It represents an excellent beginning on which others may build. To that end, Malin LaVon Walther's bibliography, the most comprehensive to date on Hopkins, will be immeasurably useful for future work on this writer. Its inclusion makes this volume even more valuable. A serious frustration that scholars now encounter is lack of information on Hopkins's life. While those who have uncovered what is now known about her should be highly commended for rescuing her from obscurity, there is a need for a full-scale biographical project to fill in the large empty spaces surrounding her life. There are many things we need to know about Hopkins, including her relationship with other black activists between the 1890s and 1916 when she dropped from public view. In the era of the black women's club movement, with many of the most influential leaders located in the Boston area, did Pauline Hopkins know and associate with these women? Who were the young black writers with whom she was acquainted? The recent publication of several excellent new biographies of black women and men, such as those on W. E. B. Du Bois and Nella Larsen, are models for the kind of scholarly investigations that are absolutely necessary if there is to be a full recovery of the lost or hidden lives of writers like Pauline Hopkins.

NOTES

1. Although Cooper was born in 1859, before Emancipation, the conditions of chattel slavery were not part of her conscious life.

2. The Hyers Sisters, Anna Madah and Emma Louise, won great acclaim for their striking soprano and contralto voices, beginning with their debut at the Metropolitan Theatre in Sacramento, California, in 1867. To the high acclaim of critics, they later made concert tours in the northern and western states (Southern 254ff.).

3. On the cover of its first issue, *CAM* announced that it was "devoted to Literature, Science, Music, Art, Religion, Facts, Fiction and Traditions of the Negro Race." It sold for fifteen cents per copy or $1.50 for a year's subscription. *CAM* has been called the first significant African American journal in this century.

4. Hazel Carby points out that in the early 1900s it was impossible for a black magazine or any such publication to survive if it depended solely on black readers to support it. With no more than 2,500 black college graduates in the country by 1900, and large numbers of others still not sufficiently literate to form a strong core of support, or not being fully aware of the meaning of the print media, *CAM*, under a leadership that insisted on its black nationalist politics, could not succeed.

5. Black women in America have long used journals to make themselves heard. Examples include Maria Stewart, the well-known feminist abolitionist who in 1832 contributed black feminist abolitionist essays to William Lloyd Garrison's *Liberator*. In 1862, Charlotte Forten Grimké, granddaughter of (black) abolitionist businessman James Forten, Sr., published her experiences working with former slaves on the Sea Islands in Garrison's newspaper as well. Two years later, her two-part essay, "Life on the Sea Islands," appeared in the *Atlantic Monthly*. In the late 1850s, black women wrote for such publications as the *Repository of Religion and Literature and of Science and the Arts* (an African Methodist Episcopal Church journal) and the *Anglo-African* magazine. They were correspondents and reporters for newspapers like the *India-*

napolis Freeman and the *Boston Advocate.* They changed the nature of print discourse as they interrogated in these publications the racial and sexual conflict/oppression of women. During Reconstruction they wrote on self-reliance, temperance, education, and the place of freed blacks in society. By the turn of the century many black women and men were contributing to magazines like *Harper's, Bookman, Century Magazine,* and *Atlantic Monthly,* and black women launched several magazines of their own: the *Woman's Era* (Boston), the first newspaper published by a black woman, Josephine St. Pierre Ruffin, and *National Notes,* which served the National Association of Colored Women, edited by Margaret Murray Washington.

WORKS CITED

Campbell, Jane. "Hopkins, Pauline Elizabeth (1859–1930)." *Black Women in America: An Historical Encyclopedia.* Vol. 1. Ed. Darlene Clark Hine, with Elsa Barkley Brown and Rosalyn Terborg-Penn. Brooklyn: Carlson, 1993. 577–79.

Carby, Hazel. Introduction. *The Magazine Novels of Pauline Hopkins.* By Pauline Hopkins. New York: Oxford University Press, 1988. xxix–l.

Cooper, Anna Julia. *A Voice from the South.* 1892. New York: Oxford University Press, 1988.

Franklin, John Hope. Foreword. *Crusade for Justice: The Autobiography of Ida B. Wells.* By Ida B. Wells-Barnett. Ed. Alfreda Duster. Chicago: University of Chicago Press, 1970. ix–xi.

Johnson, Abby Arthur, and Ronald Maberry Johnson. *Propaganda and Aesthetics: The Literary Politics of Afro-American Magazines in the Twentieth Century.* Amherst: University Massachusetts Press, 1979.

Mossell, F. N. *The Work of the Afro-American Woman.* 1894. New York: Oxford University Press, 1988.

Porter, Dorothy B. "Hopkins, Pauline Elizabeth (1856–1930)." *Dictionary of American Negro Biography.* Ed. Rayford W. Logan and Michael R. Winston. New York: W. W. Norton, 1982. 325–26.

Shockley, Ann Allen. *Afro-American Women Writers, 1746–1933.* New York: New American Library, 1988.

Southern, Eileen. *The Music of Black Americans: A History.* New York: W. W. Norton, 1971.

Yarborough, Richard. Introduction. *Contending Forces: A Romance Illustrative of Negro Life North and South.* By Pauline Hopkins. New York: Oxford University Press, 1988. xxvii–xlviii.

ONE

Slavery, Sexuality, and Genre: Pauline Hopkins and the Representation of Female Desire

KATE MCCULLOUGH

> The names by which I am called in the public place render an example of signifying property *plus*. In order for me to speak a truer word concerning myself, I must strip down through layers of attenuated meanings, made an excess in time, over time, assigned by a particular historical order, and there await whatever marvels of my own inventiveness. The personal pronouns are offered in the service of a collective function.
> —HORTENSE J. SPILLERS

Slavery, Sexuality, and the Sentimental Novel

Hortense Spillers's words, taken from her 1987 article, "Mama's Baby, Papa's Maybe: An American Grammar Book," point to the importance of self-representation for contemporary African American women writers and to the urgency of the need to articulate identity through a discourse which, if not one's own, might be temporarily appropriated as such. Implicated in this process, her statement suggests, is a confrontation with the "attenuated meanings" assigned to African American female identity by the American "historical order." Spillers's formulation charts a relationship between African American female identity and history, putting into relief the historical impact of slavery on the formation of African American identity.[1] Placing Spillers's argument into a historical context, I would suggest that we can use her formulation to help us understand both post-Reconstruction African American female writers' efforts toward self-representation and, at the same time, the *literary* history which has read (or misread) these writers.

Spillers contends that within slavery, even prior to differentiation on the basis of gender, there operated a differentiation between human and nonhuman, what she calls "body" and "flesh" (67). I would suggest that African American women writers like Pauline Hopkins used the sentimental novel (and specifically the figure of the mulatto heroine) not only as a means of extracting themselves from the category of "flesh," in order to claim human subject status, but also as a means of extracting themselves from the category of "body," in the sense that the body had come to signify for African American women a stereotype of the sexually voracious and immoral female sexed body. Hopkins, like many post-Reconstruction African American women writers, was engaged in multiple but overlapping arguments with historical constructions of black womanhood, struggling in her novel, *Contending Forces,* to avoid being reduced to the body while also struggling to recode that body, reclaiming a space for African American women as embodied humans by grounding her representations of gendered identity in a reworked notion of erotic and maternal desire.

Particularly for African American women writers, history dictated more than one of what Spillers has dubbed an "attenuated meaning" for sexuality: under slavery, African American women were both stripped of the role of mother and burdened with the role of the hypererotic. Given that slave women had no legal right to their children, who were routinely torn from their mothers to be sold as valuable property by their white, male owners and sometimes fathers, maternity would necessarily have meant something structurally and affectively different for late nineteenth-century African American women—often ex-slaves and daughters of ex-slaves—than what it meant for white women. Thus while turn-of-the-century Anglo American women worked to refigure their own sense of white female identity against the backdrop of true womanhood, African American women faced not only this dominant white image but also its inverse image: the stereotype described by Mary Helen Washington as the "immoral," "licentious and oversexed" black woman with "insatiable appetites" (73). As the cultural repository of all of the white bourgeois lady's denied sexuality, the stereotype of the black woman was seen as the true woman's direct opposite, her Other, thus disqualifying the black woman from occupying the space of virtuous Victorian lady.[2]

Reading in the context of this historical formation, literary critics agree that the post-Reconstruction fiction of African American wom-

en such as Hopkins and Frances E. W. Harper reflects a desire to "uplift" the race by offering self-representations that refuted the multiple
received stereotypes of African American women. Critics have also
agreed that to this end these authors use the vehicle of the sentimental
novel, producing heroines who celebrate domesticity, marriage, and
motherhood, and who reflect a dominant white model of virtuous
womanhood. But here the critical consensus ends in ongoing disagree-
ments over the use and valence of both the sentimental novel and the
mulatto heroine.

Certain early critics of African American fiction and, more surprisingly, some critics in the 1990s chastise writers like Hopkins for their
use of the sentimental novel, either because these authors use the sentimental novel form at all—a form long dismissed as "feminine" and
trivial—or because they attempt to use it as a form of political protest.
In this first line of criticism, the sentimental novel is viewed as a degraded form, a white literary convention that inculcates white bourgeois values, so that Hopkins becomes guilty of buying into white ideology, using a white literary form to argue for assimilation. In the
second, related line of criticism, the sentimental novel remains a degraded form but one that Hopkins and her sort misuse by trying to
import an overlay of political protest. Early critics have thus taken
Hopkins (and other nineteenth-century African American novelists) to
task, arguing variously that the sentimental novel is bad art, white art,
bourgeois art—or all three—and that it is, moreover, incompatible with
political protest fiction. More recently, Richard Yarborough has articulated this argument in slightly different terms, equating protest fiction
with realism and reading *Contending Forces* in terms of early African
American fiction writers' efforts to "discover a vehicle that would satisfy their urge toward realism without undermining their adoption of
popular literary forms" (xxxvi).

Even more curious than this assessment's appearance in the introduction to the prestigious Schomburg Library edition of *Contending Forces*
is Houston Baker's recent dismissal of Hopkins and her contemporaries. Baker criticizes both the use of a mulatto heroine and the form of
Contending Forces, arguing that Hopkins panders to a white audience,
fails to represent a black southern community of women, and produces a form of "white-faced minstrelsy" (26). He calls the novel a "cour-
tesy book for a new era" that preaches "strict moral rectitude, white-
faced mannerliness, and black northern achievement" (28). Critics such

as Baker and his forerunners thus read the mulatto as the model of middle-class white lifestyles and values, a sell-out to white America encoded in the white bourgeois genre of the sentimental novel,[3] thus linking black post-Reconstruction authors' use of a middle-class popular form, the sentimental novel, to those authors' alleged espousal of white middle-class values.[4]

But of course these lines of argument fail to take into consideration feminist work on the uses of the sentimental novel as well as specifically African American feminist readings of Hopkins's work. Respected African American feminist critics, including Hazel Carby, Barbara Christian, Deborah E. McDowell, Claudia Tate, and Mary Helen Washington (only a few among many), have shown how African American women writers like Hopkins used the sentimental novel politically. Deborah McDowell, for instance, has argued that "imaging the black woman as a 'whole' character or 'self' has been a consistent preoccupation of black female novelists throughout their literary history" (283). These critics have situated Hopkins in a line of African American writers—Hopkins's contemporary Frances E. W. Harper or her predecessors Harriet Wilson and Harriet Jacobs, for instance—who use sentimental forms as a means of cultural intervention, and they have shown how Hopkins used sentimental forms in part because they were among the culturally available and familiar forms of her time; that is, her audience would have known how to read the sentimental signifiers in her work—an important goal given the didactic aim of *Contending Forces*.

This move by contemporary African American feminist critics is linked to a more generalized reevaluation of the sentimental novel as a political and cultural form by feminist critics, both African American and Anglo American. Following earlier feminist work by critics such as Jane Tompkins (work that, for instance, used Harriet Beecher Stowe's *Uncle Tom's Cabin* to demonstrate that an inherent distinction between sentimental and political fiction is specious [see Tompkins, *Sensational Designs* and "Sentimental Power"; Fetterley, Introduction]), ongoing critical attention to the sentimental as a broad cultural form continues to interrogate easy alignments of the sentimental with either "radical" or "conservative," preferring instead to locate the sentimental as a complicated "operation or a set of actions within discursive models of affect and identification that effect connections across gender, race, and class boundaries" (Samuels 6).[5]

In this light, I will discuss Hopkins's use of the sentimental novel and the mulatto heroine. For while her later magazine fiction would address different literary forms and offer less hopeful visions, in *Contending Forces* Hopkins links sexuality to racial identity in ways that variously challenge and reinforce dominant notions of both black and white womanhood but that ultimately serve to stake a claim for a new model of African American womanhood.[6] On the one hand, Hopkins celebrates maternity and the bourgeois domestic sphere, both elements of the middle-class white Cult of True Womanhood. On the other hand, by foregrounding the question of race, she shifts the meaning of both true womanhood and the generic form, the sentimental novel, used here to express it: placing the issue of miscegenation in a domestic realm necessarily redefines that realm. That Hopkins, an African American, is writing what the subtitle of her novel identifies as a "Romance Illustrative of Negro Life North and South" is itself a radical move that must by necessity have ramifications on the sentimental tradition since she is appropriating a form that was constituted in part by the absence of black women authors and heroines from its pages: true womanhood was, by definition, not African American. Therefore, to chronicle an African American true woman whose identity was based partly in erotic desire constitutes a double reshaping of the sentimental novel: such a heroine embodies both nonwhite and nonpassionless virtue. Hopkins thus doubles the stakes in representing female erotic desire through her struggle concurrently to refute and to offer an alternative to both the passionlessness of the model of true womanhood and the lasciviousness of the stereotype of the African American woman.

Meanwhile, by rewriting the "mulatto" narrative to foreground white male rape rather than African American lust as the source of miscegenation, Hopkins counters the post-Reconstruction racist, white, supremacist appropriation of the mulatto figure. She also resists a Booker T. Washingtonian politics of emulation by resituating the mulatto in the context of master-slave relations. Using rape in place of "passing" as a figure for relations between the races, Hopkins self-consciously underscores the ways in which the white American imagination had linked sexuality to racial identity and had, moreover, figured a racial "threat" in sexual terms.[7] Thus, she both addresses and redresses the discursive terms used to construct African American womanhood and in so doing exhibits not a post-Reconstruction African American drive toward assimilation but an emphasis on the historical construction of race relations and how they are sexually configured. As Hazel

Carby notes, "Hopkins wanted to emphasize those sets of social relations and practices which were the consequence of a social system that exercised white supremacy through the act of rape" (*Reconstructing Womanhood* 140; for an alternative reading, see Dearborn). To this end, the mulatto was clearly an ideal narrative choice.

The terms of such an enterprise are clearly complicated and involve a reevaluation of the very grounding of gendered identity. Hortense Spillers points out that, given the legacy of slavery, "we could go so far as to entertain the very real possibility that 'sexuality,' as a term of implied relationship and desire, is dubiously appropriate, manageable, or accurate to *any* of the familial arrangements under a system of enslavement, from the master's family to the captive enclave. Under these arrangements, the customary lexus of sexuality, including 'reproduction,' 'motherhood,' 'pleasure,' and 'desire' is thrown into unrelieved crisis" (76). This crisis of "the customary lexus of sexuality" was inherited by postbellum African American writers like Hopkins, who struggled in both her fiction and her work at the *Colored American Magazine* (*CAM*) to find the words and literary forms to articulate what had not been sayable under slavery.

Hopkins herself recognizes that her use of the sentimental effects a shift in this "lexus of sexuality": in her preface to *Contending Forces,* as she explains her motives for writing the novel, she underscores this shift. Her explanation, with a disclaimer common to nineteenth-century women's fiction in general, deflects a charge of greed or personal pride and emphasizes the moral and didactic motivations behind her writing: "In giving this little romance expression in print, I am not actuated by a desire for notoriety or for profit, but to do all that I can in an humble way to raise the stigma of degradation from my race" (13). Like her specifically African American predecessors, she goes on to identify racial "uplift" as her goal, a goal reiterated by *CAM*'s editors in attributing to Hopkins "a heartfelt desire to aid in everyway possible in uplifting the colored people of America, and through them, the world" (*CAM*, Sept. 1900, 64). While Hopkins devoted four years to this aim in working for *CAM* as both contributor and editor, she clearly viewed fiction as the preferred means of achieving this goal.[8] In her preface she also asserts:

> The colored race has historians, lecturers, ministers, poets, judges and lawyers,—men of brilliant intellects who have arrested the

favorable attention of this busy, energetic nation. But, after all, it is the simple, homely tale, unassumingly told, which cements the bond of brotherhood among all classes and all complexions.

Fiction is of great value to any people as a preserver of manners and customs—religious, political and social. It is a record of growth and development from generation to generation. *No one will do this for us; we must ourselves develop the men and women who will faithfully portray the inmost thoughts and feelings of the Negro with all the fire and romance which lie dormant in our history,* and, as yet, unrecognized by writers of the Anglo-Saxon race. (13–14, emphasis in original)

Hopkins identifies the need for self-representation, for reclaiming and redefining the terms used to define African Americans, and links this need, through fiction's uses, to community building. In order to envision a collective cultural identity, she implies, one needs representations of the self. Thus her fiction stands not only as a supplement to "Anglo-Saxon" self-representations, or even as a corrective to prior misrepresentations of the African American by the "Anglo-Saxon race," but as an independent moment in the present of African American culture, a present moment necessary to the envisioning of that culture's future.

Not surprisingly, the identity that Hopkins concentrates on representing in *Contending Forces* is that of an African American woman, figured here by the mulatto heroine, a fragmented self which the plot moves toward unifying. By bringing into concert the racial, gender, and regional components of her identity, the novel not only displaces the racist literary and cultural heritage that linked African American women's sexuality to rape, but also emphasizes this African American woman's integrity as a human being as well as the power of her unique status *as* an African American woman.[9] What Hopkins produces, then, is not, as critics have implied, merely a white bourgeois tale in blackface but a new narrative with a new kind of heroine, a narrative that reworks racial and gendered identity to claim a narrative space for the representation of a new version of African American womanhood.

Essentially Reconstructed Womanhood

The main plot of *Contending Forces* focuses on the "mulatto" Smith family—Ma Smith, her daughter Dora, and son Will—and their lives in a post-Reconstruction, middle-class, Boston boardinghouse. The novel opens, earlier in the century, with an account of how the Smiths' white ancestors, the Montforts, fell from being Bermuda slave-owners to American slaves, the two sons eventually escaping slavery to marry into a free black northern family and an aristocratic white English family. While part of the plot traces the reuniting of the lost British side of this family with the American side, the main plot, set in post-Reconstruction Boston, traces the courtships of two mulatto heroines. The first courtship is that of Dora Smith by her two suitors: the eventually rejected villain John Langley and the ultimately victorious and noble Dr. Arthur Lewis. The second courtship is between Will Smith and the mysterious Sappho Clark (a couple whose very names alert us that they are Hopkins's ideal pair, the two who unite the willpower of the head with the love of the heart). Though the novel concludes by bringing together both couples, the heroines confront the history of American race relations along the way. Sappho, in particular, must deal with her past—her status as an "impure" woman and unwed mother as a result of her rape by her white half-uncle. Much of the plot thus concerns the working out of historical legacies and blood lines as affected by slavery.

While Hopkins's novel chronicles the lives and loves of two mulatto heroines, Dora and Sappho, it is in the depiction of the women's sewing circle, in the chapter of the same name, that Hopkins's general picture of African American female identity emerges. Recent critics have called attention to this chapter for its portrayal of the women's club movement and the domestication of political issues that this movement entailed (Campbell, *Mythic Black Fiction* 33, 39; Tate, "Hopkins" 58–59). Here, literally, the domestic realm of sentimentalism becomes the forum for political debate, as the women meet to sew and "to go over the events of interest to the Negro race which had transpired during the week throughout the country," as well as to listen to Mrs. Willis give "a talk upon some topic of interest" (143).

In the character of Mrs. Willis, Hopkins sets forth the woman of the public sphere, a character who is her spokesperson on the "woman question" but who also, because of her public position, evokes an anxiety in Hopkins's narrative. Left a widow without financial support, Mrs. Willis is forced to

hunt for the means to help her breast the social tide. The best opening, she decided . . . was in the great cause of the evolution of true

womanhood in the work of the "Woman Question" as embodied
in marriage and suffrage. She could talk dashingly on many themes.
. . . The advancement of the colored woman should be the new
problem in the woman question that should float her upon its tide
into the prosperity she desired. And she succeeded well in her plans:
conceived in selfishness, they yet bore glorious fruit in the formation of clubs of colored women banded together for charity, for
study, for every reason under God's glorious heavens that can better
the condition of mankind. (146–47)

While Mrs. Willis thus embodies the self-glorification and self-aggran-
dizement dangerously inherent in woman's entrance into the public
sphere, the exploitation of the public for private gain, she also views
public discourse as a means of curing society's ills. She justifies her
entrance into this discourse on moral grounds: self-interest and collective benefit merge harmoniously. And by working for the "advancement
of the colored woman," Mrs. Willis serves both women and the larger
cause of "Negro uplift."

Hopkins uses Mrs. Willis and the sewing circle to stage a discussion
of the "place which the virtuous woman occupies in upbuilding a race"
(148), a discussion that provides Hopkins with the opportunity to
define a virtuous woman and to foreground the importance of African
American female sexuality in historic constructions of race. Mrs. Willis opens by raising the specter of the immoral, sexually lascivious African American woman, charging the young women of the circle with
the responsibility of "refut[ing] the charges brought against us as to
our moral irresponsibility, and the low moral standard maintained by
us in comparison with other races" (148). This refutation is a common
enough sentiment for African American writers of Hopkins's day: what
is more uncommon are the means by which the women are to muster
their defense of their sex. For when Sappho asks if "the Negro woman in her native state is truly a virtuous woman" (148), Mrs. Willis
asserts that "travelers tell us that the native African woman is impregnable in her virtue." When Dora suggests that they have sacrificed that
virtue in the acquisition of "civilization," Mrs. Willis clarifies her position still further by stating,

No, not "sacrificed," but pushed [to] one side by the force of circumstances. Let us thank God that it *is* an essential attribute peculiar to us—a racial characteristic which is slumbering but not

lost. . . . But let us not forget the definition of virtue—"Strength to do the right thing under all temptations." Our ideas of virtue are too narrow. We confine them to that conduct which is ruled by our animal passions alone. It goes deeper than that—general excellence in every duty of life is what we may call virtue. (149)

Hopkins goes beyond merely defending African American women's potential to emulate a white model of true womanhood to lay claim to both an inherent "animal passion" and a wide-ranging, inherent, essential purity specific to African womanhood. Moreover, Hopkins's use of "impregnable" signals implicitly what will later be articulated explicitly: that African American women in the past cannot be held responsible for what the dominant culture would term their "compromised" moral state. That is, we must read "impregnable" not in literal terms: if African women are generally "impregnable," African American women, although physically pregnable by their masters, remain at the same time *morally* impregnable.

This question of moral culpability for rape is raised by Sappho, herself the victim of a white man's rape, when she asks Mrs. Willis if "Negro women will be held responsible for all the lack of virtue that is being laid to their charge today? I mean, do you think that God will hold us responsible for the *illegitimacy* with which our race has been obliged, as it were, to flood the world?" (149). Using the same religious terms of justification, Mrs. Willis claims that "we shall not be held responsible for wrongs which we have *unconsciously* committed, or which we have committed under *compulsion*. We are virtuous or non-virtuous only when we have a *choice* under temptation" (149). She thus retains a white bourgeois model of female purity—these women *have,* in these terms, committed a "wrong"—but through religious rhetoric and a claim of essential purity Mrs. Willis exempts the victimized African American women from blame—it is a wrong for which the women are not responsible.

While Hopkins delineates this naturally pure African American woman, however, she also attributes to her a natural "passion," defining passion as broadly as she does virtue but with somewhat more ambivalence, thus offering several models of womanhood. Standing as the passionless foil to Sappho, for instance, Dora, the mulatto happy in the domestic sphere, claims she hasn't enough sentiment "to make love a great passion" (119) and notes that her lack of a sense of eter-

nal love makes her feel *"unsexed"* (122, emphasis in original). In this
context, passion as definitive of femininity seems to mean both romantic
love and a sense of individuated desire, whether emotional or physical. But Hopkins goes beyond this model of womanhood, granting
Sappho a passion that is actively erotic but marked as positive. In the
sewing circle scene, however, the connotation of passion is more negative, reflecting a fear that grows out of historical circumstance. For
historically, of course, African American female erotic desire was often used as an excuse for white male "passion" in the form of rape.

In the sewing circle, passion is conventionally defined as Christian
sin and returns the women to the question of responsibility. Sappho,
unable to distinguish what a woman can and cannot control, asks Mrs.
Willis, "How are we to overcome the nature which is given us? I mean
how can we eliminate passion from our lives, and emerge into the purity
which marked the life of Christ? So many of us desire purity and think
to have found it, but in a moment of passion, or under the pressure of
circumstances which we cannot control, we commit some horrid sin,
and the taint of it sticks and will not leave us, and we grow to loathe
ourselves" (154). The passive voice of "the nature which is given us"
allows for two readings of this passage: we might read this nature as
the stereotype of the passionate nature assigned to African American
women by the dominant culture, or we might read it as an innate passion "given" to African American women by God or nature. In either
case, this nature troubles Sappho, who reads passion as lust, that which
prevents access to a Christ-like life. More strangely, the difference between desire and coercion disappears, and the autonomous agent becomes a sexual victim, as Sappho's rhetoric conflates passion with rape
(the "circumstances which we cannot control"), and desire becomes
possession.

Mrs. Willis, however, broadens the definition of passion to include
not only "animal passions" (149) but also any sort of governing interest. Here Hopkins both grants women an essential "passion"—sexual
and nonsexual—and cautions against its dangers, counseling self-control. Passion, Mrs. Willis explains, "is a state in which the will lies
dormant, and all other desires become subservient to one. Enthusiasm
for any one object or duty may become a passion. . . . Passion may be
beneficial, but we must guard ourselves against a sinful growth of any
appetite. All work . . . needs a certain amount of absorbing interest to
become successful, and it is here that the Christian life gains its great-

est glory in teaching us how to keep ourselves from abusing any of our human attributes" (154). Both passion as sexual desire and passion as a metaphor for obsessional interest are contained here through the imposition of Christian self-control, the same self-control convention-ally recommended to contain the abuse of "human attributes." More-over, African American women, by virtue of their innate "purity," are responsible for raising not only themselves but also their male compan-ions. Mrs. Willis tells Sappho that "most men are like the lower ani-mals in many things—they don't always know what is for their best good" (156). Similarly, much later in the novel, the narrator comments that "time and moral training among the white men of the South are the only cures for concubinage" (332), a moral training presumably in the hands of women. Thus, if Hopkins grants her heroines innate desires, she also demands that they be strictly monitored, limited, and directed toward the moral good of the race.

This model of innate desire displaced into cultural service informs one of the two marriages that resolve the plot action of *Contending Forces*: the marriage of Dora and Dr. Arthur Lewis. Claudia Tate has persuasively argued that marriage in general operates as liberational in nineteenth-century African American women's sentimental texts, as a new civil right that confirms the ex-slave's legal status as human rather than chattel ("Allegories" 102, 103). It also, of course, confirms a model of humanity that is specifically bourgeois. Within this model, "court-ship is devoid of all ardent sentiment that does not arise from noble admiration. Respect kindles love, and mutual commitment to advanc-ing the race engenders love" so that "the emphasis falls on explaining how the couple plans to live out their married life actively engaged in working for racial progress" (117). Dora clearly fits this pattern, be-ing filled with "respect" for Lewis (360), a character, modeled on Book-er T. Washington, who runs an industrial school in Louisiana. She agrees to marry him with no stronger feeling than that of "peace and contentment" (361). Like Frances E. W. Harper's heroine, Iola Leroy, Dora enters a marriage of spiritual partnership, leaving with her new husband for "his far off Southern home to assist him in the upbuild-ing of their race" (381).

Yet this regulatory vision of female desire erased or displaced into moral service, this narrative strategy to avoid reducing woman to body, does not represent the final word on passion in the novel, for Hopkins certainly represents Sappho as bearing erotic desire for Will, the hero marked by the narrative as Sappho's rightful husband. In the end Hopkins sanctions that desire by bringing the two together in marriage. This recoding of the body and desire is accomplished through an emphasis on choice rather than coercion. After Sappho has fled from Will to spare him her sexual "disgrace," she reclaims her son and finds a comfortable position as governess/companion. Yet she remains unhappy. The narrator explains that Sappho "tried not to allow herself to think upon the past; but when night came she lay awake hungering for the sight of a face, the touch of a hand, the glance of an eye. Sometimes the craving grew almost too powerful to be resisted, and once she started to dress, resolved to return to Boston, find Will, and trust all to his love" (354). Such desire, originating in Sappho rather than forced upon her, is ultimately contained in marriage and coexistent with the desire "to work together to bring joy to hearts crushed by despair" (401), but is nevertheless clearly both erotic and offered by Hopkins as a prototype of a model marriage.

Of course, Sappho must traverse miles, years, and seemingly endless pain in order to reach this happy ending, and this journey, as much as its end, constitutes Hopkins's refiguring of African American female identity. In Sappho, Hopkins has created what Spillers describes as the African American woman's position in general: "a meeting ground of investments and privations in the national treasury of rhetorical wealth" (65). Sappho is the mulatto version of the white bourgeois heroine, "tall and fair, with hair of a golden cast, aquiline nose, rosebud mouth, soft brown eyes veiled by long, dark lashes which swept her cheeks . . . a combination of 'queen rose and lily in one'" (107). Men and women alike are struck by her beauty, but she is quiet and reserved, a living refutation of the stereotype of the immoral, sexually unrestrained African American woman. While a domestic ideal, she is also a New Woman, a stenographer who "picks up a good living at home" with her typewriter (89). Clearly a model for the independent woman, she has, as Mary Helen Washington notes, "one of the first nonnurturing professions black women have in fiction" (80), a profession that Hopkins herself fell back on at various points in her life. In addition, Sappho secretly supports dependents and is capable of arranging her own affairs, from renting a room in Ma Smith's boardinghouse to taking a long train journey alone. In her friendship with Dora, Sappho discusses politics, proving that the domestic could be the sphere of politics and explicitly dismissing Arthur Lewis's Washingtonian position of conciliation in favor of Hopkins's own support of Du Bois's position (a position also represented in the novel by Sappho's future husband, Will). Learning that Lewis "thinks that women should be seen and not heard, where politics is under discussion," Sappho, not short on opinions, labels him an "insufferable prig" (126).

But Sappho's friendship with Dora is a showcase for more than just Sappho's political views. It is the first indicator of what the sewing circle comes to represent: a united community of women. Dora, we are told, "did not, as a rule, care much for girl friendships, holding that a close intimacy between two of the same sex was more than likely to end disastrously for one or the other. But Sappho Clark seemed to fill a long-felt want in her life, and she had from the first a perfect trust in the beautiful girl" (98). Whether we read the original Sappho as the forerunner of the modern lesbian or merely as the leader of a spiritual community of women, Hopkins's use of the name to signify friendship, love, and community among women is explicit. Indeed, throughout the novel Sappho and Dora trust in and support each another, in the face of duplicitous lovers and blackmailers. Given that she was raised in and set her novel in the home of the "Boston marriage," Hopkins may well have been offering this friendship as a model of what critic Carroll Smith-Rosenberg has called the "female world of love and ritual," a world in which women's affectional ties (whether physically enacted or not) were often considered at least as important and sustaining as their ties to men.[10]

This friendship also provides an arena for Hopkins's discussion of "Negro Life North and South." Dora embodies the spirit of liberty that the Maine-born, Boston-raised Hopkins attributes to the North: "Into Sappho's lonely, self-suppressed life the energetic little Yankee girl swept like a healthful, strengthening breeze" (114), the narrator comments, aligning Dora with Boston, the city where "in the free air of New England's freest city Sappho drank great draughts of freedom's subtle elixir" (115). Invoking both the North's abolitionist past and New England's revolutionary principles, Hopkins aims her narrative at a northern audience, implicitly looking to them for support in the cause of racial justice.

In contrast, Hopkins figures the South as the site of reactionary and often violent racial politics, often downplaying Boston's racist employment practices in order to emphasize southern lynching and rape.[11] She also invokes the stereotype of the exotic, sensuous South in contrast to a more Puritan legacy in the North. Ophelia Davis and Sarah White, the two laundresses in Ma Smith's boardinghouse, for instance, assume that Sappho is from the South because of her great beauty, speculating that Louisiana is her home. When Sappho confirms this judgment, Mrs. White crows, "I knowed it. . . . Ol' New Orleans blood will tell on itself anywhere. These col'-blooded Yankees can't raise nuthin' that looks like thet chile; no, 'ndeed!" (108).

Meanwhile, Dora complains that her suitor John Langley "said that he had not met a decent-looking woman who was Northern-born, and that when he did see a pretty colored girl on the street he knew without asking that she was a Southerner" (180). Langley himself takes this notion of regional beauty to its furthest extreme, conflating it with sensuality and an implied moral laxness. Confronting Sappho with her past, Langley not only blames the victim but frames her status as regionally based. Replying to her protest that she was an "innocent child" when raped, he comments, "I know . . . but girls of fourteen are frequently wives in our Southern climes, where women mature early. A man as supercilious as Will in his pride of Northern birth could take no excuse, and would never forgive" (319). Langley here implies both that southern women are sexually precocious in comparison with northern women and that northern men hold "their" women to higher moral standards than southern men do.

While the South is credited with racial evils and moral impurities, Hopkins does not settle for simply projecting all of the country's evils onto that region: the North may be liberty loving but it also reveals racism deeply inscribed in both its economic and social practices. Thus, while Hopkins structures the novel around a North-South divide, she also articulates a racial divide, calling for unity among blacks, northern and southern, against racist whites nationwide. Ma Smith reminds Dora "that sectional prejudice has always been fostered by the Southern whites among the Negroes to stifle natural feelings of brotherly love among us. Dissension means disunion" (181).

Moreover, in case any reader has missed her point, Hopkins has Ophelia Davis, one of her working-class characters, an ex-slave now enjoying the "liberties" of Boston, compare race relations North and South through a discussion of her ex-employer. Davis comments,

> Lor', chile, but Mis' Mason's a lady borned; she don't know how
> to be like some o' yer Northern people. Sho! these ladies up here

are so 'fraid thet the black'll rub off. Down South the big white
folks has nussed so meny black mammies that they don't know
nuthin' else fer their chillun. It don' matter how black you is ef yer
willin' to keep in the mud. Up here it's diffurunt; you can do all
right and live all right, but don't put yer han' on a white man or
woman, or they'll have a fit fer fear the black'll rub off." (192)

Hopkins delineates the many faces of racism, underscoring that economic and social equality or proximity are not inherently linked: northern blacks might be economically stable while southern blacks lived "in
the mud," but at the same time there might be a greater social distance
between races in the North than in the South.[12]

Hopkins's work shows considerable sophistication as well as a large
measure of compassion in analyzing the "contending forces" at work
against African Americans in both the African American and the Anglo American communities. In her contributions to the *Colored American Magazine* she displays a complex understanding of the ways in
which gender and regional oppressions can cut across race as well as
be inflected by it. An article in Hopkins's "Famous Women of the Negro
Race" series entitled "Club Life among Colored Women," for instance,
chronicles the women's club movement she also writes about in *Contending Forces*. In the article she depicts the white club movement's
betrayal of the black club movement, tracking "the race battle in wom-
en's clubs" (274), as it was played out at the Sixth Biennial of the General Federation of Women's Clubs in Los Angeles, a battle that resulted in a vote which "practically closes the federation to colored clubs"
(275).

Hopkins reads this vote as a result of northern white women defer-
ring to southern white women in order to maintain unity among the
ranks of the white club members. Again resorting to the rhetoric of
liberty, Hopkins claims, "Thrice before in the history of our country
the 'spaniel' North has grovelled before the South, but, thank God, the
time came when the old New England spirit of Puritanism arose and
shook its mane and flung off the shackles of conservatism" (277). The
evocation of the New England "spirit of Puritanism" allows the defense
of a specifically African American female liberty to be subsumed within a more generalized American spirit of independence. Hopkins thus
replaces a vision of regional factions with one of national panracial

unity, which is rhetorically summoned here and elsewhere in *Contending Forces* through images of American patriotism and particularly through the incipient sense of the national identity that provoked the American Revolution.

Hopkins goes beyond this race- and region-based analysis to offer an astute reading of the southern women's motives, a reading that adds gender to the equation and ultimately points to southern white men as a force dividing women, both northern and southern, and Anglo and African American:

> We grant that the Southern woman has given us a terrible blow. . . . Granted conditions are hard for a certain class of Southern white women; but the results of profligacy are the same in any case no matter whether white or black are the partners. Certainly the rapid life of society everywhere at present, among white and black, is not suggestive of absolute purity, and the black is no worse than his environment. . . .
>
> But if this thing [white men sexually exploiting African American women] be true . . . it is but the result of conditions forced upon a helpless people, and not their choice. . . . Meanwhile, tears and sorrow and heart-burning are the Southern white woman's portion and like Sarah of old, she wreaks her vengeance on helpless Hagar. Club life has but rendered her disposition more intolerable toward the victims of her husband's and son's evil passions. (277)

In a tradition dating back at least as far as Harriet Jacobs, Hopkins thus traces southern white women's animosity toward African American women to the system of sexual oppression in which they are both implicated: the "thing" which Hopkins posits as "true" is the fact of white male exploitation of African American women and white women's complicity with white men in the subsequent blaming of the victim. Hopkins's fiction clearly draws on the insight exhibited in this article: the recognition of the complex set of forces—race, region, gender, and their myriad intersections—that determine the shape of late nineteenth-century American racism. She also, however, replicates in *Contending Forces* the hope found in her article, where she characterizes African American women as survivors, exhorting them to hope despite "these sad short-comings" (277).

"Impregnable" Virtue and Mulatto Mothers

In Sappho, she draws a portrait of a victim yet a survivor, a woman who serves as a synthesizing force. For in the end, it is Sappho who is the meeting ground of North and South; Sappho, who is really Mabelle Beaubean; Sappho, who is southern-born but northern-settled; Sappho, who as the victim of southern racial violence is cast as the fallen woman but who also embodies northern purity and liberty; Sappho, who stands for both racial and gender solidarity and reveals the southern white man and the environment that produced him as the true enemy.

In the narrative of Mabelle's rape and its aftermath, Hopkins establishes the complex nexus of forces shaping African American women's identities, drawing race, gender, region, and historical legacy into play on the body of the African American woman. Hazel Carby reads Sappho as Hopkins's "paradigm of the historical rape of black women" (*Reconstructing Womanhood* 138). Viewed in this light Sappho provides the narrative space for the voicing of an African American woman's elided history. Her story not only establishes her as guiltless, "a victim! an innocent child!" (219), but also demands that the African American woman, even the raped, unmarried mulatto mother, be accorded full human and female subject status. This accession to full human female status requires that Sappho come to terms with the historical legacy which at once imposes the erotic and the reproductive functions on the African American female body while at the same time alienating that body from the cultural privileges of the maternal.

After the mulatto child Mabelle is abducted, raped, and left pregnant in a brothel by her white half-uncle, the half-uncle explains himself to the grief-stricken father by stating, "Whatever damage I have done I am willing to pay for. But your child is no better than her mother or her grandmother. What does a woman of mixed blood, or any Negress, for that matter, know of virtue? It is my belief that they were a direct creation by God to be the pleasant companions of men of my race. Now, I am willing to give you a thousand dollars and call it square" (261). This statement quite explicitly follows the ideology of slavery. In its terms, Mabelle "follows the condition" of her mother, a "quadroon" (258), and is to be considered by the white man as chattel, property, not as a human. As a nonwhite woman, she cannot embody the white bourgeois ideal of female virtue but must occupy the space of the lascivious black woman. As such, Mabelle/Sappho is fair game for white male lust, and her half-uncle considers himself exceedingly fair in offering a good price for her virtue. The scene stands as a searing indictment of the sexual politics of slavery and, further, indicates that these sexual politics have outlasted the legal system of slavery in the United States: Sappho's rape, echoing Grace Montfort's symbolic rape, shows that if the laws have changed since the Civil War, the ideological beliefs and investments fueling them have not (for a discussion of Montfort's symbolic rape, see Carby, *Reconstructing Womanhood* 132).

In America, rape is linked to lynching, both historically and in terms of Hopkins's narrative. Alleged rapes of white women by black men served to deflect attention from the real rapes of black women by white men and were used as the justification for lynching black men. Will Smith, Hopkins's Du Bois character and one of her favored mouthpieces, argues that "lynching was instituted to crush the manhood of the enfranchised black. Rape is the crime which appeals most strongly to the heart of the home life. Merciful God! Irony of ironies! *The men who created the mulatto race, who recruit its ranks year after year by the very means which they invoke the lynch law to suppress,* bewailing the sorrows of violated womanhood!" (270–71, emphasis in original). Both lynching and rape operate as acts of racial terrorism, whereby African American men and African American and Anglo American women are kept subservient by the threat of violence: the same violence that reinforces white male privilege (on the use of rape as terrorism, see Hall).

In addition, as a political weapon, rape strips the African American woman of her right to "motherhood," to a voluntary and nonalienated relationship to her offspring, placing her in the same cultural space as her enslaved foremothers. Since the rape of a woman, in the ideological terms of the time, disqualified her from the right to occupy the domestic ideal of true woman and mother, the rape of African American women by white men can be seen not only as a violent denial of their human status but also as a disruption of the African American family. Hopkins counters this use of rape by reworking the notion of redemptive maternity and domesticity. If, as Claudia Tate has argued, marriage was a liberatory event for a newly freed African American people, I would argue that we must also read the creation of a domestic sphere as equally liberatory and radical for the African American woman. Stripped of maternal and familial rights in slavery, the African American woman must of necessity have viewed these rights as more than just a white bourgeois space, so that claiming them could be viewed as a form of empowerment, even if an empowerment strictly within the terms of a middle-class liberal humanism. In this light, Hopkins's use of the seemingly conventional trope of redemptive maternity becomes not so conventional.

Hopkins's original use of the trope employs a predictably Christian rhetoric. When Sappho has been exposed as Mabelle Beaubean by the villain Langley and has fled from Will, she is suddenly struck with regret at her abandonment of her illegitimate son. The narrator tells us that Sappho "fancied . . . that Conscience spoke in condemnation of her neglect of her child. She had felt nothing for the poor waif but repugnance. Her delicate nervous organization was naturally tinged with superstition, and she felt that God had sat in judgment on her willingness to forget her child. . . . At length she rose from that seat resolved that come what would she would claim the child and do her duty as his mother in love and training. She would devote her life to him. They would nevermore be separated" (342). This is a straightforward use of redemptive maternity, an invocation of a moral mother-love and its transformative powers. Indeed, once Sappho acts on this decision, she finds that her "mother-love chased out all the anguish that she had felt over his birth" (346) and that "this new and holy love . . . was the compensation for all she had suffered" (347).

Hopkins codes this redemptive love not merely as imitative of a white woman's model but also as an answer to the disruption of the family effected by slavery. As Sappho reclaims her son from her aunt, the narrator records her thoughts in revealing rhetoric: Sappho "gazed on the innocent face with mingled feelings of sorrow and regret as she thought of the lonely, loveless life of the child. She had been so wicked to put him from her. It was her duty to guide and care for him. She would do her duty without shrinking. . . . She gazed with new-found ecstasy at the rosy face, the dimpled limbs, and thought that *he was hers*. Her feeling of degradation had made her ashamed of the joys of motherhood, of *pride of possession* in her child. But all that feeling was swept away" (344–45, emphasis added).

Although at first glance it looks as if, in putting "him from her," Sappho has unwittingly replicated the separation of slave mothers and their children, a denial of both her motherly rights and duties, in fact there is an important difference between the two acts. Indeed, Sappho can be read here as resisting slavery's model of maternity, for Sappho *chose* to put her son from her, rejecting the white man's child she was forced to bear. She exercises an agency that would not have been possible under slavery and uses it to reject the manifestation of her oppressor's power. Reclaiming her son then becomes a similar act of resistance, since it too is based on choice, a choice Sappho makes to reclaim the child as hers, not her rapist's. Sappho identifies the joys of motherhood as involving "possession," the knowledge that her son is "hers." Thus, she rejects a disenfranchisement of the emotions, claiming her legal, moral, and emotional bonds to her son, the fact that he "belongs" both to and with her. As a result, the novel offers a revised version of motherhood; Sappho reclaims not merely an illegitimate child, but an illegitimate child born of rape. Unchosen maternity—motherhood resulting from rape—is thus transformed from its status as a sign of dispossession. Through reclaiming both her son and her right to occupy the space of the maternal, Sappho transforms unchosen maternity into an assertion of self and kin. The mind/body split caused by the rape—the body creating a child who is rejected by the mind—is thus healed by this new version of maternity, a white bourgeois model of maternity now expanded to include the "fallen woman" and the African American woman. That Hopkins ends her narrative by making Sappho both wife and mother—rewarding her with her destined partner Will—only reinforces Sappho's status as virtuous woman and her place within her new family structure.

Yet a discourse of maternal "possession" in this context must also raise the specter of the slave-owners' "possession" of the slave. Critics such as Spillers and Tate have argued that the structural lack of the black father under slavery and his replacement by the white slave-owner have had profound implications for the notion of "family" among African Americans (Spillers 66, 80; Tate, "Allegories" 121). Accordingly, Tate concludes that "the mother's law is dominant" (121), a reading that certainly describes the privileged status of motherhood in *Contending Forces*. The absence of the all-powerful patriarchal father visibly changes the nature of the family: the Smith family, even when all its long-lost members are reunited at the novel's close, contains no fathers.[13] This absence, Tate suggests, "diminishes the importance of excessive patriarchal demands for feminine piety, purity and property, as well as mitigates feminine prescripts for absolute deference to male authority" (121), both of which reinforce an increased maternal power. But if this new version of motherhood is privileged, it is also by virtue of its power potentially dangerous, a position of authority that might be either used or abused. The lingering linguistic traces of slavery in Hopkins's description of maternity might thus be read as a warning, a caution against the misuse of a newly acquired power. We might also read it as a reminder that the liberatory force of claiming the white bourgeois family structure grows out of an embodied, historically specific position: in post–Civil War America, the family, for African Americans, offers radical possibilities, but possibilities that carry the weight of other times and spaces wherein the family operates as a conservative or even oppressive structure.

There are thus several levels of discourse occurring simultaneously in Hopkins's discussion of the strong African American mother. She refigures a white bourgeois model of true womanhood in two ways, by taking the "others" against whom this model defines itself and incorporating them into the model. She expands the notion of true womanhood to include both the "fallen woman" (the true woman's polar opposite in terms of class and sexual purity) and the African American woman (the model's opposite in racial terms). While Hopkins remains within the white bourgeois discourse on womanhood, her recasting of the strong mother as an African American "fallen woman" uses a bourgeois model to radical ends and marks a step forward in the representation of African American female identity. At the same time, however, this challenge to dominant gender ideologies can and has been appropriated by the dominant culture and used against African American women. For in a culture that privileges the father (both symbolic and literal), a family structure that lacks a father and offers a strong mother is criticized or dismissed or even, as, for instance, in the *Moynihan Report*, used to produce the stereotype of the superpowerful emasculating African American woman.[14]

Thus, while Hopkins's "Romance . . . of Negro Life North and South" works for the "uplift" of her race in general, it also concentrates more specifically on refiguring African American female identity. Inheriting a veritable national thesaurus of terms for black and white womanhood, Hopkins reclaims both passion and virtue for the African American woman. By redefining both passion and virtue in terms that relocate them within, rather than at odds with, conventional notions of "pure" womanhood, Hopkins both affirms the human status of her African American female subject and appropriates on her behalf a reworked version of maternity and family. By using the sentimental novel to confront the historical effects of rape on African American female identity, Hopkins powerfully refocuses sentimentalism's categories of home, family, domesticity, and marital love, and locates a new version of female desire within these terms. Spillers looks to the future by stating, "Actually *claiming* the monstrosity (of a female with the potential to 'name'), which her culture imposes in blindness, 'Sapphire' might rewrite after all a radically different text for female empowerment" (80), a comment implying that African American women might finally be able to claim a space in discourse, articulating their own lives and selves rather than being the object represented by someone else's narrative. Hopkins, by reworking the sentimental novel to provide a space for Sappho, begins to do just that.

NOTES

I would like to thank Eva Cherniavsky, Catherine Gallagher, Anne Goldman, Sandra Gunning, Lori Merrish, Carolyn Porter, Judith Rosen, and the members of my autumn 1992 English 390 seminar for help in thinking through the issues in this article.

1. Spillers has done some of the most important work to date on theorizing black women's subjectivity, and her argument significantly informs this essay. I am grateful to Victoria Smith for her extremely helpful discussion of this text and my argument as a whole.

2. Thus, the black woman occupied a space in the nineteenth-century white middle-class American imagination analogous to that of the prostitute in the nineteenth-century white middle-class British imagination. For a further discussion of stereotypes of black women as they appeared specifically in fiction, see Christian, *Black Women Novelists,* and Carby *Reconstructing Womanhood.* For more on Victorian Britain's "angel in the house," the middle-class white lady of leisure who stood as the dominant ideology's ideal woman, see, for example, Vicinus, *Suffer and Be Still,* and *A Widening Sphere.* For an analysis of the more literary effects of such a construct, see Gilbert and Gubar, *The Madwoman in the Attic.* For discussions of the American version of this gender ideal and its ideological function, see Cott, *The Bonds of Womanhood,* and Welter, "The Cult of True Womanhood."

3. The mulatto was, of course, a character frequently invoked in postbellum fiction by both black and white writers, a figure whose "mixed blood" seemed to literalize the cultural dilemma of how the two races were to coexist in America. The mulatto was seen by nineteenth-century readers as embody-

ing the possibility of racial intermingling or even, in the hysterical "plantation fiction" of Thomas Dixon, for instance, the possibility of a "threat" by African Americans to white cultural hegemony.

As William L. Andrews frames the issue, to "countenance miscegenation or the relaxation of political, economic, or social barriers to it was to threaten the principle of racial purity on which not only Southern race pride but social and political order in the post-war South were based," with the result that "the issue of black rights did not come down to a matter of abstract politics but rather of sexual politics in which miscegenation became the ultimate political act of triumph for blacks over the restraints of Southern civilization" (14). Andrews's statement points out that miscegenation was itself a symptom of racial conflict coded in sexual terms. In its most virulent application, post-Reconstruction white supremacists used the threat of miscegenation as justification for the lynching of black men, by means of a redefinition of miscegenation in terms of black male rape of white women. Thus, postbellum white supremacists transferred the site of miscegenation from its historical origin—the rape of slave and ex-slave black women by white men, before, during, and after the Civil War—to a new site, a phantasmagorical site on which dangerous postbellum black men ravished white southern womanhood in an effort to topple white power, while mulattos "passed" as white in order to infiltrate and corrupt white society.

4. For charges of assimilation in *Contending Forces,* see Bone, *The Negro Novel;* Elder, *The "Hindered Hand";* Campbell, *Mythic Black Fiction;* and Bruce, *Black American Writing.* Brooks's afterword to *Contending Forces* comes to mind here as an example of what I would read as a historically grounded misreading of Hopkins's text. That is, Brooks, speaking out of the historical context of 1978, charges Hopkins with "assimilationist urges" (437), as well as "a touching reliance on the dazzles and powers of anticipated integration" (434). And while she grants that Hopkins "was understandably a daughter of her time" (436), she criticizes what she sees as Hopkins's lack of anger and cites Hopkins's use of a mulatto heroine as evidence that Hopkins "consistently proves herself a continuing slave, despite little bursts of righteous heat" (434). While Brooks's reading of Hopkins might be used to support an argument that Hopkins had internalized some of her culture's racism, Brooks's holding Hopkins to the standards and issues of the 1970s rather than Hopkins's own time does a disservice to Hopkins's work. For charges of "nonrealism" or sentimentalism, see Loggins, *The Negro Author;* Gloster, *Negro Voices;* and Bone, *The Negro Novel.*

5. The sentimental novel, of course, should be read as both radical and limited or generically constrained. As a genre, this "domestic fiction" was used by nineteenth-century American writers to lay claims to (among other things) female spheres and powers, a radical cultural intervention in terms of gender

roles. At the same time, however, these spheres and powers were absolutely middle-class and participated in the consolidation of middle-class cultural hegemony—hardly a radical undertaking. Thus, while it is important to collapse Yarborough's (and others') dichotomy between sentimental and political novels, it is also important to remember that "political" can mean many (conflicting) things at once.

6. For extremely helpful readings of Hopkins's later "magazine fiction," see Ammons, *Conflicting Stories;* and Tate, *Domestic Allegories* (chap. 7).

7. Gloster points out that in plantation fiction "the Mixed blood is portrayed as the embodiment of the worst qualities of both races and hence a menace to the dominant group. To these propagandists the mulatto woman is the debaser of the white aristocrat, while the mulatto man is the besmircher of white virginity" (12). Thomas Dixon and Thomas Page, for instance, two of the most important authors of the plantation school, conflated the racial with the sexual to figure black men and women as animalistic and inferior to the white man.

8. Between 1900 and 1904, Hopkins served as editor of the Women's Department, literary editor, and, evidence suggests, unacknowledged editor-in-chief of *CAM*. For details of her involvement at *CAM,* see Campbell, "Hopkins"; Lamping, "Hopkins"; Shockley, "Hopkins"; Carby, Introduction; Johnson and Johnson, *Propaganda and Aesthetics;* and Braithwaite, "Negro America's First Magazine."

9. Harriet Jacobs makes an analogous political use of sentimental conventions, although she employs them within the slave narrative.

10. Boston marriages, a phenomenon of late nineteenth-century America, took their name from the popular perception that they flourished in Boston, although historical evidence suggests that they existed all over America. Romantic friendships between two women, Boston marriages were long-term relationships viewed by the women involved as their primary emotional commitments. Some involved physical erotic love while others involved a more spiritual notion of love. Although Hopkins does not fully develop the relationship between Dora and Sappho, her statement that Sappho fills a "long-felt want" in Dora's life as well as her choice of Sappho as the name of her heroine suggests a homoerotic bond between the two women. This bond might be read as yet another way in which Hopkins refigures both African American female identity and representations of African American female desire. For more on Boston marriages, see Faderman, *Surpassing the Love of Men.*

11. While Hopkins clearly portrays southern racism as more overtly violent than the economic racism of the North, she certainly chronicles northern racism. The white racist Colonel Clapp, for instance, tells John Langley that he never hires African American clerks, claiming, "I have had a number of your best men tried in clerical positions, and you always fail to compete favorably

with an ordinary white clerk. You can't ask the people to pay for ignorant incompetents" (232).

12. Hopkins's choice of Ophelia Davis as the speaker here underscores her point: as an ex-slave now occupying the place of a working-class free northern woman, Davis would be able to make an informed comparison of northern and southern life. While Richard Yarborough, in his introduction to *Contending Forces,* argues that "Hopkins's own elitist views mar her treatment of lower-class black characters like Sarah Ann White and Ophelia Davis" (xli), I would suggest that Davis (and to a lesser extent White) plays an important role in the novel and, ultimately, occupies a position of respect, providing yet another representation of a strong, autonomous African American woman. She beats out her church rival in a spirited fashion, and it is she who takes over Ma Smith's boardinghouse when Ma Smith gives it up to go live with Dora and her new husband at the novel's close.

13. Of course Will, as the husband of Hopkins's model African American family of the future, does figure as a symbolic or adoptive father to Sappho's child, but Hopkins leaves this relationship totally unexplored.

14. As a white feminist reading Hopkins, I believe it is crucial to remain aware both of her radical use of the figure of the mother and of the ways in which dominant culture has both romanticized this figure and turned it against African American women, attempting to recontain its radical potential. Contemporary uses of the stereotype of the powerful black matriarch conflate racial and gender attacks by casting the African American matriarch as too powerful (i.e., masculine) and, consequently, casting the absent African American patriarch as powerless (i.e., emasculated or feminized), so that the African American woman simultaneously becomes a threat to both African American and white culture. For an extremely perceptive reading of the effects of the *Moynihan Report* on contemporary American constructions of African American female subjectivity, see Spillers, "Mama's Baby."

WORKS CITED

Ammons, Elizabeth. *Conflicting Stories: American Women Writers at the Turn into the Twentieth Century.* New York: Oxford University Press, 1991.

Andrews, William L. "Miscegenation in the Late Nineteenth-Century Novel." *Southern Humanities Review* 13.1 (1979): 13–23.

Baker, Houston A., Jr. *Workings of the Spirit: The Poetics of Afro-American Women's Writing.* Chicago: University of Chicago Press, 1991.

Bone, Robert A. *The Negro Novel in America.* New Haven, Conn.: Yale University Press, 1958.

Braithwaite, William Stanley. "Negro America's First Magazine." *Negro Digest* 6.2 (Dec. 1947): 21–26.

Brooks, Gwendolyn. Afterword. *Contending Forces*. By Pauline Hopkins. 1900. Carbondale: Southern Illinois University Press, 1978. 433–37.

Bruce, Dickson D. *Black American Writing from the Nadir: The Evolution of a Literary Tradition, 1877–1915*. Baton Rouge: Louisiana State University Press, 1989.

Campbell, Jane. *Mythic Black Fiction: The Transformation of History*. Knoxville: University of Tennessee Press, 1986.

———. "Pauline Elizabeth Hopkins." In *Afro-American Writers Before the Harlem Renaissance*. Vol. 50 of *Dictionary of Literary Biography*. Ed. Trudier Harris and Thadius M. Davis. Detroit, Mich.: Gale Research, 1984. 182–89.

Carby, Hazel V. Introduction. *The Magazine Novels of Pauline Hopkins*. By Hopkins. New York: Oxford University Press, 1988. xxix-l.

———. *Reconstructing Womanhood: The Emergence of the Afro-American Woman Novelist*. New York: Oxford University Press, 1987.

Christian, Barbara. *Black Women Novelists: The Development of a Tradition, 1892–1976*. Westport, Conn.: Greenwood Press, 1980.

Cott, Nancy F. *The Bonds of Womanhood: "Woman's Sphere" in New England, 1780–1835*. New Haven, Conn.: Yale University Press, 1977.

Dearborn, Mary V. *Pocahontas's Daughters: Gender and Ethnicity in American Culture*. New York: Oxford University Press, 1986.

Elder, Arlene. *The "Hindered Hand": Cultural Implications of Early African-American Fiction*. Westport, Conn.: Greenwood Press, 1978.

Faderman, Lillian. *Surpassing the Love of Men: Romantic Friendship and Love between Women from the Renaissance to the Present*. New York: Morrow, 1981.

Fetterley, Judith. Introduction. *Provisions: A Reader from 19th-Century American Women*. Ed. Judith Fetterley. Bloomington: Indiana University Press, 1985. 1–40.

Gilbert, Sandra, and Susan Gubar. *The Madwoman in the Attic: The Woman Writer and the Nineteenth-Century Imagination*. New Haven, Conn.: Yale University Press, 1979.

Gloster, Hugh M. *Negro Voices in American Fiction*. Chapel Hill: University of North Carolina Press, 1948.

Hall, Jacquelyn Dowd. "'The Mind that Burns in Each Body': Women, Rape, and Racial Violence." In *Powers of Desire*. Ed. Ann Snitow, Christine Stansell, and Sharon Thompson. New York: Monthly Review Press, 1983. 328–49.

Hopkins, Pauline E. "Club Life among Colored Women." *Colored American Magazine*, Aug. 1902, 273–77.

———. *Contending Forces: A Romance Illustrative of Negro Life North and South*. 1900. New York: Oxford University Press, 1988.

Johnson, Abby Arthur, and Ronald Maberry Johnson. *Propaganda and Aesthetics: The Literary Politics of Afro-American Magazines in the Twentieth Century.* Amherst: University of Massachusetts Press, 1979.

Lamping, Marilyn. "Pauline Elizabeth Hopkins." In *American Women Writers: A Critical Reference Guide from Colonial Times to the Present.* Vol. 2. Ed. Linda Mainiero. New York: Frederick Ungar, 1980. 325–27.

Loggins, Vernon. *The Negro Author: His Development in American to 1900.* New York: Columbia University Press, 1931.

McDowell, Deborah E. "'The Changing Same': Generational Connections and Black Women Novelists." *New Literary History* 18 (Winter 1987): 281–302.

Samuels, Shirley. Introduction. *The Culture of Sentiment: Race, Gender, and Sentimentality in Nineteenth-Century America.* Ed. Shirley Samuels. New York: Oxford University Press, 1992. 3–8.

Shockley, Ann Allen. "Pauline Elizabeth Hopkins: A Biographical Excursion into Obscurity." *Phylon* 33 (Spring 1972): 22–26.

Smith-Rosenberg, Carroll. "The Female World of Love and Ritual: Relations between Women in Nineteenth-Century America." In *Disorderly Conduct: Visions of Gender in Victorian America.* New York: Alfred A. Knopf, 1985. 53–76.

Spillers, Hortense J. "Mama's Baby, Papa's Maybe: An American Grammar Book." *diacritics* 17.2 (Summer 1987): 65–81.

Tate, Claudia. "Allegories of Black Female Desire; or, Rereading Nineteenth-Century Sentimental Narratives of Black Female Authority." In *Changing Our Own Words: Essays on Criticism, Theory, and Writing by Black Women.* Ed. Cheryl A. Wall. New Brunswick, N.J.: Rutgers University Press, 1989. 98–126.

———. *Domestic Allegories of Political Desire: The Black Heroine's Text at the Turn of the Century.* New York: Oxford University Press, 1992.

———. "Pauline Hopkins: Our Literary Foremother." In *Conjuring: Black Women, Fiction, and Literary Tradition.* Ed. Marjorie Pryse and Hortense J. Spillers. Bloomington: Indiana University Press, 1985. 53–66.

Tompkins, Jane P. *Sensational Designs: The Cultural Work of American Fiction, 1790–1860.* New York: Oxford University Press, 1985.

———. "Sentimental Power: *Uncle Tom's Cabin* and the Politics of Literary History." In *The New Feminist Criticism: Essays on Women, Literature, and Theory.* Ed. Elaine Showalter. New York: Pantheon, 1985. 81–104.

Vicinus, Martha, ed. *Suffer and Be Still: Women in the Victorian Age.* Bloomington: Indiana University Press, 1972.

———. *A Widening Sphere: Changing Roles of Victorian Women.* Bloomington: Indiana University Press, 1977.

Washington, Mary Helen. *Invented Lives: Narratives of Black Women, 1860–1960.* Garden City, N.Y.: Anchor, 1987.

Welter, Barbara. "The Cult of True Womanhood: 1820–1860," *American Quarterly* 18 (Summer 1966): 151–74.

Yarborough, Richard. Introduction. *Contending Forces*. By Hopkins. xxvii–xlviii.

TWO

"To Allow No Tragic End":
Defensive Postures in
Pauline Hopkins's *Contending Forces*

LOIS LAMPHERE BROWN

On August 25, 1899, after more than fifteen years' leave from a high-ly visible playwriting and public performance career in Boston and the New England area, Pauline Hopkins registered a copyright for her first novel, *Contending Forces: A Romance Illustrative of Negro Life North and South*. Like many of the short stories and serialized novels that Hopkins would soon write for the Boston-based *Colored American Magazine* (*CAM*), *Contending Forces* addressed two frequently dis-cussed issues of the time: the repercussions of racially motivated sexu-al violence against women of African descent and the attempts of Af-rican Americans to build and defend a cohesive family. As Hopkins imposes these two signature concerns of nineteenth-century African Americans upon the sentimental novel form, she radically alters the form in a number of ways. One of the most apparent changes occurs when Hopkins attempts to integrate female empowerment and domes-tic goals with the ambitions and prerogatives of the central male char-acter. As a result of her revisionary efforts, Hopkins creates new liber-ating paradigms of female empowerment and male self-realization.

In this essay, I will focus on the ways in which Hopkins's consider-ations of African American female sexuality, sexual trauma, and racial uplift lead her to modify not only entrenched Anglo American symbols of sentimental female power but also rigid social codes governing fe-male desirability, permissible sexual histories, and the extent to which that history may be made manifest. In closing, I will discuss the mod-ernized male narrative that emerges in Hopkins's racially progressive rendering of the sentimental novel form. Like the female narrative centered around Sappho Clark, Hopkins's male narrative also subverts conventional codes that govern behavior and dictate one's racial place and inherent allegiances. In *Contending Forces,* Will Smith, the mixed-race male who alternately symbolizes the bourgeois social and educational potential of African Americans, is not an errant young man but a dutiful son who is in complete harmony with his female-governed household. The harmonious relations sustain the central, though tempered, matricentric influence of Smith's mother and sister. Though Smith is undoubtedly the hero of this text, his role as such is predicated upon his mother's history and interracial legacy. Often woman-authored texts in the sentimental tradition require that the hero must undergo social and religious conversion, a process usually conducted by the young woman upon whom the mantle of female power is being transferred. Hopkins nullifies that potential source of conflict and swiftly reorients the African American matriarchy, its concerns, and domestic achievements toward an empowering, ennobling European patriarchal origin.

In *Contending Forces,* Hopkins refashions the sentimental form so that it does not impinge upon her configurations of race, subjectivity, and female agency. As a result, race and gender become extremely malleable, metamorphic entities. Hopkins deems such fluidity and spontaneity essential, especially if the enigmatic mixed-race woman is to be saved from her past sexual abuse and if the abiding threats to her womanhood are to be contained. In the male narrative, the consistent advancement and levels of success achieved by Will Smith constitute an impressive metamorphosis into manhood. Through the evolutions of Sappho Clark, Will Smith, and the Smith family, Hopkins gives life to and endorses a dramatic transformative history—one that offers a set of stirring alternatives within the domains of American sentimental fiction in general and the African American sentimental tradition in particular.

* * *

> She would rise above maddening fears, penance for involuntary wrongs, the sack-cloth and ashes of her life, and be as other women who loved and were beloved.

> Poor soul! poor starved and storm beaten heart! Something of life that was dead leaped again into existence and loosened the icy hand that had for years locked

up the fountain of youthful joy. She felt drawn out of
herself.
      —PAULINE HOPKINS, *Contending Forces*, 1900

The central female figure of *Contending Forces* is Sappho Clark, a
mysterious mixed-race woman whose physical beauty and aura en-
trances many of the people she meets in late nineteenth-century Boston. Yet behind Sappho's charming demeanor, independence, and per-
spicacity lies a tragic tale of childhood abuse. As a young girl of fifteen,
she was abducted by her mulatto father's white half-brother who raped,
imprisoned, and abandoned her in a southern brothel. Ultimately, a
child was born of the rape. By the time the young girl appears in Boston, she has assumed the new name of Sappho Clark, and there are
enough details to hint at the great pains she has taken to elude her past,
forestall social censure, and otherwise survive that awful experience.
Hopkins suggests that Sappho's narrative is, by virtue of Victorian codes
about sexuality, one that cannot be disclosed. Replete with her experiences of torture, displacement, bereavement, salvation, relocation, and
secrecy, Sappho's life story is posited as an encapsulated text, which is
surrounded by the trappings and fixtures of a reinvented self and new
life that she continues to make for herself. It then follows that Sappho
must retain the shroud of secrecy about both the figure of Mabelle
Beaubean, the defenseless young female subject who endured the horrible events, and the modernized figure of Sappho Clark who has been
generated in response to those events.

One of the chief tensions in *Contending Forces* arises because Sappho Clark attempts to contain her volatile past. Hopkins complicates
Sappho's life even further by transforming Sappho's narrative from a
psychological script into an embodied text—the chief sign of which is
Sappho's illegitimate son Alphonse. The politics of self-representation
become increasingly pertinent to Sappho as other subplots of *Contending Forces* introduce community-based social and religious projects,
women's advancement, and public forums convened to protest racial
violence. Sappho has access to women's groups, moves in the same
circles as dedicated churchgoers and local ministers, and attends public meetings on lynching. Her story, a firsthand account of racially
motivated sexual abuse, incest, and illegitimacy, as well as mob violence and lynching, is in principle the master text to the very groups in
which she moves.

Hopkins writes within a tradition in which African American authors often dedicate their texts to the uplift of the race and reform of the nation. In fact, the opening lines of Hopkins's preface, in which she explains that she publishes *Contending Forces* "to do all that I can in an humble way to raise the stigma of degradation from my race" (13), seem eerily pertinent to Sappho's situation. Given Hopkins's own authorial dedication, Sappho's "text" is one that Hopkins could rightfully appropriate and that Sappho's African American community in Boston could use to fuel its various racial protests and reform efforts. Yet, as we shall see, Hopkins refrains from making what would be in this case an aggressive move. The life story that Hopkins unveils links the explicit nature of Sappho's adolescent experience with not only her dogged efforts to survive the ordeal but also the potential aftermath of cultural shame as well as her personal shame and anguish. For Hopkins to use Sappho's past as a lesson in the present would, based on Hopkins's preferred method of gradual disclosure, constitute another unfeeling and ruthless violation. Sappho would once again become an unwilling racial subject. Yet because Sappho's story is central to Hopkins's text about African American sexual history and racial progress, it must be told.

Hopkins solves this dilemma of Sappho's private anguish and what she deems to be the public's need to know by encapsulating it within a compromise—in this case, the arena of compromised race politics. After news of another violent southern lynching of an African American man reaches Boston, the executive committee of the American Colored League convenes a public forum for its concerned African American members in the New England area. The speakers scheduled to address the crowd include a prominent, coercive white judge named Clapp; the mixed-race villain of the story, John Langley; Dr. Arthur Lewis, whose speech is modeled after the accommodationist recommendations of Booker T. Washington; and Sappho's sweetheart and the hero of the text, Will Smith. The first three men defend particular American "institutions" such as sectionalism, separatist structures of class based on race, the South's sanction of sexual abuse of women of color, and the right to continued agitation about race issues. The disappointing contributions of Judge Clapp, Dr. Lewis, and John Langley are dismissed by the narrator and endured by the audience. Before the last speaker, Will Smith, can address the group, a man rises from the audience and is invited to take the stage and address the crowd.

A man of "very black complexion" (254) whose bearing induces the narrator to think that he "might have been a Cromwell, a Robespierre, a Lincoln" (255), Luke Sawyer testifies about two violent episodes that he witnessed and survived as a young man in the South. The second story he shares is the tale of Mabelle Beaubean. It was Sawyer who rescued Mabelle from the brothel and, after the half-brother's assault on her family's home following her rescue, it was Sawyer who took Mabelle to a convent in New Orleans where she bore her illegitimate son, Alphonse. Will Smith, the next and final speaker, is unaware that Luke Sawyer has just resurrected and reported the early life of his sweetheart Sappho Clark. In righteous tones, Smith summarily characterizes the young girl's experience of interracial and incestuous sexual relations as a crime of prejudice. He then segues into a much less personalized debate about interracial sexual relations. It is now that his noble rhetoric emerges, and he defines such relations as a "social crime" and lambasts those African Americans who regard interracial union as a tool for class advancement.

Having fainted upon hearing Sawyer's testimony, Sappho is no longer part of the crowd as it applauds Smith's strident maxims and call for racial solidarity. Her absence is important to note, especially since it suggests that Smith has yet to consider, or see, the realities of the philosophy he espouses. Though his address moves the crowd to tears, his remarks seriously diminish American slavery's legacy of sexual violence directed against women of African descent. It is here that the tortures inflicted upon Grace Montfort, Smith's great-grandmother, take on even greater significance. Hazel Carby was the first to read the whipping of Grace as a metaphorical rape; if we follow Carby's reading, we can see that Smith may have to grapple with overwhelming generational female distress. Not only has his love interest suffered a brutal sexual assault, but Smith is himself distantly related to such distress. Within the African American community, Sappho and her story are appropriated for political purposes—her story and then her body is subjected to the gaze and interpretation of others. Smith's remarks fail to offer her any adequate political or rhetorical defense some fifteen years after her assault. As a result of her story's disclosure, and, one could argue, its unwitting dismissal by Smith, she is eventually threatened with new sexual compromise and forced to flee Boston and abandon the life she had established for herself there. The legacy of sexual compromise, illicit desire, and dishonored family bonds is thus revisited upon the Smith family through Sappho, the most likely woman to continue the Mont-fort-Smith family line.

* * *

In writing Sappho Clark's story, Hopkins challenges those nineteenth-century white American authors who Nina Baym identifies as "unwilling to accept, and unwilling to permit their readers to accept, a conception of women as inevitable sexual prey" and who, in genteel fashion, "insisted that male-female relations could be conducted on a plane that allowed for feelings other than lust" (26). As Hopkins and her African American female peers alter this principal feature of nineteenth-century women's writing, other essential characteristics of the Anglo American form become problematic and are replaced by more pertinent racial realities. For instance, a mixed-race woman like Sappho may be revered for her angelic nature and apparent purity, but Hopkins suggests that this image and its accompanying esteem are temporary. Even though the Smiths do not lose respect for Sappho after they learn of her tragic circumstances, Sappho flees from their house, believing that she will only bring shame to her sweetheart Will Smith, who has recently proposed marriage. After recounting Sappho's blackmail by a lustful John Langley, her sudden departure from the Smith household, and the Smiths' dismay at discovering her true circumstances, Hopkins's narrator makes a dreary philosophical pronouncement: "We may right a wrong, but we cannot restore our victim to his [*sic*] primeval state of happiness. Something is lost that can never be regained. The wages of sin is death. Innocent or guilty, the laws of nature are immutable" (332). The compelling image of purity that is a "natural" part of the white heroine's destiny often looms as wishful thinking for the mixed-race heroine. What is a privileged, unquestioned, and fiercely introverted reality for white heroines is a battle against entrenched political and social doctrine for women of African descent.

The Anglo American sentimental novel is especially powerful in its redefinition of young women as the individuals best trained to save both the men they love and the domestic matriarchy to which they belong. The image of the delicate and pious sentimental heroine conflates virginal purity with a steely moral strength. The establishment of domestic matriarchy, ideals of "true womanhood," and neatly resolved endings are among the chief characteristics of the popular nineteenth-century sentimental novel and romance. As the cult of true womanhood emerged, the sentimental form began to evolve and the seduction plot, central to early texts such as Susanna Rowson's *Charlotte Temple,* subsequently fell away. Emerging instead were conservative codes with rigid directives for female behavior. Underlying these directives were visionary domestic guidelines meant to maximize a female influence based within the home. The Anglo American sentimental novel form espouses an empowered domestic and matrifocal arena that results in movement toward interiority for the heroine. Though the heroine's self is emerging and being nurtured, her development is geared toward containment, within both domestic politics and influence, and marriage and its ensuing responsibilities. Baym asserts that "by the novel's end, [the white heroine] has developed a strong conviction of her own worth as a result of which she does ask much from herself. She can meet her own demands and inevitably, the change in herself has changed the world's attitude toward her so that much that was formerly denied her now comes to her unsought" (19). The dominant Anglo American form of the sentimental novel denotes a social and cultural utopia that central female characters of early African American literature cannot achieve.

The African American sentimental narrative tradition, with which Hopkins has been associated, values some of the principal aspects of the Anglo American form—namely, modesty and virtue, though the latter is often more in principle, owing to the awful slavery experiences of many African Americans. Religious practice, domestic order, organized communities, and adherence to traditional family roles are also central to these texts. Portions of these African American "narratives of liberation" (Tate, "Allegories" 107) are decidedly optimistic. Authors urge their readers to believe that the race could sustain an economic, educational, and psychological recovery from slavery. As we shall see, however, Hopkins suggests a more pessimistic scenario for individuals of African descent in postslavery America. Hopkins's reconfiguration of the white sentimental form not only requires extreme resourcefulness from its marginalized female character but pushes the character to highly imaginative enterprises and willful reinterpretations of the social order. In *Contending Forces,* Hopkins challenges the propriety and design of both white and African American sentimental forms when she boldly reconstructs episodes of sexual abuse inflicted upon women of African descent.

Like Harriet Jacobs and Frances E. W. Harper, Hopkins uses the sentimental novel form to address issues such as the sexual exploitation of female slaves, the pervasive practice of lynching, the difficulties of life for mixed-race individuals in both slavery and postslavery American society, and the need for postslavery programs of uplift within African American communities. Yet, unlike Jacobs's and Harper's narratives, the victimized female character in Hopkins's works is increasingly removed from African American communities such as the one Sappho joins in Boston. Indeed, Sappho is a woman who survives her trauma and is enterprising enough to attempt to make a future for herself. Yet she is also a woman who is haunted by her past, which is presented as capable of endangering Sappho's new identity and preventing her from ever fully joining an African American community. In an attempt to save her, Hopkins must distance Sappho from her abusive emotional, physical, and psychological childhood experience. In doing so, Hopkins increasingly suggests that mobility is simply not enough if Sappho is to maintain her hard-won state of recovered grace and apparent virtue.

Within the white sentimental design, an African American woman would not be able to exert a powerful female influence if there was even the slightest hint of sexual impropriety on her part or within her family history. Moreover, unlike their fictional white counterparts, nineteenth-century African American female characters would not likely be members of any kind of honorable and empowering family bond. Sappho is not a member of the close-knit Smith family but that is quickly rectified. She soon becomes more than a tenant in their boarding house—she is swiftly embraced as friend and confidante. After some seemingly insurmountable circumstances are set aside, by the novel's end she also becomes wife and daughter. Nonetheless, Sappho's intimacy with the Smiths cannot erase the fact that she is an orphan, that she lost her family to racially motivated mob violence, and that, for an extended period of her past, she could not acknowledge her son because she found his birth heinous, shameful, and otherwise problematic. In Hopkins's text, tragic circumstances threaten the female character with severe isolation. Indeed, the circumstances of the female's distress become insurmountable within the traditional sentimental paradigm: the redemptive promise of the Anglo American scenario is obscured by the shameful alienation of Hopkins's African American sentimental heroine.

In many nineteenth- and turn-of-the-century African American narratives, the heroine is threatened with sexual compromise, never recov-

ers from the shame of such compromise, fears that her community and/
or family will exile her, or refuses to ever fully admit the details. In her
works, Hopkins emphasizes that African American women are besieged
in ways that exceed the parameters allowed by the Anglo American
sentimental form. Both self-expression and self-determination, two
components closely monitored within the white sentimental form, are
more likely to be choked by the African American woman's undying
and traumatic past. Dianthe Lusk in Hopkins's *Of One Blood* (1902–
3) and Marie Leroy in Frances E. W. Harper's *Iola Leroy* (1892) both
suffer from the weight of their unexpressed mental anguish. Yet in *Contending Forces* and in Harriet Jacobs's *Incidents in the Life of a Slave
Girl* (1861), we see two female characters committed to not only re-
covering their voices but preserving their bodies as well. Although this
type of self-awareness may suggest a wholly independent female figure,
Linda Brent and the troubled women of Hopkins's texts rely heavily
on others for their recovery.

The traumatized mixed-race women that Hopkins places in the foreground of her works have often endured rape, the birth of illegitimate
children, rejection in love relationships, and the destruction of their
immediate families. Hopkins does not automatically empower these
women, as the white and African American forms of the sentimental
novel often do, nor does she offer these mixed-race women futures that
satisfactorily contain their horrible pasts. Instead, Hopkins grants their
pasts a formidable primacy that constantly threatens their new lives,
love interests, and self-development. As these characters contemplate
the stigma of their pasts and imagine the social prejudice that they will
likely endure in white and African American circles, they are further
driven into an induced interiority. The more unfortunate women in
"Talma Gordon," *Hagar's Daughter,* and other of Hopkins's works
may seem to be on the brink of rescue but their circumstances become
increasingly bewildering; they are exiled, silenced, or driven to death.

Some of Hopkins's central female characters, such as Sappho Clark,
are given the chance to counter such unabating, debilitating introspec-
tion. They are offered bodily protection and legitimate social standing
by men who have considered their own potential ruin and married the
women nonetheless. Although women such as Sappho, Hagar Enson
in *Hagar's Daughter,* and others are rescued and then ensconced within an exclusive, self-sufficient group, Hopkins's characters neither turn
to nor receive this protection from African American communities. In

addition, they do not invest themselves in the programs of uplift found in many nineteenth-century African American women's sentimental narratives. Unlike other African American women writers of the time, Hopkins denies her American mixed-race characters the strength derived from immersion in work relating to racial uplift. Although Claudia Tate has recently suggested that Sappho is indeed a part of essential race work within the African American community, she also recognizes the limitations of Sappho's public contributions. According to Tate, Sappho is "an important though subtle political mouthpiece" whose voice is "restricted to private space, preventing her penetration into the public sphere of influence" (*Domestic Allegories* 161).

Like Sappho, other Hopkins characters are unable to penetrate "the public sphere of influence" that Tate refers to. Talma of the 1900 short story "Talma Gordon," Judah of *Winona* (1902), Dianthe Lusk and her mother Mira in *Of One Blood* (1902–3), and Luke Sawyer of *Contending Forces* (1900) are individuals whose experiences legitimize the concerns of the "public sphere" yet whose narratives are denied the agency and social power that they rightly deserve. Like Sappho, these individuals have endured racially induced physical and sexual violence during slavery or the post-Reconstruction years. In addition, these male and female characters are willing to challenge prevailing patriarchal law through military aggression, espionage, and emotionally charged testimony when necessary. Yet, men such as Judah and Luke Sawyer, who have personally opposed slavery and attempted to counter its sanctioned aggression, have limited access to the African American public and never achieve legitimate leadership positions within American or African American society.

Dianthe Lusk, her mother Mira, and Talma experience slavery and its abiding stigma in ways that seem to impede their entry into public campaigns for justice as well. Sappho's ability to speak, create a new identity for herself, and be self-sufficient is in stark contrast to the more beleaguered, disqualified male and female candidates for community leadership positions in *Contending Forces* and Hopkins's later works. Yet, the success that Hopkins allows Sappho is tempered by Sappho's past, an uncontained, unresolved narrative. Like Mira in *Of One Blood*, Sappho's sexual trauma could become a heinous American legacy, part of a perverted matricentric American history. The tragic southern experiences of Grace Montfort and her distant descendant by marriage Sappho Clark suggest that there is a legacy of sexual abuse, a tragic female history that will be continually reenacted in America. The failure of characters to construct viable postslavery African American racial identities in America thus becomes a recurring and distinctive motif in the works of Pauline Hopkins.

In *Contending Forces,* one episode in particular clearly illustrates Hopkins's belief that certain forms of abuse endured by women of African descent are simply not compatible with African American communities intent on postslavery success. As a single woman, Sappho becomes a candidate for the regimented feminist and race-conscious programs of Mrs. Willis, the "bright widow of a bright Negro politician" (143). As a widow, and as a woman with a stern sense of her responsibilities to the younger generation, Mrs. Willis is reminiscent of the matriarchal figures who prevail in the Anglo American sentimental paradigm. Sappho approaches Mrs. Willis and, without admitting her own experiences, asks whether "Negro women will be held responsible for all the lack of virtue that is being laid to their charge today? . . . Do you think that God will hold us responsible for the *illegitimacy* with which our race has been obliged, as it were, to flood the world?" (149, emphasis in original). Sappho submits her questions to Mrs. Willis, one of two women that Claudia Tate credits for imposing in the novel a "mother's law" that "centers a black matricentric morality[,] . . . privileges a female centered ethical context, and serves as a broader basis for redefining a virtuous woman other than on the grounds of sexual chastity" (*Domestic Allegories* 174). However, it seems that this new mother's law, though a radical replacement of patriarchal law, is limited and not necessarily its accommodating, liberating antithesis.

The way in which Mrs. Willis answers Sappho thrusts the onus of self-examination upon Sappho. Unable to apply the tenets of mother's law, Sappho is unable to neutralize her history and remains plagued by her question. She does not seem able to believe that she did not comply with her attacker or "commit some horrid sin" whose "taint . . . sticks" like bloodstains upon the hands of Lady Macbeth "and will not leave" (154). At this crucial moment, Sappho is unable to use Mrs. Willis's new matricentric principle to redefine her status and thus clear the way for her full participation in Mrs. Willis's gatherings.

Sappho's preoccupation with morality was shared by nineteenth-century African American women involved in suffrage and uplift—yet Hopkins presents Mrs. Willis and her uplift program as highly autocratic, militaristic, and disinclined to debate the moral issues facing its young women. Thus, the program and its leader seem unsuitable for women with emotional scars like Sappho's. Hopkins could have seized this incompatibility as a chance to make Sappho an active defender of such concerns. Instead, she prefers to use this short-lived exposure to uplift as a moment in which Sappho can express, rather than repress, her revulsion for matters having to do with her rape and the self-serving, unprofessional interest that Mrs. Willis has in the story. Mrs. Willis makes her last overture to Sappho, inviting her to share her troubles. However, "just as the barriers of Sappho's reserve seemed about to be swept away, there followed, almost instantly, a wave of repulsion toward this woman and her effusiveness, so forced and insincere. Sappho was very impressionable, and yielded readily to the influence which fell like a cold shadow between them. She drew back as from an abyss suddenly beheld stretching before her" (155). By using language that suggests a romantic interlude, writing that Sappho's reserve is almost "swept away," that she experiences a "wave of revulsion," is "impressionable," and "yield[s] readily" to a disembodied influence, Hopkins daringly reiterates the sexual nature of Sappho's dilemma and complicates our understanding of her interactions with Mrs. Willis.

The imagery that charts Sappho's response is much more lyrical and fluid than the descriptions of the militaristic manner in which Mrs. Willis guides her young female charges. When the young girls convene with Mrs. Willis, "by two o'clock all the members [are] in their places," the meetings involve the tabulation of facts pertinent to "the Negro race" and end promptly at six o'clock. The young women then take "refreshment in squads of five" (142–43). Sappho's life, replete with heroic rescues, assumed identities, and an illegitimate child, exceeds the pace of these weekly uplift exercises. Indeed, the nineteenth-century African American female culture that Hopkins displays prides itself on its order and controlled uniformity. Hopkins appears to ask how such an arena could accommodate the level of independence, emotional chaos, and imprinted difference that Sappho represents. Sappho has moved from defensive attempts to secure female interaction—best illustrated when she locks her bedroom door so that she and Dora Smith can converse and indulge in gaiety—to suspicion of any formal exchange between herself and her supposed female mentors and role models. In other words, Sappho has moved from limited interaction to necessary disengagement—a decision that costs her important female friendships and a nurturing home environment that values such sentimental bonds. By the end of *Contending Forces,* Hopkins has consistently demonstrated that Sappho, her experiences, situation, and responses, cannot be integrated into the African American community.

Sappho's abuse at the hands of her white half-uncle clearly symbolizes suffering at the hands of the white patriarchal order and revives the popular narrative element in African American sentimental fiction whereby mixed-race individuals—usually women—suffer threats, disenfranchisement, or personal ruin at the hands of a white relative who fears the mixed-race character's encroachment upon legitimacy and family inheritance. Hopkins incorporates this paradigm of betrayed family allegiance, which appears in Harper's *Iola Leroy,* into both *Contending Forces* and her first serialized novel *Hagar's Daughter: A Story of Southern Caste Prejudice.* In both texts, Hopkins explores the ramifications of desecrated family bonds and paves the way toward her third serial novel, *Of One Blood; or, The Hidden Self,* in which she presents her most frightful rendition of incestuous relations.

In *Contending Forces* Hopkins introduces another insidious threat from within the larger African American community. When John Langley, a powerful local mulatto politician, attempts to blackmail Sappho, her already tenuous relationship to the African American community is jeopardized. To some degree, Hopkins mutes the racial element when she blames Langley's deplorable nature on his coarse eighteenth-century white ancestors—one of whom, incidentally, contributed to the murder and destruction of Will Smith's British relatives, the Montforts. Nonetheless, Hopkins renders the African American community of Boston as a place that threatens to compromise Sappho and prevent her from overcoming her previous subjugation and sexual distress.

After Langley approaches Sappho and threatens the anonymity on which she depends and the virtue she has reconstructed, Hopkins swiftly counters his actions. Hopkins immerses the adult Mabelle Beaubean in an intense redemptive process that enables her to figuratively transcend her past sexual abuse. Sappho disappears and reappears on Easter Sundays, seeks refuge with the same order of nuns who nursed and sheltered her after her sexual abuse, is respectfully, but unsuccessfully, courted by a wealthy man, and is finally reunited with Smith with whom she enjoys "happy love—a love sanctified and purified by suffering" (398). Sappho's proximity to the nuns' holiness, chastity, and institutionalized purity seems to be the only effective antidote to slavery's desecration of women of color. When Sappho marries Smith and leaves New Orleans, her reinstated virtue is maintained, since she and Smith become ready-made parents without having sexual relations. Indeed, her son Alphonse is presented as such an angelic figure of whiteness that he seems to reiterate the image of his mother's restored purity.

Newly established as a representative of treasured womanhood, Sappho seems to have reached a position that transcends even the most holy version of Anglo American true womanhood. Because of the extreme circumstances of her past and present, Sappho is that much more inaccessible to those among whom she lives. This complicates the Anglo American paradigm that would demand that she now save and restore the lost souls about her. If Hopkins were writing in accordance with that sentimental paradigm, Sappho would have to contend with widespread Anglo American male depravity and moral chaos, involving a national mindset and history, rather than just one man. She would be obligated to reform a man who despises rather than cherishes her, or who believes that she can easily be treated as chattel and can find public sentiment that justifies such belief. In either of these cases, it is difficult to imagine a sentimental narrative in which such a man would believe Sappho the representative of a useful domestic order or be inclined to believe that his incorporation into her family would make him a better man. Thus, Sappho's fate must be quite different from that of Ellen in Susan Warner's *The Wide Wide World,* Mary Scudder in Harriet Beecher Stowe's *The Minister's Wooing,* or even Cassy in Stowe's more popular *Uncle Tom's Cabin.*

As *Contending Forces* comes to a close, Sappho does not embrace the African American condition and move on to perform the type of mediatory functions that critics such as Hazel Carby have outlined as one of the traditional routes for female mulatto characters in sentimental fiction. Sappho's harassment by the mulatto villain John Langley, the family's impending introduction into the British upper class, and the prestige of Will Smith's Ivy League and European education make it difficult to impose a traditional sentimental conclusion—even an African Americanized conclusion—upon the text. Sappho is first incorporated into a bourgeois Negro family that has no peer in the novel. Later, it is revealed that Sappho is a descendant of a sophisticated, though illegitimate French American bloodline, and finally, Sappho is established within the bonds of marriage to a Harvard-educated, well-traveled debonair man who has increasingly chameleon-like racial identities that progressively move him closer to a white European lineage. Although Sappho is ultimately incorporated into an African American family, the Smiths are last portrayed leaving America on a voyage to trace their own traumatic family history that will unavoidably intensify their non-American and thus non–African American identities. It is evident that Hopkins believes that for women like Sappho purity can be maintained or successfully reinstated only by eluding the prevailing American patriarchal chaos. Ultimately, Hopkins suggests that if Sappho remains in America, she may face additional racial injustices, which could in turn jeopardize her newly constructed purity.

* * *

> We shall *be* what we make of ourselves by the force
> and determination within us.
> —PAULINE HOPKINS, *New Era Magazine*, 1916

The success of the sentimental heroine is usually gauged by her ability to transform a godless man into a more spiritual being or by the degree to which she is able to counter the external patriarchal order with her newly politicized domestic order. Hopkins succeeds in setting different standards for a reader's appraisal of Sappho, not only because of the singularity of Sappho's experience, but also because of the character with whom she is ultimately paired. Once Sappho Clark becomes the wife of Will Smith, she is more firmly ensconced within a family whose class position is on the brink of substantial metamorphosis. In addition to their material gain and potential class advancement, the Smith family is, as the book comes to a close, drawing closer to their own European heritage. Though these circumstances are brought about by Ma Smith's direct family relations, Will Smith is best able to capitalize upon these fortuitous circumstances. Once again, Hopkins's modification of the sentimental novel paradigm defies prevailing literary convention. Rather than presenting a couple who dedicate themselves to uplift or relegating her heroine to a marriage whose chief passion is directed toward her people, Hopkins positions these central figures on the threshold of a valuable, gentrified, and un-American experience.

One of Hopkins's most dynamic characters, Will Smith resembles the learned figure of W. E. B. Du Bois; Smith espouses progressive doctrine, promotes and embodies self-development, and represents his race within various circles of the dominant white culture. As she shapes Smith's character, Hopkins blends images from traditional nineteenth-century sentimental fiction with the new ideals of her reformed sentimental paradigm. Will Smith is a man who stands ready to defend his loved one(s) and who eventually wanders from home to pursue his own goals, which are supported and financed to a great extent by his mother and sister. Yet Smith differs from most of his male predecessors in both the white and African American sentimental traditions. He is neither a renegade like James Marvyn of Stowe's *The Minister's Wooing*, an ineffective would-be hero like St. Clare in *Uncle Tom's Cabin*, or even the proper African American hero Dr. Latimer with whom Iola is paired at the end of Harper's *Iola Leroy*.

Will Smith does not rebel against the church or family, has no qualms about crossing the Victorian boundaries concerning gender roles within the home, and occupies the same home in which the novel's heroine seeks refuge. These details and others in the text suggest early on that Will Smith is party to the visionary sentimental plot that Hopkins is developing with respect to Sappho. As the text proceeds, he becomes increasingly valuable. It is Smith who provides Sappho access to the legitimating role of wife and mother. Finally, it is Smith who provides Sappho with the chance to truly distance herself and her son Alphonse from America. Because she is Will Smith's wife, the British relatives and others will likely regard Sappho as a representative African American woman. Throughout the text, however, Hopkins has established that Sappho is decidedly unrepresentative. By including Sappho in the Smiths' journey, Hopkins reinforces her belief that the African American identity must not be essentialized.

According to Judith Berzon, many early African American authors "used the mulatto character in order to emphasize his superiority, to show white America that some blacks could succeed within the framework established by the dominant white majority, and to attack American society for not recognizing the worth of some members of the non-Caucasian group" (52). Indeed, Hopkins does "use" Smith to "emphasize his superiority"—she indicts America for its failure to appreciate its African American citizens. Susan Gillman extends Berzon's thesis when she proposes that these novelists focus on "race mixture" and interracial realities "as a means of negotiating the social tensions surrounding the formation of racial, national, and sexual identity in the post-Reconstruction years" (222). Berzon's emphasis on the confrontational use of the figure and Gillman's sense of the strategic value of developing such figures lead us to a crucial element in Hopkins's refiguring of the African American sentimental paradigm. Just as Hopkins uses Sappho to enact a vital redefinition of the sexualized sentimental heroine, she uses Will Smith to explore African American destinies in Europe.

In her first published novel, Hopkins apparently makes Smith light-skinned to ensure his ability to overcome American race prejudice and repeated political compromise. He is described as "destined to shine in the future in the *world* of science" and as one who "sought to *expand* his faculties and illuminate his mind by *seeking* a *clearer* perception of the interest relation which weak humanity bears to the *glorious* mysteries of life and the *grandeurs* of creation" (166, 220, emphasis added). The discourse of liberation is sustained by Smith's own acquisitive desires as well as his impressive intellectual quest. This discourse of desire is synonymous with his identity and appetites—this glorious enterprise will therefore not only lead him into the world but also beyond an all-encompassing American blackness. In the passage above, Hopkins reinvents the image of the American pioneer. More importantly, she justifies the idea that her heroes must become refugees from American prejudice or sacrifice their potential and be wholly preoccupied by their attempts to combat it.

Hopkins designs the plot of *Contending Forces* so that its outcome hinges on Will Smith's mixed-race identity. Early in the text, as the narrator analyzes the most likely contenders for Sappho's affections, it is apparent that Hopkins will not be locating heroic development within an unmixed African identity. The noticeable blackness of Luke Sawyer, the first hero in Sappho's life, his lapse into a self-deprecating manner, and the dreadfully unappealing terms in which he couches the description of his feelings for Sappho, eliminate him and others like him. Once Will Smith is chosen over John Langley, another light-skinned African American, as the proper object for Sappho's affections, Hopkins unabashedly grooms Smith for the role and prepares readers to accept him. The narrator emphasizes his whiteness and in this way begins to displace the African background that would align him more closely to Luke Sawyer and separate him from the fair-skinned Sappho. The grandson of the white runaway slave Jesse Montfort, Smith is described as "tall and finely formed" with features that are "almost perfectly chiseled" (90). The narrator makes special mention of his hair having "just a tinge of crispness to denote the existence of Negro blood" (90). The use of the words "almost," "just," and "tinge" exaggerate his whiteness, suggesting that his blackness is practically insignificant but present in amounts that will allow him access to Sappho Clark, whose racial makeup is described in similar terms.

Hopkins endows Smith's heroic identity with a specific racial component and by so doing also reveals that the heroic identity is one she deliberately confers upon certain characters. Yet Hopkins's claims that Smith is of a mixed-race background seem somewhat engineered. His mother, the child of a white man named Jesse Montfort and an African American woman named Elizabeth Whitfield, is actually a mulatto; her children are once removed from the pseudo-scientifically defined mulatto identity and thus more likely simply to be designated Negro. Since Mrs. Smith married a "free-born Southern Negro—a Virginian" (82)—and the narrator does not imply or mention any mixed-race heritage on his part, Will and his sister Dora have a racial mix that makes them more biologically "black" than "white." Nonetheless, our attention is directed to the visual signs of Smith's physical form, and Hopkins proposes that his appearance is proof of his whiteness.

Hopkins's distress about America's treatment of individuals of African descent requires that she pursue some substantial course of (re)action. For both her heroes and heroines, then, mobility is essential. Sappho Clark is a self-confessed transient who carries home furnishings with her and finds that she can "make [herself] very comfortable in a short time with their help" (99). As *Contending Forces* comes to a close, Hopkins resurrects the ill-fated trans-Atlantic move from England to Bermuda of the Smith family's British predecessors. When we consider the mixed-race identity that Hopkins stresses for the Smith family, it seems that with Sappho they are a unit that can be successfully, and perhaps rightfully, separated from the American violence that has plagued her family and the Smiths' eighteenth-century ancestors. Hopkins's emphasis upon the racial identities of the Smith family ultimately gives way to a seeming racial mobility as they explore and recognize the substantial monetary and racial legacy bequeathed to them by Charles Montfort and his sons. Consequently, Hopkins's text is saturated with malleable racial identities. Perhaps the most contorted of these identities is that of Jesse Montfort who goes from being a rich white child, to an enslaved "black" person, to a self-declared and self-emancipated white man, to a husband of an African American woman and father of interracial offspring. Such flexible racial histories and personas enable Hopkins's figures, male and female, to escape America's rigid racial codes and avoid being constrained within the limited sociopolitical and educational circles of the American Negro.

One of the most problematic results of Hopkins's manipulation of blackness and her decision to sustain important European links for her main African American characters is that she is then unable to depict a stalwart African American hero who develops within his community and the nation at large. Unlike Luke Sawyer, Sappho's childhood rescuer, Smith limits his goodwill to his immediate family. He is not involved in any other subplots in the text and is never identified as having extended himself on behalf of the larger African American community. When he is a guest at the elite white Canterbury Club in Boston, members there celebrate him at the expense of other seemingly worthy individuals of color. This celebration further distances him from the very community he supposedly champions. At the American Colored League meeting, Smith's African American audience regards him as an honorable race representative. Yet this communion amounts to little more than a momentary fervor and race-identification that may or may not develop. Hopkins is increasingly intent on making the Montfort-Smith connection viable. As a result, the whiteness and the promise of renewed family bonds begin to overwhelm the already tenuous links that Will Smith has had with the African American community, as well as temper the central roles that Ma Smith and Dora have played in the community.

Smith's African Americanness becomes more and more diluted as *Contending Forces* comes to a close. The sentimental journey that the Smiths embark upon will take them to England as well as to the one-time slaveholding haunts in Bermuda that belonged to their British patriarch, Charles Montfort. Sappho and Will Smith, both of whom have existed on the edge of various racial communities, are about to be separated from the African American community by the fact of Smith's Montfort lineage, which Sappho, as Smith's bride, now shares. It is at this moment that Hopkins's text illustrates how difficult it is to predict or designate a site from which racial protest or uplift must begin. In her sentimental narratives, Hopkins constantly juxtaposes her heroes, villains, victims, and survivors. By doing so, she effectively validates the final choices that she makes in her stories. Though married, Sappho Clark is still attempting to define her methods of survival and healing; Will Smith has yet to apply the fruits of his education or choose his community, be it racial, familial, or social. Like the Smiths, Hopkins's turn-of-the-century readers are on the threshold of new societies and are invited to dream of unexplored lands that have a direct, though previously unimagined, connection to their own existence.

* * *

In *Contending Forces,* Pauline Hopkins invites us to consider that the African American sentimental narrative—which African American authors frequently used to depict effective community organizing, racial solidarity, and sociocultural and economic advancement—may have its own insidious utopian bent. Indeed, *Contending Forces* suggests that in this particular African American tradition progress and uplift often can be enacted only at the cost of certain personal repression. As Hopkins uses the figures of Sappho Clark and Will Smith to illustrate, racial identity is no longer synonymous with one's supposed American racial community, nor is one's sexualized racial identity always compatible with the visions and programs of either the oppressed or dominant group. As a result, Hopkins's first novel becomes a striking, racialized sentimental narrative that is significantly different from previous African American sentimental novels. She utilizes only certain portions of the Anglo American form, and she does not adopt the racially reoriented tactics of sentimental empowerment introduced by her African American peers.

In *Contending Forces,* Hopkins establishes her belief that within the African American sentimental paradigm, women of color are only able to achieve a fragile purity that is inconsequential either to the society they inhabit or to the American feminist and political agendas they might espouse. To mitigate the pernicious influence of a patriarchal and racist society, Hopkins creates a central male character who becomes the vital link between this besieged domestic order and an empowered family honor. Hopkins is unapologetic as she staunchly advocates self-protection and defensive action. Both her authorial stance and final recommendations prevent us from presuming that her texts and characters will be traditional representatives of African American experiences.

WORKS CITED

Baym, Nina. *Woman's Fiction: A Guide to Novels by and about Women in America, 1820–1870.* Ithaca, N.Y.: Cornell University Press, 1978.

Berzon, Judith. *Neither White nor Black: The Mulatto Character in American Fiction.* New York: New York University Press, 1978.

Carby, Hazel. *Reconstructing Womanhood: The Emergence of the Afro-American Woman Novelist.* New York: Oxford University Press, 1987.

Gillman, Susan. "The Mulatto, Tragic or Triumphant? The Nineteenth-Century American Race Melodrama." In *The Culture of Sentiment: Race, Gender, and Sentimentality in Nineteenth-Century America.* Ed. Shirley Samuels. New York: Oxford University Press, 1992. 221–43.

Harper, Frances E. W. *Iola Leroy; or, Shadows Uplifted.* 1892. New York: Oxford University Press, 1987.

Hopkins, Pauline. *Contending Forces: A Romance Illustrative of Negro Life North and South.* 1900. New York: Oxford University Press, 1988.

Jacobs, Harriet. *Incidents in the Life of a Slave Girl.* 1861. Ed. Jean Fagan Yellin. Cambridge, Mass.: Harvard University Press, 1987.

Rowson, Susanna. *Charlotte Temple.* 1794. New York: Oxford University Press, 1986.

Stowe, Harriet Beecher. *The Minister's Wooing.* 1859. Hartford, Conn.: Stowe-Day Foundation, 1988.

———. *Uncle Tom's Cabin; or, Life among the Lowly.* 1852. Ed. Ann Douglas. New York: Penguin, 1981.

Tate, Claudia. "Allegories of Black Female Desire; or, Rereading Nineteenth-Century Sentimental Narratives of Black Female Authority." In *Changing Our Own Words: Essays on Criticism, Theory, and Writing by Black Women.* Ed. Cheryl A. Wall. New Brunswick, N.J.: Rutgers University Press, 1989. 98–126.

———. *Domestic Allegories of Political Desire: The Black Heroine's Text at the Turn of the Century.* New York: Oxford University Press, 1992.

Warner, Susan. *The Wide Wide World.* 1850. New York: Feminist Press, 1987.

THREE

Inherited Rhetoric and Authentic History: Pauline Hopkins at the *Colored American Magazine*

C. K. DORESKI

> We know that there are able publications already in the field, but the pang that has set our active world a-borning is the knowledge that the colored man has lost the rights already won because he was persuaded and then bullied into lying down and ceasing his fight for civil liberty.
> —*New Era Magazine*, FEBRUARY 1916

> We are sparing neither time nor money to make this Magazine the most authentic historian of the race's progress.
> —*New Era Magazine*, MARCH 1916

More than a decade after her severance from Boston's *Colored American Magazine* (*CAM*), Pauline Hopkins retained a politically charged philosophy of African American arts and letters as evidenced by her pronouncements heralding the publication of the *New Era Magazine*. Colleagues from *CAM* might have been surprised by the stridency of her call for action, but none would have been shocked by its insistence upon community-based, collective action. By the time of this final acknowledgment of the collaborative nature and resultant power of the periodical press, Hopkins had resolved the earlier problematic issue of the relationship between the public self and history. For black America the periodical press could not afford to be ephemeral; it had to consciously shape and nurture its nascent history. In her culminating effacement of self as historian, Hopkins ceded authority to the magazine and, by extension, to the African American periodical press at large. The move from author of individual significance (a concern of her transcendentalist forebears) to author as a community force serving a larger historical project began for Hopkins during her formative years as editor of *CAM*.

Throughout her tenure at *CAM* (1900–1904), Hopkins acknowledged her obligation not simply to cultivate but to create an audience for her revisionist race history. She assumed the authority of race historian and mediated between the issues of race and gender to incite a readership to pride and action (on the race and gender split, see Stansell). Even *CAM*'s title page claimed agency and responsibility by appealing to that segment of the population that W. E. B. Du Bois would soon call the "Talented Tenth" (Meier 207–47; Bruce, *Black American Writing,* esp. chap. 5). This monthly (not unlike such nineteenth-century bourgeois cousins as the *Atlantic Monthly* and *Putnam's Monthly*) schooled its readers in arts and manners, hoping to provide that surface of success expected in the emerging middle class. But it also advanced a politically charged, cultural agenda in its challenge to the status quo and its commitment to the discovery and preservation of African American history. The shadow of compromised citizenship cast by *Plessy v. Ferguson* (1896) necessitated an urgent commitment to the recovery and perpetuation of race history.

Hopkins transcended the journal's arts context by writing for "those who never read history or biography."[1] She hoped that, through the imitative commodified culture of the magazine, ideas of the marketplace could become a marketplace of ideas. Visually sharing qualities associated with weekly newspapers in advertisements for products ranging from Frederick Douglass watches to cosmetics, *CAM* offered a product-intense, textual world in which even biography and history might become marketable commodities. Thoroughly attuned to the intertextual power of the emulative matrix of the press, she knew that her historical portraits could gain power when read through the animated and often competing texts of each issue. She wrote in the certainty that her biographical texts would inform her fiction and social notes, even as they were informed by the larger textual whole. In this way, Hopkins wrote in that grander nineteenth-century tradition identified by one critic as one in which "criticism . . . was closely allied to history and novel writing, and was also the vehicle for all sorts of ideas about the purpose and destiny of human life in general" (Wilson 122–23).

While Hopkins the novelist has recently earned deserved attention, Hopkins the biographer has attracted only passing interest. Curiously, despite a commitment from scholars to African American autobiography that includes the restoration of "the black slave's narrative to its complex status as history and as literature" (Davis and Gates iii), the significant role of biography as a means of shaping race history through public lives has received comparatively little attention.[2] An intertextual reading of Hopkins's historical counternarratives (fictional and biographical) in *CAM* suggests how she constructs history and challenges conventional generic distinctions by conflating discourses of history, biography, fictional narrative, race, and gender in order to shape a rhetorical self to counter the absence of a reliable race history.[3]

The validation of Hopkins as an authentic historian through her role as biographer demands exploration of her reliance on and divergence from the New England regional tradition of biography as the spiritually or ideologically informed presentation of exemplary lives. Comfortable with the tradition she seeks to deconstruct, she advances the cultural and racial history of slavery into present-tense instruction applicable to this era of imperiled citizenship. In so doing, her biographies and fictions find authentication through life stories that derive their significance from the ability to inspire in the individual reader what Emerson calls the "unattained but attainable self" ("History" 239). Her Emersonian emphasis that "all history is . . . but biography"[4] stems from the belief that in order to translate, as William Andrews says, "word into act" (71), readers must sense the historical possibilities of daily life. Hopkins's belief that history is firmly embedded in individual narratives would seem to accord with Hayden White's definition of narrative as "a solution of how to translate *knowing* into *telling,* the problem of fashioning human experience into a form assimilable to structures of meaning that are generally human rather than culture-specific" ("Value of Narrativity" 1; Goody). But while such "fashioning" into universals might have some appeal to a fiction writer in search of a broad audience, such grandiose universalizing would be anathema to Hopkins as race historian.

Far more ambitious than the familiar quest for totalizing fictions (whether we call them fiction or history), her portraits, like Emerson's, share the didactic ends of that distant rhetorical ancestor from the Puritan great migration: exemplary biography. Sacvan Bercovitch, in discussing exemplary biography and its "organizing metaphors," argues that this kind of biography "transmutes history itself into a drama of the soul" (*Puritan Origins* 8). Not unlike the Cotton Mather of *Magnali Christi Americana*—who saw "*Biography,* provoking the *whole World,* with vertuous Objects of Emulation" (89)—Hopkins sought a biographical form that would incarnate history. Her preoccupation with the translation of representative lives into authentic history begins with two series of biographical sketches written for *CAM.* Appearing monthly from November 1900 to October 1902, "Famous Men of the Negro Race" and "Famous Women of the Negro Race" constitute her own experiments in historiography and biography as they harness this once sacred impulse for secular service. Attending to the spirit of this world, she composes history from exemplary lives in the hope of "elevat[ing] the image of the entire race" (McDowell, "Changing Same" 95).

The formulaic inheritance of the representative biographical sketch, which denies the literary or historical uniqueness of these lives, reiterates and extends the grander, antebellum historical context of slavery so that it informs the citizenship crisis of her day.[5] Like Lydia Maria Child, whose *The Freedmen's Book* (1865) had isolated "the power of character over circumstances" as the core didactic end of such insistent representative lives, Hopkins transformed race icons into players in a history requiring authentication through participation (Child 218).[6] She translated the familiar lives of Toussaint-Louverture, Frederick Douglass, Sojourner Truth, and Harriet Tubman into participatory, exemplary texts, and in so doing relaxed into the conventions of the established genre and obligations of essential biography, wherein the life described becomes an extended allegory (on social versus essential biography, see Bercovitch, *Puritan Origins* 149). Her challenges to this rhetorical inheritance would include figures about whom Hopkins felt ambivalent (e.g., Booker T. Washington), less famous and more local personages better served by a social biography (wherein the life is but a microcosm of its historical context of great events), and professional women whom she saw as embodiments of a community rather than as individual heroes. The personalized flexible organization of these sketches allows Hopkins to accommodate the aesthetic dimension of emplotment (employing vignette and dialogue to animate the life) as well as the cognitive historical obligation to argument (exposing the greater moral imperatives of history).[7] Drawing upon what Hazel Carby has called "an idealized concept of her New England past" (*Recon-*

structing Womanhood 121), Hopkins sought to enlighten and inspirit readers into a kindred abolitionist fervor by using social and cultural exemplars to nullify competing racist ideologies. Unlike her transcendentalist models, she sought not to privilege the individual but to celebrate an evolving sense of historical integrity and community. This essay explores Hopkins's move from the inherited rhetoric of the representative biographical sketch to a culturally defined, intertextually enriched vision of the way in which all history *is* biography.

* * *

Committed to the "wonderful deeds and brilliant achievements which have been accomplished by men of color throughout the world," "Famous Men of the Negro Race" declares its historical project by delineating an audience "denied its history and distinguished only as the former slave[s] of the country" (*CAM*, Nov. 1900).[8] This project is one of recovery as well as commemoration and offers the "truth" that will give African Americans "the history of a patriot, a brave soldier, the defender of the country from foreign invaders, and God fearing producer of the nation's wealth" (*CAM*, Nov. 1990). The role call of local heroes insists upon emulative public life and active citizenship as a prerequisite to mentorship as well as historical significance.

While ostensibly "preserving the fascinating individual personality of each man," Hopkins subverts the unique in favor of the cumulative contribution to a public genealogy and restorative kinship in order to invent history. Reading real events (i.e., the strict chronology of the men's lives) as paradigms for the larger cultural narrative, Hopkins, like any post-Hegelian historian, accepts her role as interlocutor, using anecdote (see Fineman) and narrative emphasis to lend structure to lives and events as she mediates between the individual heroic soul and the grander racial and cultural tapestry.

Of the dozen portraits composing "Famous Negro Men," three representative men constitute the larger cultural matrix and inheritance of the series: Toussaint-Louverture, Frederick Douglass, and Booker T. Washington. These exemplary cultural heroes invest the series as a whole with a vaguely Emersonian stature, while the less defined and more local exemplary lives derive their historical coherence and resonance within the larger context of these three historically centered, slave-defined cultural heroes. Readers familiar with Emerson's *Representative Men* (1850) and Child's *The Freedmen's Book* would see these

lives as obligatory cultural markers as well as history. Appearing individually in *CAM*, these lives predicate a revisionary sense of how the
representative biography might embody the political agenda of the
magazine itself. The force of the collective cultural sweep—from the
distant and unrecorded (other than by the enemy) trials of Toussaint-
Louverture, to the meticulously historicized and self-fashioned lives of
Douglass, to the contemporary and self-chronicled life of Washington—
approximates Hopkins's personal commitment to the relationship of
life's detritus to the embracing context of history. Each biography challenges her to exploit the exchange context of the magazine without
sacrificing the integrity of her fashioned lives.

With "Toussaint L'Overture" (*CAM*, Nov. 1900, 9–24), Hopkins
grounds her enterprise in a history of slave revolt while acknowledging the Emersonian rhetorical tradition she both inherits and modifies.
A prefatory note displaces the expected invocation and announces a
larger contextualizing project. The despoilment of a garden paradise
mirrors the destruction of its inhabitants as Hopkins reinvents the
competing histories of old and new worlds in terms of the history of
her race. She expands the power of descent discourse to include the
recovery of Haiti's proper history.

Ever mindful of historical resonances, Hopkins displaces historical
claims and certainties by calling attention to their arbitrary and transient natures. Authenticating historical documentation supplants received historical fact in a chain of calling and renaming, which loosely
anchors the evidence of position or place. In order to emphasize the
link between native servitude and American slavery, Hopkins resorts
to fictional strategies and the literary, Christian discourse of the garden. Hispaniola becomes an Edenic place of temperate climate, "always
laden with fruit and covered with flowers" (10). To capture the preco-
lonial and prelapsarian state of this virginal place, a place literally
without commodities, she describes it as a land in which "gold, silver,
and copper mines abound" (10) although such metals have no exchange
value there. The garden as trope yields to an accelerated Genesis tale
of fall and expulsion in which African slaves replace the aborigines, who
had been "driven into a cruel and barbarous servitude by the Spanish
adventurers" (10). Slavery quickly turns into a "many-headed monster"
(10) that not only casts the race into servitude but confuses the racial
line: "From the mingling of the whites and blacks the mulattoes had
sprung" (10). From this island issues what Hopkins calls the "voice of

history . . . the point of interest for all Negroes" (10). The embodiment
of that voice is Toussaint-Louverture.

Signifying on Emerson's *Representative Men,* Hopkins extends her
characterization to include the implications for race history as she en-
visions Toussaint as "Napoleon's black shadow," a man "who made
and unmade kings and formed governments anew" (11). She exhorts
her readers to accept that "races should be judged by the great men
they produce, and by the average value of the masses" (11), and then
supplies a historical narrative that constructs a Haitian perspective on
the revolution. Throughout this new history, readers engage in alternative readings of race biography and history: "Such was the beginning of a revolt that ought to have a world-wide fame. It stands without a parallel in history,—the successful uprising of slaves against their
masters, and the final establishment of their independence" (14). The
authorial "ought" intensifies Hopkins's claim to revisionary history.
The effacement of what should have been "world-wide fame" prompts
her reconstruction project. Yet as the collective history of the island is
recalled, it "seems merged in the exploits of one man, L'Overture" (14).
Securing the relationship between the collective "uprising of slaves" and
the individual "exploits of one man," Hopkins at once privileges the
hero while suspending his deeds in a collective matrix. This larger cultural impress enables a historical narrative to blossom from the life of
a "Negro [who] left hardly a line for history to feed upon" (14).

In the absence of autobiographical testimony, Hopkins, suspicious
of the "reluctant testimony of [Toussaint's] enemies," resorts to narration to depict this Senegalese "Negro of unmixed blood" (15). She
acknowledges his slave origins while stressing his literacy and classical training, thus bridging origins and circumstance for contemporary
readers. In a sharp role reversal, Hopkins's heroic slave assumes mastery "at the head of the newly freed, leading them from victory to victory for France under Bonaparte" (15). Toussaint, conforming to what
Claudia Tate has labeled the "gender conservatism" of the era (*Domestic Allegories* 161), assumes the lineaments of regal patriarch and "under his paternal administration, laws, morals, religion, education, and
industry were in full force, while commerce and agriculture flourished"
(17).

A dialogic interface of history and biography, kindred to that of her
openly historical fiction, draws authenticity from its intertextual relationship with excerpts from journals and letters of Toussaint's "ene-

mies." Anxious for readers to appreciate the significance of this representative man, Hopkins plots the arc of his career parallel to that of his bête noire, Napoléon. The ideological rivalry inscribed in the figures of Toussaint and Napoléon corresponds to Emerson's own sketch of Napoléon. When at last it becomes evident that Napoléon is determined to crush the spirit of liberty in the blacks of St. Domingo, Toussaint evolves into the intrepid leader who obeys to the letter the stern mandates of war.

In an unexpected inversion of the slave narrative, death rather than birth is "shrouded in mystery" (23). Under Napoléon's hand, Toussaint dies off the record, at least in Hopkins's hagiography. Hopkins, willing to compensate for that historical silence, interjects: "We know not the exact manner of his taking off, but that he was cruelly murdered *there is no doubt*" (23, emphasis added). Clearly under the sway of Thomas Carlyle and William Wordsworth's romantic projections of the hero as she insists upon Toussaint's "grandeur of a great moral heroism" (19), Hopkins nonetheless relies upon a rhetoric of disengagement with her European models as she details that hero's fatal flaw: "The ruin of Toussaint was due in great measure to his loyalty to France and his filial feeling for Bonaparte" (16).

Hopkins's depiction both recovers a lost historical perspective and sustains an essential biography, placing Toussaint and Haiti in a historical continuum of race history for African Americans. Effecting closure with a historical sweep from Thermopylae to Fort Wagner, Hopkins as visionary historian sanctifies the record through an act of Pan-African revelation: "History recorded these deeds, and they shall be known; God intends it so! Therefore the history of the Island of St. Domingo is interesting to the Negroes of the United States; brothers in blood, though speaking different languages, we should clasp our hands in friendship when we look back upon our past" (24). Toussaint draws significance from the embracing Pan-African vision of Hopkins's newly constructed historical record, insisting as it does upon a shared history as well as a common destiny.

Unlike the unwritten history of Toussaint-Louverture, Frederick Douglass's thrice-chronicled life challenged Hopkins to sculpt received narratives, lending biographical contours to a dauntingly familiar autobiography (*CAM*, Dec. 1900, 121–32). Challenged with making the mythically familiar new, Hopkins expands Douglass's shifting frameworks of the ideal (especially in his *Narrative*), searching for historical and cultural referents in her biography aimed at a contemporary audience of marginally enfranchised citizens. Here she tranforms the autobiographical, "I-centered" slave narrative into a mediated biography available to the new African American citizen by sharing not only great deeds but the potential of a larger collective force, the "citizen" always moving toward that constituent whole of "citizenry." The broader sense of race obligation as well as history suggests the influence of Du Bois's 1897 articulation of "the real meaning of Race" (815) in "The Conservation of Races."[9] Within this lingering Emersonian context, Hopkins imagines (in Du Bois's words) that representative men "were but epitomized expressions" (817) of a race of great men and great women drawn together by the civilizing force of culture (Moses, esp. chap. 5).

Hopkins, relying upon the familiarity of Douglass's own "lives," draws his autobiographically constructed past(s) into the readers' present. Douglass's Emersonian auto-American-biography (Bercovitch, *Puritan Origins,* esp. chap. 5) contextualizes a social biography of urgency and purpose as his life becomes an exemplum for African Americans in general. The historical resonance of slavery, bondage, and freedom echoes throughout the naming rituals familiar to readers of slave narratives. Genealogy and history coalesce in Hopkins's Pan-African speculation that "in the veins of this man ran the best blood of old Maryland families mingled with the noble blood of African princes." Drawing readers anew into the drama of Douglass's narrative, Hopkins transforms a capsule history of chattel slavery into a contemporary narrative of citizenship: "Later in the evening *our invited friend* from New Bedford, *the fugitive slave (Frederick Douglass),* came to the platform" (123, emphasis added). This associative series of competing social designations prompts a complex chain of reader response: The phrase "our invited" invests the friend with a larger society and an assumption of equality; "the" as definite article intensifies the internal conflict (i.e., a "slave" reacting to the very condition of slavery by becoming a "fugitive") in both designation and legal category; and "(Frederick Douglass)," embedded as it is in parentheses, signals both a construct (Douglass creating his own selfhood) and a public identity—albeit delivered sotto voce.

While honoring the features of Douglass's own lives, Hopkins subverts her inherited text and redirects readers to trample what Emerson would call "any fence of personality" that keeps them from self-discovery and action (*Representative Men* 631). Successive waves of biography and history fabricate the news of the day as figures and events recapitulate the past while predicating the future. The epilogue returns readers emphatically to the anxieties of the hour, redesignating slavery from fact to metaphor to metonym. Slavery persists in the lynch laws, race murders, and the convict-lease system: "To-day we have again the rise of slave-power, for the old spirit is not dead" (128). Douglass's autobiographical selves, in Hopkins's biography, coalesce into "an example of possibilities which may be within the reach of many young men of the rising generation" (132).

Unlike Child's sketches of Toussaint and Douglass, which stress the family-centered, private "capabilities of Black Men" (83), Hopkins's biographies revitalize the heritage by insisting upon public biographies as the intimate ground of history. Passages celebrating the family possibilities of the emancipated sphere—Douglass discovering in New Bedford "the colored people owning their comfortable little homes and farms, schooling their children and transacting their business" (123)— yield to the larger framing emphasis on the didactic ends of biography and history.

The inherited rhetorical demands of the representative life served Hopkins well when she dealt with figures she deemed heroic. The received structure, however, broke down rather early, necessitating reconstruction along different lines, as she began to cope with the eccentric nature of her "representative men." The Booker T. Washington sketch (*CAM*, Oct. 1901, 436–41), which concludes the series, offers insight into the problematic nature of the genre for Hopkins as she turns nineteenth-century heroic conventions on her contemporary and rival. By its very nature, biography demands belief in the subject-embracing rhetoric, and this portrait must bear the polemical weight of the entire series. While Toussaint's and Douglass's lives seemed divinely inspired, Washington's (in his autobiography as well as Hopkins's sketch) seems decidedly secular, deliberate, and forced.

Her strict accounting of this representative man is perfunctory from the start. Public presence and authority do little to animate this "subject of [a] sketch" whose influence in "words and acts on the future history of the Negro race will be carefully scrutinized by future generations" (436). Hopkins's intricate and personalized rhetoric slips into the indifferent air of an all-too-familiar biography. The exceptional qualities of Washington's *The Story of My Life and Work* are nullified by her strained indifference: "No one will question the assertion that Dr. Washington and Tuskegee are one. . . . Tuskegee Institute is the soul of the man outlined in wood, in brick and stone" (436). Hopkins refuses to animate this "outlined" man, withholding both dramatic narration and fictional dialogue. Rather, she allows him to condemn himself by his own tide of accomplishments and honors, divorced from a larger sense of community. Halfheartedly she notes, "Dr. Washington's public career as a speaker is full of interest" (439). The absence of the expected generic elements contribute to the sense of diminished form and compromised rhetoric.

Hopkins concludes with a lifeless, cautionary epilogue in which "motives" turn suspect in the harsher light of history: "When the happenings of the Twentieth Century have become matters of history, Dr. Washington's motives will be open to as many constructions and discussions as are those of Napoleon today, or of other men of extraordinary ability, whether good or evil, who have had like phenomenal careers" (441). Readers recalling the series' initial depiction of Toussaint's subversion by Napoléon were certain to hear the ironic weight of the equivocating—"whether good or evil"—judgment on Washington. Embedded in this invocation is Hopkins's unwritten warning, which seems like a revision of Emerson: if Washington is the race, it is because the people he sways are little Washingtons.

The suspension of authorial moral judgment is but one way that Hopkins signals her ambivalence toward Washington and his prescription for black America. The collapse of rhetoric in this sketch suggests the power of biography, when aesthetically charged, to sustain the representation. It also serves to intensify the sense of peril for contemporary readers. The accomplishment of the series is not simply that it emphasizes the triumph of race heroes over slavery, but that it encourages those survival traits as a means of securing full citizenship. The withdrawal of authorial passion in the Washington sketch italicizes the persistent subtext of the series: that these life stories are "interwoven inseparably with the political history of the United States in the most critical period of its existence" (*CAM*, Feb. 1901, 301). Portraits of more regional "famous men" demonstrate her skillful adaptation of the genre, favoring those with the moral complexity, fervor, and capacity that she considers worthy of visionary race models.

Of the remaining nine portraits, all but one share Boston roots or obligations and most of the careers originate in the Oberlin-Boston nexus of reform and abolitionist fervor. As Hazel Carby has noted: "The history of abolition was a constant reference point for Hopkins; the possibility of the revival of such a force for political change was the source of her political optimism" (*Reconstructing Womanhood* 121). Not only was this invocation of regional history essential to capturing her audience, but it informed the dominant rhetoric of each sketch. Hopkins relied upon the intertextual resonance of these portraits to deconstruct for her readers the received history of place and origins so that they might find the life of history itself in their own genealogy.[10] Through the rhetorical reiteration of slave ancestry, readers might recover the inventive passion of the abolitionist movement as these regional figures are invested with historical weight, circumstance, and obligation. Their public lives, when subjected to the art of biography, turn exemplary as well as historical. They become a lens through which history appears both perceivable and participatory.

Experimenting with authenticating history through these exemplary lives, Hopkins—biographer and mediating voice—moves beyond history as a static past to that great force which is "literally present" in our actions, as James Baldwin would later claim.[11] Readers inspired by the opening portraits of Toussaint and Douglass could turn to these successive sketches of citizens seemingly in their midst to chart a course for their own improvement, their own contributions to the race. Hopkins exploited her fictional talents to lend dramatic narration and enlivening dialogue to her biographies. She wrested African American history from the "maelstrom of slavery" and situated it in a larger cultural continuum (*CAM*, Jan. 1901, 236). Unlike the portraits of the cultural icons, those of Hopkins's less "Famous Men" rely upon rhetorical and narrative strategies that introduce the notion that race history precedes and empowers individuals. They also emphasize the precarious nature of African American citizenship in their insistence upon participation in history through public roles.

"Lewis Hayden" is a stylistic case in point (*CAM*, Apr. 1901, 473–77). Reinvoking and then upsetting the conventions of hagiography, Hopkins begins with an insistence of Hayden's spirituality in the face of his seemingly unexceptional nature. Though not "great as a scholar, nor one gifted with eloquent speech," he nonetheless "consecrated all that he had" to the Lord's work (473). Readers insert themselves into the biographical space made apparent in the ordinariness of the unfolding life. After an Emersonian meditation on the nature of "ge-

nius," Hopkins concludes: Hayden "coveted no man's genius, but did
the best with his own special gifts, and at his death held the respect of
all persons—white and black—from the governor down to the lowli-
est citizen of the grand old commonwealth of Massachusetts" (473).
Hopkins targets the public life as a means of integrating the representative man with his history. For those of less than heroic stature, rec-
ognizable patterns of service authenticate their lives.

Conventions of the slave narrative enable Hopkins to establish a
framework within which to confront her anxiety of influence. She must
recover the vitality of the received form of the antebellum slave narrative and put it into the service of her contemporary representative lives:
"Mr. *Hayden* was born in *Kentucky,* but the date is lost in the dark
annals of slavery. He escaped with his wife, *Harriet,* when quite a young
man. It was the usual thrilling story of hiding in barns, swamps, and
forests by day, and travelling by night ever toward the North Star, then
the beacon-light in the travail that preceded the birth of liberty" (473,
emphasis added). From "the dark annals of slavery" biography rescues
the specific and the general trials of race history: from chattel slavery
to flight to Oberlin to Boston.

Hopkins multiplies these familiar dramatic effects through dramatic narration and fictional dialogue, italicizing authorial exhortations
to readers. In her sketch, Hayden's life was one of fictional imperatives—"adventures," "sacrifices," and "events"—inscribed on the tab-
lets of public (because verifiable) history. Cascading layers of specific
reference inform the more recent Boston history—"having a store on
Cambridge Street, just above North Anderson Street (then known as
Bridge Street)" (474)—privileging the local in its creation of an intimate dialogue with the readers. She expands the local context beyond
the immediate neighborhood to the state house where Hayden was a
member of the Massachusetts Legislature and, "at the close of his public
career," Secretary of State. This trajectory of public success is confirmed
by the fact that state offices closed for the "funeral exercises" of this
public servant (474).

The epilogue militantly announces the relevance of race history and
welfare to African Americans: "The deeds of men of a past generation
are the beacon lights along the shore for the youth of today. We do not
rehearse deeds of riot or bloodshed from a desire to fire anew the public mind, but because our traditions and history must be kept alive if
we hope ever to become a people worthy to be named with others. We

must pause sometimes in the busy whirl of daily life and think of the past, and from an intelligent comprehension of these facts read the present signs of the times" (476). Advancing the private mind into the public arena, Hopkins seeks coherence and immediacy in her biographical histories. The twin axes of slave history and citizenship recur in each profile but are explicit in Hayden's sketch: "The question then was: Has the Negro a right to resist his master? We settled that in the Civil War. The question now is: Has the Negro a right to citizenship? This last question cannot be settled by strife" (477). The impersonalized generalizations concluding Hayden's biography characterize the way in which Hopkins moves quickly from history to the urgent, present tense citizenship implications with the collective authorial voice "we." The recurrent emphasis throughout these narratives remains that history for black America is what *is*, not what *was*.

While the "Famous Men" series forms a relatively uniform rhetorical chorus, it is more than simply a race miscellany. Hopkins sought figures whose newly emerging public roles underscored their moment in race citizenship and history. This necessitated a departure from prior models like Emerson's *Representative Men* where every figure is canonical. Although *CAM* exploited the serial nature of these biographies (to enhance readership), contemporary critics committed to the expansiveness and depth of Hopkins's historical grasp need to appreciate the intertextual subtlety of her collection. For example, the literacy and authority of William Wells Brown would "stimulate the soul thirsting for the springs of knowledge" (*CAM,* Jan. 1901, 236); the Emersonian self-reliance of state representative Edwin Garrison Walker would illumine the "thrilling occurrences . . . [and] sacrifices made of money and of personal safety by the colored men of New York and New England for the amelioration of their race" (*CAM,* Mar. 1901, 361); the valor of Sargeant William H. Carney, volunteer in the Massachusetts 54th Infantry Regiment, would incarnate New England's noble African American history when, as color-bearer, he "held the emblem of liberty in the air" at Fort Wagner (*CAM,* June 1901, 87).

Senators, jurists, soldiers, and authors form a human bridge of historical recovery and continuity, embodying the "benefits of sacrifices, hopes and prayers . . . for future Afro-American[s]" (*CAM,* June 1901, 89). Authentic history originates in the biographies of just such standard-bearers. In an echo of her fictional project, Hopkins muses on the genealogical import of race history: These lives "are about all we can claim as absolutely our own; we are of one blood, and of one kind with them" (*CAM*, Sept. 1901, 337). Yet, uneasy with a celebration of merely individual paths, Hopkins decided to expand her representative kinship into a community notion of race biography and history in her "Famous Women of the Negro Race."

* * *

Although "Famous Women of the Negro Race" (Nov. 1901–Jan. 1903), like its predecessor, historically and culturally anchors readers through familiar iconographic portraits—in this instance, Sojourner Truth and Harriet Tubman—it departs significantly from the earlier series (with its reliance upon the representative individual) in favor of group portraits of community endeavor, privileging the public and spirited contributions of African American women to culture and society. The series begins with one such collective portrait, "Phenomenal Vocalists," as if to signal a radical departure from Hopkins's earlier representative individual strategy. The restricted, public historical focus of the "Famous Men" series proved inadequate to the needs of previously marginalized contributions of African American women.

By inaugurating her new series with a collective portrait, Hopkins inserts a contextualizing group identity that informs even the heroic figures of Sojourner Truth and Harriet Tubman, transforming them from indecorous race heroines (women deemed excessively public and opinionated for the day) into exemplars of a race history and ongoing community. As Claudia Tate notes in her incisive discussion of the turn-of-the-century revision of patriarchal texts and models in African American fiction: "Even though the black Victorian model permitted professional activity outside the home for the wife and other females of the household, modesty and reserve were essential. Those middle-class women (like Mary Church Terrell and Ida B. Wells-Barnett) who asserted positions of leadership, thus resisting that decorum, were often regarded as aggressive and immodest" (*Domestic Allegories* 151–52).

"Sojourner Truth: A Northern Slave" (*CAM*, Dec. 1901, 124–32) occasions an immediate revision of life in the abolitionist North and an attendant challenge to Hopkins's own generation of readers. Moving swiftly from a globalized capsule history of slavery to a regional account, Hopkins advances the theory that Truth's life is "remarkable because she experienced that Northern slavery of which we know so

little at present" (125). This "Ethiopian Sybil" is the very incarnation
of what her biographer finds most difficult to capture without yielding to contemporary clichés of women's spirituality. Lacking the fictional spurs of characterization and plot, the sketch grounds its discussion
of the revelatory spectacles of one "who knew religion only by revelation!" (131) in a sequence of domestic framings of personal and racial
family history.

Ever conscious of the bourgeois probity of her audience, Hopkins
as mediating biographer enables this life to emerge as both family narrative and assertive self-construct. She sanctions even as she subverts
the "append[ed] certificate of character given Sojourner Truth by men
. . . as a guarantee of the authenticity of this woman's statements" by
privileging the subject herself: "The subject of this biography, Sojourner
Truth, as she called herself—but whose name was originally Isabella—
was born between the years of 1797 and 1800" (125). While the culturally significant subject of "this biography" is the woman who "called
herself" Sojourner Truth, not the one who "was named" Isabella, the
sketch must still account for her chattel history.

Sojourner Truth joins Hopkins's established pantheon of male race
heroes (Douglass, Toussaint, Langston, Washington, and Elliott), who
seem equal when seen through the leveling experience of slavery.
Through this reiteration of secular saints, Hopkins (now bound by race
and gender) deconstructs received history as she reconstructs the essential narratives of representation and history in the black community. Here the biographical project depicts an ongoing race history as the
complementary revelation of domestic dramas: Sojourner Truth as sexual victim under slavery, as mother of five children, as rescuer of her
son. These fictionally embellished escapades (familiar to readers of
Uncle Tom's Cabin) sound the reassuring notes of turn-of-the-century
domestic fiction. But within the blurred genres of history, fiction, and
biography, we can detect the subtext of a black heroine, which announces what Tate identifies as "domestic allegories of political desire." Under
the genteel surface beats an aggressive and assertive life.

Unlike the slavery thresholds in the "Famous Men" sequence, this
historical antecedent risks generalizing Isabella's experience of sexual,
emotional, and physical trauma to the condition of slave women.
Marriage, motherhood, and morals "suffered" because slaves were not
allowed to have those social roles and characteristics. In third person
narration, Hopkins makes communal Sojourner/Isabella's plight and

then turns to yet another contemporary instruction regarding southern race policies and fears of amalgamation. Neither womanly attributes nor maternal instincts assume dramatic form until the narrative turns to the authentic subject, Sojourner Truth. As in Harriet Jacobs's *Incidents in the Life of a Slave Girl,* agency resides in women as complex and complete individuals as Hopkins privileges the intimate components of this public life.

Only Truth's slave and family roots require male authentication. Hopkins liberates her from domesticity into a series of spiritual and global travels, noting that "she sent her children word of her whereabouts" (132). This nod toward maternal responsibility both acknowledges and severs Truth's connection with her family circle in order that she may perform on a grander, public stage. Traveling throughout New England, Sojourner Truth translates knowing into telling, "lecturing, preaching, and working by the day" (132). She surmounted her illiteracy with "her commanding figure and dignified manner" as she gave voice to her racial history and her gender. With her "remarkable gift in prayer and great talent in singing" (132), Truth embodies the spirituality and artistry Hopkins explores in the remaining sketches.

The subject of Harriet Tubman presented greater challenges than the lesser known Sojourner. Because Tubman (like Toussaint and Douglass) had an archetypal presence in race history, Hopkins sought to make anew "the Moses of her people," to render this already familiar cultural figure in an immediate and pertinent way.[12] In "Harriet Tubman ('Moses')" (*CAM*, Jan./Feb. 1902, 210–23), the present political struggles—"the strange Providences which have befallen us as a race" (210)—become the historical extension of Tubman's own struggle seen as parable. Evoking a "paradise lost" familiar to readers of "Toussaint L'Overture," the sketch announces its Christian correspondence to the "life of Jesus." Simultaneously a martyr, "side by side with . . . Joan of Arc, and Florence Nightengale," and a survivor, Tubman exceeds even these Christian prototypes: "for no one of them has shown more courage and power of endurance in facing danger and death to relieve human suffering than has this woman in her heroic and successful endeavors to reach and save all whom she might of her oppressed and suffering race, and pilot them to the promised land of Liberty" (212). Hopkins relies upon this image of the feminized Christ throughout the sketch as she draws Tubman through her "stations of life."

Echoing the slave narrative, Hopkins introduces a range of possibilities regarding Tubman's being named and self-naming and is herself intrigued by the fictional potential of the authorial act of naming. The catalogue of identities mimics the itinerary of her extraordinary life as it merges the domestic with the public life. As "Moses," she becomes the very idealization of motives; as "conductor," she like Christ epitomizes "the Way"; as "Moll Pitcher," she incarnates a national and racial folk hero; as Araminta, she announces the circumstance of her birth; as one who "married," she confirms self-agency and self-authority. Like Toussaint and Truth, Tubman presents no written record for the biographer Hopkins to shape, thereby liberating fictional instincts to dramatize and characterize the emerging historical record. Literal kinship is subordinate to the grander panorama of Tubman's larger racial family. So inherently dramatic is this historical record that Hopkins, as if to deny its seeming fictional excesses, stresses Tubman's humanity: "One of the most ordinary looking of her race; unlettered; no idea of geography! asleep half the time" (215).

When read against the subsequent iconographic sketches, the initiating "Phenomenal Vocalists" is grander in concept and scheme than first appears (*CAM*, Nov. 1901, 45–53). Now its affirmation of "the pathos and trueness to nature" (46) of African American music and its testimonial to the nobility and sacrifice of the African American woman must be read through the lives of Truth and Tubman, investing the sketch with larger race ambitions. Whether to appease the sensibilities of her Victorian readership or to enlarge the historical ground to include an expanded notion of family, Hopkins depicted "the achievements of Negro women who were beacon lights" (46) within a suitably decorous frame. Only the bold eccentricities of the series' icons violate decorum for Victorian women.

In the remaining generalized portraits of educators, literary workers, college elite, and club women, Hopkins explores the women's communal or "lift while climbing" cultural work. As Angela Davis has noted, during these turn-of-the-century years "a serious ideological marriage had linked racism and sexism in a new way" (121), compelling African American women to transform seemingly innocent social activities, like the Boston Women's Era Club, into politically intense circles for social change (Giddings, esp. chap 6). The national club movement, far from being a race-blind sisterhood, broke along politically practical and racially circumstantial lines.[13] While the casual reader of *CAM* might view these sketches as simple testimonials to culture and taste (offering the imitative socialization of the bourgeoisie), Hopkins invested these life studies with the broader cultural ambitions of the national club movement. An insistence upon generational continuity as well as collective identity pervades each installment. Family or name recognition was preserved while a historical race identity was proposed. Hopkins sought to displace cultural ignorance with a schooled intelligence sharpened by fragile and incomplete citizenship.

Unlike earlier portraits celebrating historical moments and individual courage, these communal portraits memorialize individuals (complete with genealogical specifics) because they categorize public work and opportunities for the race. Hopkins assumes that individual achievement is but one way to "mark an era in the progress of the race" (as she notes in "Phenomenal Vocalists" 51). In modifying received biographical strategies, she imposes on the individual life story the imperative of cultivating race consciousness through collective identity. The rising generation must draw individual and race inspiration not simply from the heroic, historically distant few but from their cultural identity as African Americans. Cognizant of her authorial duty to fulfill readers' expectations, Hopkins balances her political agenda of extolling learned and independent womanhood with a socially realized series that, at least superficially, accommodated the ethos.

If Hopkins's men embodied an instructive historical authenticity through sharply focused public lives, these "Famous Women" bridge family and culture to bring progress to the race. Salvation resides in a union of the private and public lives of women *and* men. As Hopkins asserts at the close of "Literary Workers": "Why is the present bright? Because, for the first time, we stand face to face, as a race, with life as it is. Because we are at the parting of the ways and must choose true morality, true spirituality, and the firm basis of all prosperity in races or nations—honest toil in field and shop, doing away with all superficial assumption in education and business" (*CAM*, Apr. 1902, 371). Such physical confrontation requires more than a historical regard for the exemplary: it necessitates a generational continuity with the future. Hopkins, in a manner familiar to readers of her fiction, deliberates on the race's inability to compensate for the "stress and pain of that hated past" (371). Advancement, she suggests, depends upon the construction of an authentic history that can point to, as well as lead beyond, slavery.

Awareness of such tense issues as accommodation and generation

dominate the biographer's historical review at the midpoint of her series on "Educators." Here she simultaneously seems to acknowledge the
inferiority of African American cultural contributions as she suggests the
originary force of African culture. Her historical review undercuts the
privilege accorded Anglo-Saxon "race" accomplishments in its commanding restoration of historical antecedents. Wresting "race" from its
current Anglo-Saxon moorings (A. Davis 110–26; Horsman), Hopkins
seeks originary cultural moments like the one narratized in *Of One
Blood*. Rhetorically, this reversal serves the double-voiced pattern of the
text so that the novelist can both please an accommodationist—black
or white—and inform the militant race-and-culture reader. When Hopkins's many contributions to the *Colored American Magazine* are considered intertextually, she appears more militant and savvy than either
Hazel Carby or Gwendolyn Brooks allows. What Carby labels as her
"unashamed sycophancy" (*Reconstructing Womanhood* 130) and
Brooks declares to be reverence for "the modes and idolatries of the
master" (404) seem upon further reflection to be the linguistic manipulation of a writer conversant with the signifying power of the double-
voiced narrative. This dialogic interplay allows the novelist to inform the
historian-biographer of the interplay between master and slave, polem-
icist and accommodationist.

Through these collective portraits, the biographer privileges the public roles of black women in American society over the customary celebration of "nobler women, more self-sacrificing tender mothers"
(*CAM*, Nov. 1901, 46), so that she may include them in the larger race
tapestry. Nowhere does the domestic sphere receive the attention she
would pay it in her fiction. Not only did the audience for these biographies require the sustaining citizenship instruction that public lives
provided, but the genre demanded it. The series encouraged a move
from the preoccupation with moral suasion and genteel education to
the "organized intelligence" called for in "Club Life among Colored
Women" (*CAM*, Aug. 1902, 273–77). Repeatedly asserting the "intellectual capacity" of African American women, she advanced the cause
of "a new race of colored women" (*CAM*, Oct. 1902, 446–47).

* * *

In those turn-of-the-century years at *CAM*, Hopkins as editor, biographer, historian, and fiction writer understood the intertextual potential of the periodical press. It is difficult from this historical distance to

appreciate the synergic relationship between her individual contributions and her century-distant audience. Though the single-volume re-
publication of her magazine novels makes her serial fiction readily
available to a new generation, it obscures the larger, instructive context of Hopkins's cultural mission at the magazine: to restore "the fire
and romance which lie dormant in our history" (*Contending Forces,*
14). While her biographical sketches may lack the literary "fire and
romance" of her fiction, when read individually in the pages of *CAM,*
they nonetheless significantly enhance our understanding of the ways
Hopkins, as Elizabeth Ammons has noted, "changed history" through
her revisionary reconstruction of the novel (*Conflicting Stories* 85).
Most immediately, these sketches represent an African American woman novelist's attempt (paraphrasing Hopkins) to throttle evil by invoking the power of "an upright manhood and an enlightened womanhood" (*CAM,* July 1902, 213). Though they lack the "distinctiveness
as a discourse" that Elizabeth Fox-Genovese finds critically so compelling in some black women's autobiographies, these biographies adroitly
manipulate a host of generic strategies, generating a sense of the dramatic and historical depth of the African presence in America.

Pauline Hopkins's "talented" fate committed her "to teach life" (Du
Bois, "The Talented Tenth" 861). Long before she joined the Colored
Co-operative Publishing Company and for the remainder of her life,
she wrote as a conscientious African American with a duty to her race,
her gender, and her intellectual and artistic gifts. In reconstructing the
inherited rhetorical conventions of the exemplary life, she sought to
authenticate not simply race history but also black America as an equal
partner in the larger national experience. If Mather and Emerson seem
to constitute an unlikely rhetorical inheritance for a turn-of-the-century African American woman writer, readers need only recall that
Mather's *Magnalia* and Emerson's *Representative Men* were also attempts to construct *American* history ex nihilo. For Hopkins, the appropriation of generic strategies from the dominant white culture was
not a concession to oppressive cultural values. It was a dignified and
accessible way of rendering homage to the African American past.

NOTES

1. In a promotional note for Hopkins's *Contending Forces,* a *CAM* colleague
suggests the very intensity of her authorial fervor: Her "ambition is to become

a writer of fiction, in which the wrongs of her race shall be handled as to enlist the sympathy of all classes of citizens, in this way reaching those who never read history or biography" (*CAM*, Sept. 1900, 195–96). See Carby, *Reconstructing Womanhood* (esp. chaps. 6–7) for a historical account of Hopkins
at *CAM*.

2. Certainly the work of James Olney, William Andrews, Jean Fagan Yellin, Mary Helen Washington, Elizabeth Fox-Genovese, and others has deep-
ened and expanded our sense of African American autobiography and history. The richness of this debate prompts my inquiry into the relatively ignored
realm of African American biography. Unlike the relatively commonplace jour-
nalistic efforts (e.g., *Twentieth-Century Negro Literature*, "written by One
Hundred of America's Greatest Negroes" [*CAM*, vol. 5, 1902] or Child's
sketches in *The Freedmen's Book*), Hopkins's biographies, while suffering from
the formulaic repetitiveness of the genre, demand serious treatment as literary historical acts of recovery and commemoration.

See Andrews, "Representation of Slavery" (72) for a discussion of Booker
T. Washington's preference for biography; see Bercovitch, *Puritan Origins* (esp.
chap. 5) for a suggestive account of the early nineteenth-century culture of
American biography and the ways in which it reflects Cotton Mather's attempt
to construct history through hagiography in the wake of another great migration; see also Murdock, Introduction (26–48).

3. Hopkins targeted an audience conversant with those Puritan ancestors
of Emerson and Child as well as with Frederick Douglass, Paul Laurence
Dunbar, Charles Chestnutt, and W. E. B. Du Bois. Her readers, acquainted with
the literary conventions of Washington's *Up from Slavery* (published serially
in *Outlook*, Nov. 3, 1900, to Feb. 23, 1902) as well as Du Bois's articles in
the *Atlantic Monthly* and elsewhere (soon to form the core of *The Souls of
Black Folk* [1903]), would hear the double-voiced ambition of a cultural history bonded to an authentic national context. But because African American
culture drew on experiences greatly differing from those of the Puritans and
other white New Englanders, she appropriately modified her inherited rhetoric, subverting the classical oration and its Puritan and Emersonian embellish-
ments by insinuating strategies drawn from the slave narrative, tailoring them
to meet the needs of her audience of partially enfranchised citizens.

4. Hopkins, "Edwin Garrison Walker" (*CAM*, Mar. 1901, 358); compare
with Emerson's assertion in "History" (240) and *Emerson in His Journals* (May
28, 1839 [p. 219]); see also Du Bois, "The Conservation of Races" (817).

See White, *Metahistory* (68–69) for an extended discussion of "the conception of history as the story of heroes . . . as the special achievement of the
Romantic age of the early nineteenth century"; see West, *The American Evasion* (138–50) for consideration of Du Bois's intellectual debt to Emerson and
William James; and Bruce, "W. E. B. Du Bois."

5. The recurrent generic structure as well as Hopkins's variations upon it may be recognized in several ways. Borrowing from rhetorical structures familiar to readers of Mather, Emerson, and Child, these reconstructed exemplary lives of major historical figures typically include most of the following: a classical invocation or exordium followed by narration that supplies the genealogical information characteristic of the slave narrative, information of particular interest to people forcibly deprived of their ancestry; a dramatic narration, evoking the slave narrative in its rhetorical urgency and purpose; relevant historical documentation to authenticate the drama; an exhortation reminiscent of Mather and Emerson; dialogue (a novelist's means of persuasion)—fictional, of course—to bring the subject to life; and a classical epilogue, again in the Emersonian mode, effectively summarizing the postnarrative relevance for a contemporary audience.

As Olney notes in "'I Was Born,'" readers of slave narratives are apt to be "dazed by the mere repetitiveness of it all" (148). The generic conventions of the typical exemplary biography share this lack of rhetorical variance.

6. Child appended this editorial instruction to Harriet Jacobs's "The Good Grandmother," noting: "The above account is no fiction. The author, who was thirty years in Slavery, wrote it in an interesting book entitled 'Linda.' She is an esteemed friend of mine; and I introduce this portion of her story here to illustrate the power of character over circumstances" (218).

7. See White, *Metahistory* (1–42) for definitions of emplotment and argument in history; see Tate, "Allegories" (107) for consideration of the fundamental differences between the racial discourses of black male and female narratives.

8. There is considerable disagreement in the dating of these series. Roses and Randolph in *Harlem Renaissance* date "Famous Men" from Feb. 1901; Carby in *Reconstructing Womanhood* dates "Famous Men" from Dec. 1900. *CAM*'s internal promotional indexes date the series as follows: "Famous Men of the Negro Race" (Nov. 1900–Oct. 1901); "Famous Women of the Negro Race" (Nov. 1901–Oct. 1902). A complete list of the articles in these series can be found in the bibliography at the end of this volume.

9. Du Bois writes: "This history of the world is the history not of individuals, but of groups, not of nations, but of races, and he who ignores or seeks to override the race idea in human history ignores and overrides the thought of all history. . . . [Race becomes] a vast family of human beings generally of common blood and language, always of common history, traditions, and impulses, who are both voluntarily and involuntarily striving together for the accomplishment of certain more or less vividly conceived ideals of life" ("The Conservation of Races" 817)

10. Carby also notes that this generational history informs Hopkins's historical fiction as well: "In Hopkins's fictional representation of the social re-

lations between black and white, she reconstructed a generational history across a century to situate the contemporary reassertion of the doctrine of white supremacy within a framework that demythologized the American story of origins" (*Reconstructing Womanhood* 141).

11. See Baldwin, "White Man's Guilt": "White man, hear me! History, as nearly no one seems to know, is not merely something to be read. And it does not refer merely, or even principally, to the past. On the contrary, the great force of history comes from the fact that we carry it with us, are unconsciously controlled by it in many ways, and history is literally *present* in all that we do" (410).

12. See Bercovitch, *Puritan Origins* (esp. chap. 5) for a discussion of the typological significance of Moses in American biography. From John Winthrop to Daniel Boone and Mark Twain, Americans have found Moses to be an archetype for their "errand into the wilderness."

13. See Lerner, *Black Women in White America* (575–76) for Fannie Barrier Williams's account of being shunned by a white women's club in Chicago: "Progress includes a great deal more than what is generally meant by the terms culture, education and contact. The club movement among colored women reaches into the sub-social condition of the entire race. . . . The club is only one of the many means for the social uplift of a race. . . . The club movement is well purposed. . . . It is not a fad. . . . It is rather the force of a new intelligence against the old ignorance. The struggle of an enlightened conscience against the whole brood of social miseries, born out of the stress and pain of a hated past."

WORKS CITED

Ammons, Elizabeth. *Conflicting Stories: American Women Writers at the Turn into the Twentieth Century.* New York: Oxford University Press, 1991.

———, ed. *Short Fiction by Black Women, 1900–1920.* New York: Oxford University Press, 1991.

Andrews, William. "The Representation of Slavery and the Rise of Afro-American Literary Realism, 1865–1920." In *Slavery and the Literary Imagination.* Ed. McDowell and Rampersad. 62–80.

———. *To Tell a Free Story: The First Century of Afro-American Autobiography, 1760–1865.* Urbana: University of Illinois Press, 1986.

Baldwin, James. "White Man's Guilt." In *The Price of the Ticket: Collected Nonfiction, 1948–1985.* New York: St. Martin's, 1985. 409–14.

Bender, John, and David E. Welbery, eds. *Chronotypes: The Construction of Time.* Stanford, Calif.: Stanford University Press, 1991.

Bercovitch, Sacvan. *The Puritan Origins of the American Self.* New Haven, Conn.: Yale University Press, 1975.

————. *The Rites of Assent: Transformations in the Symbolic Construction of America.* New York: Routledge, 1993.

Brooks, Gwendolyn. Afterword. *Contending Forces.* By Hopkins. 403–9.

Bruce, Dickson D., Jr. *Black American Writing from the Nadir: The Evolution of a Literary Tradition, 1877–1915.* Baton Rouge: Louisiana State University Press, 1989.

————. "W. E. B. Du Bois and the Idea of Double Consciousness." *American Literature* 64 (June 1992): 299–309.

Carby, Hazel V. Introduction. *The Magazine Novels of Pauline Hopkins.* By Hopkins. xxix-l.

————. "The Quicksands of Representation: Rethinking Black Cultural Politics." In *Reading Black, Reading Feminist.* Ed. Gates. 76–90.

————. *Reconstructing Womanhood: The Emergence of the Afro-American Woman Novelist.* New York: Oxford University Press, 1987.

Child, Lydia Maria. *The Freedmen's Book.* 1865. New York: Arno, 1968.

Davis, Angela Y. *Women, Race, and Class.* New York: Vintage, 1981.

Davis, Charles T., and Henry Louis Gates, Jr., eds. *The Slave's Narrative.* New York: Oxford University Press, 1985.

Du Bois, W. E. B. "The Conservation of Races." 1897. In *Writings.* 815–26.

————. *The Souls of Black Folk.* 1903. In *Writings.* 357–547.

————. "The Talented Tenth." 1903. In *Writings.* 842–61.

————. *Writings.* New York: Library of America, 1986.

Emerson, Ralph Waldo. *Emerson in His Journals.* Ed. Joel Porte. Cambridge, Mass.: Harvard University Press, 1982.

————. *Essays and Lectures.* New York: Library of America, 1983.

————. "History." 1841. In *Essays and Lectures.* 236–57.

————. *Representative Men.* 1850. In *Essays and Lectures.* 615–761.

Fineman, Joel. "The History of the Anecdote: Fiction and Fiction." In *New Historicism.* Ed. Veeser. 49–76.

Fox-Genovese, Elizabeth. "'My Statue, My Self': Autobiographical Writings of Afro-American Women." In *Reading Black, Reading Feminist.* Ed. Gates. 176–203.

Gates, Henry Louis, Jr., ed. *Reading Black, Reading Feminist: A Critical Anthology.* New York: Meridian, 1990.

Giddings, Paula. *When and Where I Enter: The Impact of Black Women on Race and Sex in America.* New York: Morrow, 1984.

Goody, Jack. "The Time of Telling and the Telling of Time in Written and Oral Cultures." In *Chronotypes.* Ed. Bender and Wellbery. 77–98.

Hopkins, Pauline E. *Contending Forces: A Romance Illustrative of Negro Life North and South.* 1900. Carbondale: Southern Illinois University Press, 1978.

————. *The Magazine Novels of Pauline Hopkins.* New York: Oxford University Press, 1988.

Horsman, Reginald. *Race and Manifest Destiny: The Origins of American Racial Anglo-Saxonism*. Cambridge, Mass.: Harvard University Press, 1981.

Jacobs, Harriet. *Incidents in the Life of a Slave Girl*. 1861. Ed. Jean Fagan Yellin. Cambridge, Mass.: Harvard University Press, 1987.

Johnson, Abby Arthur, and Ronald Maberry Johnson. "Away from Accommodation: Radical Editors and Protest Journalism, 1900–1910." *Journal of Negro History* 62 (Oct. 1977): 325–38.

———. *Propaganda and Aesthetics: The Literary Politics of African-American Magazines in the Twentieth Century*. 2d ed. Amherst: University of Massachusetts Press, 1991.

Lerner, Gerda, ed. *Black Women in White America: A Documentary History*. New York: Pantheon, 1972.

Mather, Cotton. *Magnalia Christi Americana; or, The Ecclesiastical History of New England, Books I and II*. 1702. Cambridge, Mass.: Harvard University Press, 1977.

McDowell, Deborah E. "'The Changing Same': Generational Connections and Black Women Novelists." In *Reading Black, Reading Feminist*. Ed. Gates. 91–115.

———. "Reading Family Matters." In *Changing Our Own Words*. Ed. Wall. 75–97.

McDowell, Deborah E., and Arnold Rampersad, eds. *Slavery and the Literary Imagination*. Baltimore, Md.: Johns Hopkins University Press, 1989.

McKay, Nellie Y. "The Souls of Black Women Folk in the Writings of W. E. B. Du Bois." In *Reading Black, Reading Feminist*. Ed. Gates. 227–43.

Meier, August. *Negro Thought in America, 1880–1915*. 2d ed. Ann Arbor: University of Michigan Press, 1988.

Mitchell, W. J. T., ed. *On Narrative*. Chicago: University of Chicago Press, 1981.

Morrison, Toni, ed. *Race-ing, Justice, En-Gendering Power: Essays on Anita Hill, Clarence Thomas, and the Construction of Social Reality*. New York: Pantheon, 1992.

Moses, Wilson Jeremiah. *Alexander Crummell: A Study of Civilization and Discontent*. New York: Oxford University Press, 1989.

Murdock, Kenneth. Introduction. *Magnalia Christi Americana*. By Mather. 1–48.

Olney, James. "The Founding Fathers: Frederick Douglass and Booker T. Washington." In *Slavery and the Literary Imagination*. Ed. McDowell and Rampersad. 1–24.

———. "'I Was Born': Slave Narratives, Their Status as Autobiography and as Literature." In *Reading Black, Reading Feminist*. Ed. Gates. 148–74.

Pryse, Marjorie, and Hortense J. Spillers, eds. *Conjuring: Black Women, Fiction, and Literary Tradition*. Bloomington: Indiana University Press, 1985.

Roses, Lorraine Elena, and Ruth Elizabeth Randolph. *Harlem Renaissance and Beyond: Literary Biographies of 100 Black Women Writers, 1900–1945*. Boston: G. K. Hall, 1990.

Stansell, Christine. "White Feminists and Black Realities: The Politics of Authenticity." In *Race-ing, Justice, En-Gendering Power*. Ed. Morrison. 251–68.

Tate, Claudia. "Allegories of Black Female Desire; or, Rereading Nineteenth-Century Sentimental Narratives of Black Female Authority." In *Changing Our Own Words*. Ed. Wall. 98–126.

———. *Domestic Allegories of Political Desire: The Black Heroine's Text at the Turn of the Century*. New York: Oxford University Press, 1992.

———. "Pauline Hopkins: Our Literary Foremother." In *Conjuring*. Ed. Pryse and Spillers. 53–66.

Veeser, H. Aram, ed. *The New Historicism*. New York: Routledge, 1989.

Wall, Cheryl A., ed. *Changing Our Own Words: Essays on Criticism, Theory, and Writing by Black Women*. New Brunswick, N.J.: Rutgers University Press, 1989.

Washington, Booker T. *The Story of My Life and Work*. 1900. New York: Negro Universities Press, 1969.

———. *Up from Slavery*. 1901. New York: Penguin, 1986.

West, Cornel. *The American Evasion of Philosophy: A Genealogy of Pragmatism*. Madison: University of Wisconsin Press, 1989.

———. "Black Leadership and the Pitfalls of Racial Reasoning." In *Race-ing, Justice, En-Gendering Power*. Ed. Morrison. 390–401.

White, Hayden. *Metahistory: The Historical Imagination in Nineteenth-Century Europe*. Baltimore, Md.: Johns Hopkins University Press, 1973.

———. "The Value of Narrativity in the Representation of Reality." In *On Narrative*. Ed. Mitchell. 1–24.

Wilson, Edmund. *Axel's Castle: A Study in the Imaginative Literature of 1870–1930*. New York: Scribner's, 1969.

FOUR

Taking Liberties:
Pauline Hopkins's Recasting
of the *Creole* Rebellion

John Cullen Gruesser

> Fiction is of great value to any people as a preserver
> of manners and customs—religious, political and so-
> cial. It is a record of growth and development from
> generation to generation. *No one will do this for us;*
> *we must ourselves develop the men and women who*
> *will faithfully portray the inmost thoughts and feelings*
> *of the Negro with all the fire and romance which lie*
> *dormant in our history,* and, as yet, unrecognized by
> writers of the Anglo-Saxon race.
> —Pauline Hopkins, *Contending Forces*
> (emphasis in original)

The preceding quotation expresses two key tenets of the literary philosophy of Pauline Hopkins, the most prolific African American woman
writer and the most influential black literary editor of the first decade
of the twentieth century. Hopkins believed that an intimate relationship should exist between African American fiction and African American history. Not only could novels and short stories be an effective
means of making the race's past familiar to newly literate black Americans, but African American history, containing countless episodes filled
with "fire and romance," could offer writers material readily adapt-
able to political and artistic purposes. Hopkins also believed, however, that it was up to African American authors to exploit the didactic,
propagandistic, and artistic potential that lay "dormant" in their history. If the race did not produce a group of writers committed to the
achievement of this goal, then African Americans risked having their
past either consigned to oblivion or willfully distorted by their enemies.

Hopkins puts her ideas about African American literature into practice in "A Dash for Liberty" (1901). Published in the *Colored American Magazine* (*CAM*), this short story not only commemorates a significant moment in African American history, the 1841 rebellion on the slave ship *Creole,* but also rewrites this historical episode so that it resonates with the turn-of-the-century challenges confronting African Americans. Moreover, "A Dash for Liberty," the first twentieth-century treatment of the *Creole* revolt, can be read as Hopkins's declaration of independence from both the white historical record and earlier writing by African American and white abolitionist authors. Before turning my attention to Hopkins's story, I will provide some background information on the *Creole* affair and the nineteenth-century literary works based upon it.

* * *

Madison Washington was a Virginia slave who led a successful revolt on the slave ship *Creole* in 1841 and whose life inspired literary works by Frederick Douglass, William Wells Brown, and Lydia Maria Child in the 1850s and 1860s. Four decades later, Hopkins wrote "A Dash for Liberty," a new version of the *Creole* uprising and the life of its leader, whom she renames Madison Monroe.[1] Although a number of recent articles have discussed Douglass's "The Heroic Slave" (1853)—the earliest and longest version of the story—only Richard Yarborough has commented upon the versions by Brown, Child, and Hopkins. In addition to exploiting the patriotic and romantic potential of Washington's story, as her literary antecedents do, Hopkins incorporates into her version a theme particularly relevant to conditions that African Americans faced in 1901: the need for unified action to combat white oppression of both black men and black women.[2]

In late October 1841, the American brig *Creole* left Virginia with a cargo of tobacco and slaves bound for New Orleans. The 135 slaves on board were strictly segregated by sex: the men were held in the forward hold and the women in the rear of the vessel. The revolt began on the evening of November 7 when the overseer, William Merritt, found Madison Washington, described in the depositions as a large and powerfully built man and the head cook for the slaves, in the main hold aft with the women. Merritt and the first mate, Zephaniah Gifford, tried to grab Washington, but he broke free while another slave, Elijah Morris, fired a pistol at Gifford. Washington then called upon the other slaves to join him. A fierce battle raged between the nineteen slaves who participated in the rebellion on one side and the ten members of the crew and four white passengers on the other. By 1:00 A.M. the rebels had control of the ship; one white man was dead and some others wounded, and two slaves were seriously injured, one mortally. Washington wanted to sail for Liberia, but when Merritt, who agreed to navigate the ship, told him there were not enough provisions for such an extended voyage, Washington settled for Nassau in the Bahamas. On the morning of November 9, the *Creole* reached this British colony where slavery was illegal.

Despite the protestations of John Bacon, the American consul, the slaves who did not participate in the revolt were allowed to go free. Likewise, in defiance of American demands for their extradition, the nineteen rebels were held for a few months and then released.[3] Although abolitionists applauded the British actions, politicians in the South and North deplored what they regarded as Great Britain's unwarranted interference in a purely American affair. Daniel Webster expressed the Tyler administration's displeasure to London, and the *Creole* episode greatly complicated the negotiations that eventually led to the August 1842 Webster-Ashburton Treaty, which defined the boundary between British and American territory from Maine to Minnesota. Over a decade later, the Anglo-American Claims Commission awarded the United States $110,330 for the slaves lost in the *Creole* affair.

Although the uprising on the *Creole* figures prominently in Douglass, Brown, and Child's literary versions of the story, Madison Washington's life prior to the rebellion plays an even more important role in these works. On this subject, however, there is almost no historical record. The three nineteenth-century stories based on Washington's life were all influenced directly or indirectly by a June 1842 *Liberator* article. As speculative as it is informative, "Madison Washington: Another Chapter in His History" remains the only source of biographical information about Washington, aside from some brief references to him in some of Frederick Douglass's speeches in the 1840s,[4] Henry Highland Garnet's "Address to the Slaves of the United States," and the white abolitionist Joshua Coffin's history of slave insurrections.

Repeating earlier descriptions of Washington as a freedom fighter (and thus a patriot worthy of his name), the *Liberator* article offers a "new clue" to the character of the "hero" of the *Creole* revolt, adding a romantic dimension to his story: reports from Canadian and northern abolitionists that Washington had been free in Canada but returned to Virginia to liberate his wife. The article hypothesizes that Washington's wife might have been on board the *Creole,* which would explain his presence among the women slaves that triggered the revolt, and calls for British abolitionists to gather more information about Washington, which apparently was never forthcoming.[5] As William Andrews notes, "This effort by the *Liberator* to infer a romantic plot underlying the *Creole* incidents testifies to a strong desire of American abolitionism for *a* story, if not *the* story, about Washington that would realize him as a powerful symbol of black antislavery heroism" (28).

In contrast to the significantly shorter versions that followed it, Douglass's "The Heroic Slave," the only version published before the Civil War, runs over thirty pages. This novella, Douglass's sole foray into fiction, was written primarily for a white, northern male audience, as Andrews, Robert Stepto, and Richard Yarborough have noted. Unlike Brown and Child, Douglass divides his story into four sections. Part one emphasizes the patriotic aspect of Washington's history but also introduces the romantic. In a Virginia forest, a northern white man, Mr. Listwell, determines to become an abolitionist after overhearing Madison Washington's to-be-or-not-to-be-free soliloquy, in which he expresses both his desire to escape and his reluctance to do so because of his love for his wife Susan. In part two, Washington, now a fugitive, arrives by chance at the Listwells' home in Ohio, tells them about his escape and the five years he passed in the Virginia woods during which he was sustained only by weekly meetings with Susan, and with the abolitionist couple's help reaches Canada safely, a free man at last. In the third section, Douglass cuts short the romantic plot to focus on the patriotic. Listwell and Washington meet again in Virginia a year later, the latter having returned in an effort to liberate his wife, who is then killed in their escape attempt. Before Washington boards the slaver bound for New Orleans, Listwell slips him files with which to cut himself free. In the final section, two Virginia sailors discuss the *Creole* revolt, which one of them experienced firsthand. Like Listwell, who in part one is converted to abolitionism by Washington's words, this sailor has changed his mind about slavery as a result of witnessing Washington's bravery, leadership, and restraint during the rebellion and its aftermath.

Brown's and Child's depictions of the *Creole* episode have much more in common with each other than they do with Douglass's "The Heroic Slave." There are also significant differences between them.[6] Given literacy rates and socioeconomic conditions at the time, Brown, like

Douglass, was still writing mainly for a white audience. Nevertheless, the dynamics of the situation for African Americans in general and black writers in particular had changed greatly in the decade since the publication of "The Heroic Slave." Brown actually wrote two versions of the story: one, entitled "Madison Washington," appeared in *The Black Man, His Antecedents, His Genius, and His Achievements* in 1863; the other, "Slave Revolt at Sea," was chapter 4 of Brown's *The Negro in the American Rebellion* (1867). Apart from the deletion of the final sentence of "Madison Washington" and the addition of one paragraph to the beginning and three paragraphs to the end of "Slave Revolt at Sea," the versions are identical.

Both books in which Brown's account of Washington appeared were early attempts to write black history. More ambitious than its successor, *The Black Man* stresses continuity by beginning in antiquity and concluding with portraits of notable African Americans. In the preface to *The Negro in the American Rebellion*, Brown states that this work began as an attempt "to serve for future reference an account of the part which the Negro took in suppressing the Slaveholders' rebellion" to which he added "a sketch of the conditions of the race previous to the commencement of the war" that emphasized African American bravery and resistance (v).

In contrast to the versions by Douglass and Brown who were African Americans writing mainly for a white audience, "Madison Washington," the story by the white abolitionist, fiction writer, and essayist Lydia Maria Child, appeared in *The Freedmen's Book* (1865), an anthology of biographical sketches, poems, essays, and household tips designed to be used in advanced classes of the freedmen's schools. Although Child's aims were in part didactic,[7] she clearly regarded the volume as historically significant, referring to it in her preface, "To the Freedmen," as the "true record of what colored men have accomplished under great disadvantages."

Richard Yarborough notes that, in contrast to "The Heroic Slave," the subsequent versions not only greatly limit the role assigned to white characters in order to emphasize the nobility and bravery of the protagonist—whom they, unlike Douglass, describe as an unmixed African—but also explicitly depict the violence of Washington's rebelliousness and maximize the romantic possibilities of the story. In the versions by Brown, Child, and Hopkins, Washington—both in his attempt to liberate Susan from the plantation and in leading the slave revolt on the *Creole*—

fells his white adversaries, either with his fists or a club. Moreover, following through on the *Liberator* article's suggestion, Susan is on board the *Creole* when the uprising takes place in the three later versions.

Child opts for a surprise melodramatic ending, waiting until the last page of the sketch to reveal Susan's presence on the boat. Brown and Hopkins, however, inform the reader early on that Susan is aboard, but the husband and wife do not discover each other's presence until the morning after the rebellion. In contrast to Douglass and Brown, as Yarborough points out, Child hints that the possibility that Susan will be sexually abused in part motivates Washington to return to Virginia for her, which becomes a major theme in Hopkins's version.

* * *

Several elements make "A Dash for Liberty" unique among the literary renditions of the *Creole* affair. One of the most important of these is the fact that the story was written by a black female writer for the readers of the *Colored American Magazine,* "the first significant Afro-American journal to emerge in the twentieth century" (Johnson and Johnson 4).[8] In addition to contributing a remarkable number of essays, articles, short stories, and novels to the periodical, Hopkins played a major editorial role at the magazine. Although she was not listed as editor-in-chief on the masthead until March 1904, there is strong evidence to suggest that she may have been functioning in that capacity for a considerable period.[9] Hazel Carby has described Hopkins's editorial philosophy:

> The *Colored American Magazine* was a direct response to the political climate of the turn of the century—that is, to black disenfranchisement, Jim Crow laws, the widespread murder of black people in the South, and political apathy in the North. Hopkins viewed the journal as a vehicle for social intervention, as an attempt to replace the politics of compromise with political demands for change in social relations. The first editorial asserted that the *Colored American Magazine* "aspire[d] to develop and intensify the bonds of that racial brotherhood, which alone can enable a people, to assert their racial rights as men, and demand their privileges as citizens." (xxxii)

Hopkins was convinced that fiction could be instrumental in this struggle, as the epigraph to this essay indicates. In her introduction to *Short*

Fiction by Black Women, 1900–1920, Elizabeth Ammons underscores the key role that Hopkins's solicitation, promotion, and selection of poetry, short stories, and novels for publication in *CAM* played in the development of black literature at the start of the century. Hopkins believed that fiction could be used "to enlist the sympathy of all classes of citizens" to the injustices suffered by African Americans through its unique ability to reach "those who never read history or biography" (*CAM*, Jan. 1901, 219).

Without question, the most distinctive feature of Hopkins's version of the *Creole* episode is her decision to rechristen the main character Madison Monroe. Writers and scholars have pointed out the pivotal role that naming and unnaming have played in black experience. As Michael G. Cooke notes, African American literary texts often concern "the presence or absence of names, their status and their scope" (172).[10] A person's name holds the key to his or her identity. To rob someone of his or her name is to cut that person off from his or her ancestry, family, and history; whereas, to give someone a name situates the person within a societal, genealogical, and historical framework. As devastating as it can be for a person to be deprived of a name, being given a false one can be even more destructive. Observers since the 1840s have commented on the appropriateness of Madison Washington's name in view of the actions attributed to him;[11] however, from one perspective, it was a fictional and potentially meaningless title given to a slave of pure African ancestry, presumably by his white owner. As the writer of two extended biographical series in *CAM*, "Famous Men of the Negro Race" and "Famous Women of the Negro Race," and as a literary artist who consistently incorporated history into her novels and short stories, Hopkins would not alter the name of an early black figure in a work of fiction without careful premeditation, particularly given the historical and political repercussions of such an action.

The search for a strictly historical motivation behind the name change, while far from conclusive in itself, uncovers some interesting facts. George Washington and James Monroe (like James Madison) were presidents from Virginia who served in the Revolutionary War. They also held slaves. Neither Monroe's response as governor of Virginia to Gabriel Prosser's ill-fated slave insurrection in and around Richmond in 1800 nor his actions as president during the debate over and passage of the Missouri Compromise between 1819 and 1821 seem meritorious enough to warrant Hopkins's substitution of his name for

Washington's. On the other hand, Monroe supported emigration to Liberia, and the first settlement, which would later become the country's capital, was named in his honor by the American Colonization Society. This seems relevant given that the leader of the *Creole* rebellion is described as an "unmixed African" in all but Douglass's version of the story, that historical accounts of the uprising report that upon gaining control of the vessel Washington originally wanted to sail to Liberia, and that the whole trajectory of Hopkins's story points in the direction of Africa (as I discuss below). Lest Monroe be mistaken as an abolitionist, however, it should be noted that he has been characterized as a typical southern liberal who "became an ardent advocate of the colonization of freed slaves in Africa as the best means of resolving the problem" that he, like Jefferson, believed liberated blacks posed to the country (Ammon 189). Nevertheless, the Virginian's association with Liberia, his support—qualified though it was—of an effort by free blacks to form their own community, may account for Hopkins's decision to change her main character's name *to* Monroe.

As to the question of why she changed the name *from* Washington, even more pertinent may be the contemporary struggle within the black community between those allied with Booker T. Washington and his policy of accommodating white constraints placed on African Americans and those opposed to Washington's ideas, particularly W. E. B. Du Bois. A year earlier in her novel *Contending Forces,* Hopkins had thematized this debate through the contrasting philosophies of her characters Arthur Lewis and Will Smith. In "A Dash for Liberty," changing the name of her protagonist—who organizes a brave corps of African Americans who will lead their fellow blacks to freedom—from Washington entailed an implicit criticism of the leading black figure in turn-of-the-century America, someone whose program Hopkins regarded as inimical to the best interests of African Americans. (Whether cognizant of this subtle slight or not, the powerful Booker T. Washington would later revenge himself on Hopkins for her more overt questionings of his policies by having an ally, Fred R. Moore, buy the *Colored American Magazine* in 1904, remove it to New York from its strong base of support in Boston, and eventually fire Hopkins.)

An even more compelling explanation for the name change is that Hopkins recognized that the earlier versions of Washington's life were already consciously crafted fictions based only partly on historical fact; by changing the hero's last name she was emphasizing the fictiveness

of her version.[12] Both Robert Stepto and William Andrews have credited Douglass's "The Heroic Slave" (1853) with being the first attempt
to break out of the autobiographical-biographical mode of African
American writing rooted in oral storytelling and use fiction as a means
to convey a political message. By naming her protagonist Madison
Monroe rather than Madison Washington, Hopkins signals that she is
creating a new fiction inspired by the historical events relating to the
Creole episode that differs substantively from those that preceded it.
In contrast to the Douglass, Brown, and Child versions, written just
before, during, and immediately after the Civil War (and aimed at a
northern white and/or newly freed black audience), "A Dash for Liberty" uses the historical facts relating to the *Creole* revolt to address
issues that directly concerned her turn-of-the-century black readers.

Complicating matters, as Yarborough notes but does not comment
upon (187), the following citation is affixed to the top of "A Dash for
Liberty," between the story's title and the author's name: "Founded on
an article written by Col. T. W. Higginson, for the Atlantic Monthly,
June 1861." Thomas Wentworth Higginson's article is a sixteen-page
account of Denmark Vesey's abortive slave uprising in Charleston,
South Carolina, in 1822 that makes no specific mention of Madison
Washington or any other leader of a slave rebellion. Given the fact that
Hopkins was generally quite scrupulous in acknowledging her sources, particularly when these were African Americans and white abolitionists whose work was often little known, we can discount deliberate obfuscation on her part. Two explanations, then, come to mind:
either the headnote is a mistake or something in Higginson's description of Vesey inspired Hopkins to rewrite Washington's story.

On the one hand, there is a piece of evidence that at first glance appears to support the argument for error. *The Black Man* by William
Wells Brown, whom Hopkins met and who became a major influence
on her life and work, contains not only a sketch of Madison Washington but also one of Denmark Vesey. In an uncharacteristic move, according to his biographer William Farrison, Brown specifically cites
Higginson's *Atlantic Monthly* article at the end of the pages devoted
to Vesey. Thus, it certainly seems possible that Hopkins could have
carelessly confused the two sketches, believing that Higginson's article inspired Brown's account of Washington. But why would she cite
Brown's source rather than Brown himself?

On the other hand, it also seems possible that Hopkins, with Brown's description of Washington fresh in her mind, looked up Higginson's article after reading the account of Vesey in *The Black Man* and found something there that inspired her to write her own version of the *Creole* affair. In support of this theory, an important link exists between Washington and Vesey: both men were free when they conceived of their plans to liberate those still in bondage. According to the article in the *Liberator,* Washington had escaped to Canada but returned to Virginia to free his wife only to be captured, sold, and transported on the *Creole*. Similarly, in a sentence that according to Higginson "reveal[s] the secret soul of Denmark Vesey," a fellow insurrectionist reports that "Vesey, on first broaching the plan to him, said 'he was satisfied with his own condition, being free, *but, as all his children were slaves, he wished to see what could be done for them*'" (731–32, Higginson's emphasis). Like Brown's version, Hopkins's story begins with the free Monroe deciding to leave Canada and return to Virginia to liberate his wife, thereby underscoring his commitment to freeing others despite risks to himself. Thus, it seems not only plausible but likely that in "A Dash for Liberty" she was inspired in part by Higginson's depiction of Vesey's effort to organize blacks to fight for their freedom.

Hopkins's headnote, then, can be seen as reinforcing the "fictive" nature of "A Dash for Liberty." By citing Higginson at the start of her story, Hopkins emphasizes the uniqueness of her version of the *Creole* episode, which not only draws upon and revises the white historical record and her literary antecedents (Douglass, Brown, Child, *and* Higginson) but also addresses the situation African Americans found themselves in at the turn of the century.

Like Douglass, Hopkins divides her *Creole* story into four parts; she devotes each to a different geographic location—two American settings sandwiched between two foreign ones. Each move takes Monroe to the southeast, roughly in the direction of Africa. Moreover, as the story progresses, Monroe surrounds himself with an increasingly larger number of black people committed to freedom. Section one presents Monroe free in Canada but alone. The second section depicts Monroe trying to free his wife in Virginia. Section three is set in the North Atlantic on board the southbound *Creole,* where a black community is created that acts in concert to free themselves and the other slaves. The final and shortest section describes the slave ship's arrival in Nassau, where

the newly freed community of men and women are "offered protection and hospitality" (98/247)[13] by a predominantly black society where
slavery is illegal.

Hopkins devises a structure at once compact, rife with meaning, and
symmetrical. In the earlier versions of the story, Washington's return
to the South for his wife serves as the high point of the romantic plot
while his liberation of the slave ship functions as the climax of the
patriotic plot. Hopkins not only weaves these narrative threads into
her story, she also demonstrates the need for unified action to combat
white oppression of blacks in general and the sexual exploitation of
black women in particular, a theme that reaches its turning point in
section three at nearly the same moment as the patriotic plot.

In contrast to her literary antecedents, Hopkins places a great deal
of emphasis on the vulnerability of black women to sexual assualt by
white men in "A Dash for Liberty." Whereas Douglass, Brown, and
Child follow the *Liberator* article's lead in stressing the romantic aspect of Washington's return to the South, Hopkins stresses that Monroe acts primarily to protect his wife from sexual abuse—a justified fear
as the captain's subsequent rape attempt shows. In the first section,
Monroe tells his Canadian employer: "Imagine yourself in my place;
how would you feel? The relentless heel of oppression in the States will
have ground my rights as a husband into the dust, and have driven
Susan to despair in that time. A white man may take up arms to defend a bit of property; but a black man has no right to his wife, his liberty, or his life against his master. This makes me low-spirited, Mr.
Dickson, and I have determined to return to Virginia for my wife. My
feelings are centered in the idea of liberty" (89/243). Here, at the start
of the story, Hopkins intertwines the sexual exploitation theme with
the patriotic plot. When Monroe and his eighteen companions free
themselves and 116 other slaves in the *Creole* revolt in the second half
of the story, he unwittingly achieves his original purpose as announced
in the first section. Monroe and his men not only free his wife Susan,
who unbeknown to them happens to be on board, but their rebellion
puts a stop to the captain's attempted rape.

At this point, I must take issue with one aspect of Yarborough's oth-
erwise perceptive comments about "A Dash for Liberty." After noting
Hopkins's introduction of the theme of sexual exploitation into her
Creole story and her innovation of giving a voice and a force to Sus-

an, Yarborough then describes Hopkins's depiction of the behavior of her protagonist and his wife as stereotypically romantic:

> By having Madison fortuitously appear and interrupt the assault on Susan like some white knight rushing to the aid of a damsel, Hopkins ultimately falls back on the conventions of sentimental romance. Hopkins does succeed in reinserting the black female into a field of action dominated, in Douglass's fiction, by the male. However, in claiming for Susan a conventional role generally denied black women, she necessarily endorses the accompanying male paradigm in her depiction of Madison, a paradigm drawn from the same set of gender constructions that provides Douglass with his heroic model. (178)

Yet, as Yarborough himself acknowledges, the first act of violence performed by a black person on board the *Creole* is Susan's striking of the captain to stop his assault on her. Moreover, although there can be no disputing that in the climactic moments of section three Monroe acts while Susan waits for some kind of deliverance, Yarborough misses what I believe to be a major innovation in Hopkins's retelling of the *Creole* story: her stress on the fact that Monroe does not act independently. To substitute one figure of speech for a more apposite one, rather than bursting in like a solitary white knight rescuing a fair maiden, Monroe successfully leads a black cavalry into battle against the forces of white oppression. Douglass, Brown, and Child all create an inspiring figure who embodies the "white" values of an unswerving commitment to freedom (to match his suggestive name) and an undying love for one's spouse—the patriotic and romantic plots. In contrast, Hopkins stresses communal action—the dash for liberty—even changing the main character's last name (but not altering his circumstances) to deemphasize the individual person in favor of what he and his companions succeed in accomplishing through concerted effort.[14]

Furthermore, the inclusion of the rape scene in the third section balances the structure of Hopkins's story and underscores the importance of creating black unity because in a number of ways it parallels the depiction of Monroe's return to his former place of enslavement in the second section—with one essential difference. Both in Virginia and on board the *Creole,* Susan is separated from the other slaves because of her refinement and great beauty. As a lady's serving maid on the plantation, she sleeps in the main house away from the slave quarters. Similarly, on the slave ship she receives her own cabin because of the captain's designs on her. In both scenes Monroe takes advantage of distractions to mask his assault: in Virginia, he strikes during a party; on the *Creole*, a rainstorm enables the rebels to free themselves without being detected by the whites. In both scenes Monroe fights bravely, armed with a club. However, whereas he fails in Virginia because he acts alone, Monroe succeeds on the *Creole* because he is joined by a dozen and a half other men.

By playing on the multiple meanings of the word "dash," Hopkins's title reinforces her story's four-part structure and emphasizes the need for action to enhance black unity and defend against black women's sexual exploitation. At least five distinct "dashes for liberty" occur in the story. A "dash" can mean a sudden movement or a rush, normally on foot, and this clearly describes Monroe's escape from his Virginia plantation to Canada and freedom, which has already been accomplished before section one opens the story. Like her literary predecessors who emphasize Washington's romantic motivations, Hopkins through her title also refers to Monroe's return to Virginia to free Susan, which is the subject of the second section.

In section three when Hopkins uses the title phrase to describe the revolt, she relies on another definition of "dash," that is, the verve or spirited action Monroe and his companions demonstrate in attempting to take over the ship: "The 'Creole' proceeded slowly on her way towards New Orleans. In the men's cabin, Madison Monroe lay chained to the floor and heavily ironed. But from the first moment on board ship he had been busily engaged in selecting men who could be trusted in the *dash for liberty* that he was determined to make" (95/246, emphasis added). Moreover, because the word "dash" also denotes physical violence, the striking or smashing of someone or something, in the third section Hopkins incorporates an additional "dash for liberty" into her story—a dash by a black woman for the freedom to control her body. On board the *Creole*, Monroe's wife Susan tries to thwart the captain's attempt to rape her first by "dash[ing] his face aside" and then striking him with "a stinging blow across the eyes" (96/246).[15] A further violent "dash" for liberty occurs later in the third section when Monroe uses a capstan bar to kill a white man who has just fatally shot a black rebel. In the story's fourth section one more "dash" is recorded: the *Creole*'s landing or splash against the dock in Nassau where the slaves will find freedom.

Hopkins's illustration of the need for united action to combat various forms of white oppression made her story relevant to the conditions facing African Americans at the turn of the century and resonates with her other writing. In her nonfiction, she comments on the violence and political machinations being directed against African Americans in the 1890s and the early 1900s and advocates a unified response to combat these racist actions. For example, in *A Primer of Facts Pertaining to the Early Greatness of the African Race and the Possibility of Resoration by Its Descendants—with Epilogue,* published at her own expense in 1905, Hopkins angrily denounces the assertions being made about African Americans by the southern "plantation" writers and boldly rejects Booker T. Washington's accommodationist policies:

> Because of the desire and commands of our enemies, shall agitation stop, and shall we sit in silence while our traducers go unanswered? This question answers itself. We cannot cease from agitation while our wrongs are the sport of those who know how to silence our every complaint and plea for justice. NEVER SURRENDER THE BALLOT.
>
> The iron heel of oppression is everywhere; it has reached every section of the country, and every black citizen has a duty to perform. . . . It has reached a pass where the educated Black will handle any subject in his assemblies but politics. The South and its friends have said: "Not a word of complaint, no talk of lynching, not an offensive word, or it will go hard with you," and the race leaders have bowed to that decree in abject submission. (27–28)

Furthermore, in her fiction, Hopkins repeatedly shows a concern for black women and the fact that their relationships with white men, while often resulting in children, are rarely matrimonial. In *Contending Forces,* for instance, Hopkins deplores not only the lynching of black males by southern mobs but also the sexual abuse and concubinage that many black women were subjected to at the turn of the century. Rather than advocating amalgamation as a solution to the "tragic mulatto syndrome" and ultimately the second-class citizenship of black Americans, Hopkins believes that, as a result of slavery, miscegenation in the United States has already occurred on a massive scale. She decries white America's insane and impossible pursuit of racial purity, often used as a justification for acts as contradictory as lynchings and the sexual exploitation of black women by "chivalrous" southern men, the very group responsible for widespread amalgamation in the first place. Frequently in her novels, characters' "blood," their often hidden or unknown familial and racial ancestries, are revealed and play a major role in determining their fates.

Along these lines, I would argue that the name of the slave ship, the *Creole,* perhaps even more than Madison Washington's suggestive name (which, as noted, she deliberately changes), may have been the key factor attracting Hopkins to the slave rebellion as the subject for a *CAM* short story. Like "dash," the word "creole" has various meanings, one of which is a person of mixed white and black ancestry. Similar to Brown and Child, Hopkins describes Monroe as an "unmixed African" and his wife as a "beautiful octoroon." Moveover, in contrast to Douglass, who stresses a symbolic connection between Madison Washington and the founding fathers in the opening paragraph and elsewhere in "The Heroic Slave," Hopkins, echoing something unique to Brown's version, emphasizes a direct blood connection between Susan and one of the founding fathers:

> It was a tradition that her grandfather served in the Revolutionary War, as well as both Houses of Congress. That was nothing, however, at a time when the blood of the proudest F.F.V.'s was freely mingled with that of African slaves on their plantations. Who wonders that Virginia has produced great men of color from among the exbondsmen, or, that illustrious black men proudly point to Virginia as a birthplace? Posterity rises to the plane that their ancestors bequeath, and the most refined, the wealthiest and the most intellectual whites of that proud state have not hesitated to amalgamate with the Negro. (94/245)[16]

Instead of emphasizing how the heroic actions of the black Virginian patriot Washington link him to the white Virginian founding fathers, as Douglass does, Hopkins calls into question the honor of "the most refined, the wealthiest and the most intellectual whites" from Virginia (which Douglass takes for granted) by pointing out the extent to which these men engaged in sexual relations with slave women, thereby fathering mixed race offspring and founding a stigmatized subclass of people to which both Susan and many of the African American women suffering sexual exploitation at the turn of the century belong.

In "A Dash for Liberty," Susan, a creole, and the boat, the *Creole,* are mirror images. Thus, by liberating the one, Monroe and his companions liberate the other. It is only by failing to save Susan by himself and being retaken into slavery in Virginia in the second section that Monroe, at the head of a score of firmly committed men, can truly free her, the other slaves on board the *Creole,* and himself in sections three and four. Just as the rebels put an end to the captain's metaphorical rape of black America—the transportation of human cargo to the slave market of New Orleans—they also stop the captain's actual rape of Susan. In the process, Monroe fulfills the purpose he announced in the first section to protect his wife's virtue and thereby preserves their mixed blood marriage, itself one more and perhaps the story's most important "dash," this time referring to a blending, for liberty.[17]

* * *

In "A Dash for Liberty," Pauline Hopkins not only evokes the "fire and romance" inherent in the *Creole* revolt but also significantly rewrites this historical episode and the earlier literary versions of it to produce her own brand of sophisticated and politically engaged fiction. She implicitly argues that black America will only be fully free when its women no longer suffer sexual oppression and concubinage and that a unified response by and for African American men and women is needed to combat the lynchings, sexual exploitation, and disenfranchisement campaigns directed against them.

NOTES

1. The literary legacy of the *Creole* revolt does not end with "A Dash for Liberty." The rebellion is also the subject of Theodore Ward's four-act musical "Madison" (1956), based on Douglass's "The Heroic Slave."

2. Even today many of the facts relating to the *Creole* rebellion and its aftermath remain sketchy or unknown. Before 1970 the only detailed description of the revolt was an 1842 account in the *Senate Documents* consisting of depositions taken from white sailors and passengers involved in the incident. This remains the single most important source of information about the uprising. In the last twenty-five years, three articles on the *Creole* episode have appeared that have helped to bring the major events of the rebellion into somewhat clearer focus. See Johnson, "The *Creole* Affair"; Jones, "The Peculiar Institution"; and Jervey and Huber, "The *Creole* Affair." The summary that follows is taken from these essays and *Senate Documents.*

3. In contrast to the documented reports of the rebels being freed in Jervey and Huber's and Jones's accounts, Clinton Johnson makes the undocument-

ed assertion that the nineteen participants in the revolt were charged with pi-
racy and murder and an unspecified number of them were tried, convicted, and
executed (249).

4. See Douglass, "American Prejudice against Color: An Address Delivered
in Cork, Ireland, October 23, 1845" (1:59–70); "American and Scottish Prejudice against the Slave: An Address Delivered in Edinburgh, Scotland, on May
1, 1846" (1:243–49); "Farewell to the British People: An Address Delivered
in London, England, on March 30, 1847" (2:19–52); and "Slavery, the Slumbering Volcano: An Address Delivered in New York, New York, on April 23,
1849" (2:148–58), in *The Frederick Douglass Papers.*

5. Curiously, given the mystery surrounding Washington's life before and
after the *Creole* affair, in the only sentence of Brown's "Madison Washington"
(1863) not included in his "Slave Revolt at Sea" (1867), we are told, "Not
many months since, an American ship went ashore at Nassau, and among the
first to render assistance to the crew was Madison Washington" (85).

6. On this subject, Yarborough states, "It must be noted that there are several instances where Brown, Child, and Hopkins employ remarkably similar
phrasing. Brown had appropriated material from Child before, in the first
edition of *Clotel.* There is evidence of extensive borrowing here as well—either by Brown from an earlier version of Child's sketch or by Child from
Brown's in *The Black Man,* or by both Brown and Child from an earlier text
by another writer" (186).

7. James M. McPherson emphasizes the didactic purpose of *The Freedmen's
Book* in his foreword to the 1968 reprint: "Because many of the pupils in freedmen's schools were adults whose experiences in slavery had provided little
training for the responsibilities of freedom, Mrs. Child sprinkled the book with
advice on home economics, the raising of children, rules of good health, hab-
its of industry and morality, and the like."

8. Born in Maine in 1859, Hopkins was neither a survivor of slavery like
Douglass and Brown (both of whom actively resisted the "peculiar institution"
by escaping to the North) nor a contemporary witness to it like Child. As a
magazine editor and a literary artist—and a woman—who was most active
during the period known as the "nadir," the worst postbellum conditions facing African Americans, Hopkins necessarily approached the *Creole* revolt as
a historically significant event with particular relevance for her turn-of-the-
century black readers. A number of critics, including Claudia Tate and Mary
Helen Washington, have addressed the issue of authorial control of history
during the 1890s and early 1900s.

9. Discussions of Hopkins's editorial responsibilities and the role politics
played in the purchase and subsequent demise of *CAM* are in Braithwaite,
"Negro America's First Magazine"; Du Bois, "The Colored Magazine";

Johnson and Johnson, *Propaganda and Aesthetics;* Johnson, "The Rise of the Negro Magazine"; and Meier, "Booker T. Washington."

10. On the subject of naming and unnaming in African American literature and culture, see Ellison, "Hidden Name"; Stuckey *Slave Culture* (193–244); and Benston, "I Yam What I Am." Benston claims that "for the Afro-American . . . self-creation and reformation of a fragmented familial past are endlessly interwoven: naming is inevitably genealogical revisionism. All of Afro-American literature may be seen as one vast genealogical poem that attempts to restore continuity to the ruptures or discontinuities imposed by the history of black presence in America" (152).

11. Robert Stepto, for example, has shown the importance of the protagonist's last name to the opening and closing paragraphs as well as the very structure of Douglass's "The Heroic Slave."

12. I am using "fictive" both as it is generally understood and in the more specific sense of the term William Andrews employs in his essay on the "The Heroic Slave": "The marginal world of the earliest black American novels may be usefully termed a fictive world, in the special sense that . . . applies 'fictive' to the subjects and objects of representation in various 'mimetic artforms' like poetry, the novel, or the drama. What is re-presented in these types of literary discourse are not 'existing objects or events' but 'fictive member[s] of an identifiable class of natural ("real") objects or events'" (26).

13. Throughout this paper I will provide parenthetical page references: the first page number refers to the more accessible reprint of Hopkins's story in Ammons's *Short Fiction;* the second is from its original publication in *CAM.*

14. I do not mean to suggest that Hopkins was averse to depicting heroes in her stories and sketches or that Madison Monroe is less than heroic in "A Dash for Liberty." My argument is that Hopkins supplements (rather than supplants) the notion of the individual hero with the notion of community.

15. This presentation of the black woman's right to control her own body recalls Harriet Jacobs's vivid and effective treatment of the same theme in *Incidents in the Life of a Slave Girl* (1861), which is itself a deliberately fictionalized depiction of the author's life as a slave, a fugitive, and a free woman.

16. Susan's ancestry resembles that of the title character of Brown's novel *Clotel* (1853), who is the mulatto daughter of Thomas Jefferson. It also seems possible that in this passage Hopkins, given her emphasis on the sexual exploitation of black women, is subtly parodying the male bias, the stress on patriotism, and even some of the phrasing of Douglass's first paragraph, which reads in part as follows: "The State of Virginia is famous in American annals for the multitudinous array of her statesman and heroes. She has been dignified by some the mother of statesmen. History has not been sparing in recording their names, or in blazoning their deeds. Her high position in this respect,

has given her an enviable distinction among her sister States. With Virginia for his birth-place, even a man of ordinary parts, on account of the general partiality for her sons, easily rises to eminent stations. Men, not great enough to attract special attention in their native States, have, like a certain distinguished citizen in the State of New York, sighed and repined that they were not born in Virginia. Yet not all the great ones of the Old Dominion have, by the fact of their birth-place, escaped undeserved obscurity. By some strange neglect, *one* of the truest, manliest, and bravest of her children,—one who, in after years, will, I think, command the pen of genius to set his merits forth, holds now no higher place in the records of that grand old Commonwealth than is held by a horse or an ox" (473–74).

17. It is worth noting that this union of the light-skinned Susan and the "unmixed African," Madison Monroe, epitomizes the racial solidarity that Hopkins argues for in the story.

WORKS CITED

Ammon, Henry. *James Monroe: The Quest for National Identity.* New York: McGraw-Hill, 1971.

Ammons, Elizabeth. Introduction. *Short Fiction by Black Women, 1900–1920.* Ed. Elizabeth Ammons. New York: Oxford University Press, 1991. 3–20.

Andrews, William L. "The Novelization of Voice in Early African American Literature." *PMLA* 105 (Jan. 1990): 23–34.

Benston, Kimberly W. "I Yam What I Am: The Topos of Un(naming) in Afro-American Literature." In *Black Literature and Literary Theory.* Ed. Henry Louis Gates, Jr. New York: Methuen, 1984. 151–72.

Braithwaite, William Stanley. "Negro America's First Magazine." *Negro Digest* 6.2 (1947): 21–26.

Brown, William Wells. *Clotel; or, The President's Daughter.* 1853. New York: Macmillan, 1970.

———. "Madison Washington." In *The Black Man, His Antecedents, His Genius, and His Achievements.* 1863. New York: Arno, 1969. 75–85.

———. *The Negro in the American Rebellion: His Heroism and His Fidelity.* Boston, Mass.: Lee and Shepard, 1867.

Carby, Hazel. Introduction. *The Magazine Novels of Pauline Hopkins.* By Pauline Hopkins. New York: Oxford University Press, 1988. xxix–l.

Child, Lydia Maria. "Madison Washington." *The Freedmen's Book.* 1865. New York: Arno, 1968. 147–53.

Coffin, Joshua. *An Account of Some of the Principal Slave Insurrections.* New York: American Anti-Slavery Society, 1860.

Cooke, Michael G. "Naming, Being, and Black Experience." *Yale Review* 67.2 (1978): 167–86.

Douglass, Frederick. *The Frederick Douglass Papers. Series One: Speeches, Debates, and Interviews.* 5 vols. Ed. John W. Blassingame. New Haven, Conn.: Yale University Press, 1979–92.

———. "The Heroic Slave." In *The Life and Writings of Frederick Douglass.* 5 vols. Ed. Philip S. Foner. New York: International Publishers, 1950–75. 5:473–505.

Du Bois, W. E. B. "The Colored Magazine in America." *Crisis,* Nov. 1912, 33–35.

Ellison, Ralph. "Hidden Name and Complex Fate." In *Shadow and Act.* By Ralph Ellison. New York: Signet, 1966. 148–68.

Farrison, William. *William Wells Brown: Author and Reformer.* Chicago: University of Chicago Press, 1969.

Garnet, Henry Highland. "An Address to the Slaves in the United States." In *Walker's Appeal in Four Articles and an Address to the Slaves of the United States.* By David Walker and Henry Highland Garnet. 1848. New York: Arno, 1969.

Higginson, Thomas Wentworth. "Denmark Vesey." *Atlantic Monthly,* June 1861, 728–44.

Hopkins, Pauline. *Contending Forces: A Romance Illustrative of Negro Life North and South.* 1900. New York: Oxford University Press, 1988.

———. "A Dash for Liberty." *Colored American Magazine,* Aug. 1901, 243–47. Rpt. in *Short Fiction by Black Women, 1900–1920.* Ed. Elizabeth Ammons. New York: Oxford University Press, 1991. 89–98.

———. *A Primer of Facts Pertaining to the Early Greatness of the African Race and the Possibility of Restoration by Its Descendants—with Epilogue.* Cambridge, Mass.: P. E. Hopkins, 1905.

Jacobs, Harriet. *Incidents in the Life of a Slave Girl, Written by Herself.* 1861. Ed. Jean Fagan Yellin. Cambridge, Mass.: Harvard University Press, 1987.

Jervey, Edward D., and C. Harold Huber. "The *Creole* Affair." *Journal of Negro History* 65.3 (1980): 196–211.

Johnson, Abby Arthur, and Ronald Maberry Johnson. *Propaganda and Aesthetics: The Literary Politics of Afro-American Magazines in the Twentieth Century.* Amherst: University of Massachusetts Press, 1979.

Johnson, Charles S. "The Rise of the Negro Magazine." *Journal of Negro History* 13 (Jan. 1928): 7–21.

Johnson, Clinton H. "The *Creole* Affair." *Crisis,* Oct. 1971, 248–50.

Jones, Howard. "The Peculiar Institution and National Honor: The Case of the *Creole* Slave Revolt." *Civil War History* 21 (March 1975): 28–50.

"Madison Washington: Another Chapter in His History." *Liberator,* June 10, 1842, 1.

Meier, August. "Booker T. Washington and the Negro Press with Special Reference to the *Colored American Magazine.*" *Journal of Negro History* 38 (Jan. 1953): 67–90.

Stepto, Robert. "Storytelling in Early Afro-American Fiction: Frederick Douglass's 'The Heroic Slave.'" *Georgia Review* 36 (1982): 355–68.

Stuckey, Sterling. *Slave Culture: Nationalist Theory and the Foundations of Black America.* New York: Oxford University Press, 1987.

Tate, Claudia. *Domestic Allegories of Political Desire: The Black Heroine's Text at the Turn of the Century.* New York: Oxford University Press, 1992.

U.S. Senate. *Senate Documents.* 27th Cong., 2nd Sess., II. No. 51. 1841–42. 1–46.

Ward, Theodore. "Madison." 1956. Hatch-Billops Archives, New York.

Washington, Mary Helen. *Invented Lives: Narratives of Black Women, 1860–1960.* Garden City, N.Y.: Anchor, 1987.

Yarborough, Richard. "Race, Violence, and Manhood: The Masculine Ideal in Frederick Douglass's 'The Heroic Slave.'" In *Frederick Douglass: New Literary and Historical Essays.* Ed. Eric J. Sundquist. New York: Cambridge University Press, 1990. 166–88.

FIVE

Mammies, Bucks, and Wenches: Minstrelsy, Racial Pornography, and Racial Politics in Pauline Hopkins's *Hagar's Daughter*

KRISTINA BROOKS

> Fiction is of great value to my people as a preserver of manners and customs—religious, political and social. It is a record of growth and development from generation to generation.
> —PAULINE HOPKINS, *Contending Forces*

Choosing to "preserve" the conditions and customs of her race through her fiction, Pauline Hopkins offers for posterity a wide range of African American characters: from the tragic mulatto, to the middle-class matron, to the stereotypical mammy. Her second novel, *Hagar's Daughter: A Story of Southern Caste Prejudice* (1901–2), is a cautionary tale about the pernicious personal and national effects of "caste prejudice," or racism, on black and white Americans alike. At a time when debates over evolution, race, and the national character were at their peak, Hopkins decided to represent—and thus reinscribe—caricatures of the mammy, buck, and wench in *Hagar's Daughter*. Although her use of racial caricatures in a novel she hoped would combat racism seems inexplicable, Hopkins's representational strategy actually results in a destabilization of the concept of racial difference itself. The category of race *encompasses* difference in this narrative: not only are her central characters of mixed race, but her African American characters are represented both as subjects and—in the case of the mammy, buck, and wench—as objects. Hopkins draws a boundary of difference within the novel, not between characters identified as white or black but between southerners (who grew up within the corrupt system of slavery) and northerners who must now coexist as citizens. Through an analysis of the historical and the contemporary reader's relation to the objectified Others in the novel and an identification of the sources of pleasure or displeasure in this interaction, my reading of racial identity in *Hagar's Daughter* goes beyond condemnation or celebration to show precisely how Hopkins's racial objectifications powerfully foreground her own—and our culture's—ambivalence toward racial difference.

This essay thus offers dual interpretive perspectives, from late nineteenth-century and late twentieth-century models, on a novel that several critics have identified as a social melodrama, a genre that John Cawelti calls "the most time-bound of all the major formulas . . . because this formulaic type depends to such a great extent on the outlook and values of a particular era" (263).[1] Situating this novel in relation to contemporaneous discourses about race and evolution, I argue that Hopkins's turn-of-the-century readers would view her racially objectified characters within the context of the minstrel tradition. To late twentieth-century readers, however, Hopkins's representations of a mammy, buck, and wench might appear as racial pornography, figures objectified and denigrated solely on the basis of their racial identity. While minstrelsy is a familiar entertainment form that is receiving renewed critical attention, racial pornography is a new and under-theorized category of representation that conjoins the loaded issues of racial difference and sexuality.[2] Both of these interpretive models, however, depend upon the position of the reader or viewer to produce meaning and thus result in a range of interpretations. Rather than ascribing an overly simplified positive or negative critical judgment to the author and her novel, these models, taken together, generate both questions and answers about Hopkins's strategies and the effects of her representations on readers.

Racial Common Ground

Hagar's Daughter first appeared in the *Colored American Magazine* (*CAM*) in monthly installments from March 1901 through March 1902. The novel presents several mysteries of identity, most centrally those of Hagar and her daughter Jewel. The plot is driven by this mother-daughter relationship and the theme of maternal inheritance, which is most significant for its bestowal of racial identity. Consistent with other novels of the period by African American women, this novel's focus on strong female characters and their relations to each other relegates the male characters to the margins of the narrative.[3] Hopkins's plot expresses itself in two separate narratives, one set in the 1860s, the other in the 1880s; through their interlocking plot elements, these narratives stress the dual influences of nature and nurture on the characters' racial identities and morality.

One-quarter of the novel, the first eight chapters, takes place in Maryland in 1860–62, when southerners are becoming increasingly estranged from the Union as the section's pro-slavery position hardens. Hopkins's abbreviated vision of plantation culture and the history of racial oppression that it conveys are presented as inextricable from the present moment in race relations. Yet, the moral issue at stake in the novel is not slavery but amalgamation. Through the interrelated histories of three women of mixed race—Hagar, her daughter Jewel, and her daughter's foil, Aurelia—Hopkins foregrounds the message that "amalgamation has taken place; it will continue, and no finite power can stop it" (270). In the novel, the white and African American races are now and forever linked, at both national and familial levels, despite racist rhetoric and policies that seek to keep them apart.

The novel's central preoccupation with interracial relations determines its problematic position between a subversive agenda of attacking racial prejudice and segregation and an accommodationist one of defining success as a process of "lightening up." By countering legal, social, and literary prohibitions against relations or marriage between individuals identified as racially different, Hopkins can be viewed as a protest writer.[4] However, because she uses the literary stereotypes of the tragic mulatto and generic minstrel figures like the mammy, buck, and wench, Hopkins imperils her subversive intention. Although her strategy is to destabilize racial difference through representations of mulatto characters and interracial unions, Hopkins's objectification of racial difference in several caricatures results in a mixed message about the value of African American identity.

With the novel's mixed-race characters, Hopkins attempts to assail both contemporaneous racist dogma and enforced segregation. Her representations are rooted in an interconnected matrix of discourses about race, evolution, and nationalism, which clouded prospects for harmonious familial and national relations between African Americans and Anglo Americans. George M. Fredrickson notes that 1890 marked "the full triumph of Darwinism in American thought"; that year's (faultily interpreted) federal census supported the thesis "that blacks were failing to hold their own . . . in an inevitable 'struggle for existence' among human races" (246). To this ideological milieu Hopkins contributes a novel in which neither race, class position, nor ancestry per se is the determinant of human development. In *Hagar's Daughter,* Hopkins directs her readers to repudiate the past—the institution of slavery and those who were enslaved—and to identify instead with the text's African American subjects, the free men and women who are the readers' social contemporaries. By representing chronological racial "progress" in her novel, Hopkins counters the theory embodied in the late nineteenth-century's most influential treatise on the race question, Frederick L. Hoffman's *Race Traits and Tendencies of the American Negro* (1896), which predicted the eventual annihilation of the African American race through hereditary degeneracy (Fredrickson 249–50). Degeneracy in *Hagar's Daughter* is relegated to the past and located in the South. Following the representational strategies of countless abolitionist writers, Hopkins demonstrates that, through their willing or unwilling participation in the "peculiar institution," both slaves and masters are dehumanized.

While Hopkins holds up mixed-race characters as role models in both *Contending Forces* and *Hagar's Daughter,* she also objectifies some members of the race—in particular, the darkest members. In his introduction to the former novel, Richard Yarborough faults her for "elitist views [that] mar her treatment of lower-class black characters" and for endorsing "contemporary ideas regarding the role of race and ancestry as determinants of physical and psychological development" (xii, xxxiv). Contrary to Yarborough's assertions, however, what Hopkins affirms with her objectification of certain characters is a clear division between the racially segregated past and a racially integrated future.[5] In *Hagar's Daughter,* class position, racial identity, and ancestry are overruled by historical conditions, so that both the freeborn African American descendants of the novel's slave characters and the mulatta characters who are raised as "white" women express subjectivity.[6] Hopkins thus ultimately affirms the kinship of slaves with their free descendants but, through her racial caricatures of those who are slaves, she exacts the price of readers' dis-identification with these ancestors

by relegating them—and, more generally, the object status assigned to the African American race—to a past that must be overcome.[7]

If the past is marked by racially based slavery, the future of race relations in *Hagar's Daughter* is represented by interracial relationships and the resulting offspring, who can often "pass" as white. Hopkins buttresses her novel's interracial relationships with the theory that "'nature was stronger than prejudice'" (270). In portraying interracial relationships as being driven by the force of nature, she counters the racist theory of polygenesis, which, in positing the separate creation of the races as distinct species, served as a basis for policies of segregation and racial oppression. Hopkins claims that not only nature but God, as well, favors interracial relations; Cuthbert Sumner, a white male character who could not accept his fiancée Jewel's mixed racial heritage, is forced to recognize that "he had sinned. . . . Then it was borne in upon him: the sin is the nation's. It must be washed out. The plans of the Father are not changed in the nineteenth century; they are shown [to] us in different forms. The idolatry of the Moloch of Slavery must be purged from the land and his actual sinlessness was but a meet offering to appease the wrath of a righteous God" (283–84). Amalgamation, while countering racist doctrines, also results in "lightening up" Hopkins's primary characters, particularly the women. It is this crossing of the color line that disturbs some readers, who see in Hopkins's tragic mulatta characters traces of intraracial prejudice and a denigration of blackness itself.

This criticism has merit—given Hopkins's clear distinctions between the morality and intelligence of darker slave characters and the lighter, free African American characters—yet Hopkins's mulatta characters are not necessarily markers of an accommodationist strategy that privileges white standards of beauty. White readers, in fact, objected to Hopkins's interracial themes; one white reader of the *Colored American Magazine* canceled her subscription over the issue, complaining, "The stories of these tragic mixed loves will not commend themselves to your white readers and will not elevate the colored readers." Hopkins replied, "I am glad to receive this criticism for it shows more clearly than ever that white people don't understand *what pleases Negroes*" (*CAM*, May 1903, 399).

The appeal of mixed-race characters had been proven through narratives published by both African American and white authors: William Wells Brown, George Washington Cable, Ellen and William Craft, Frances E. W. Harper, Harriet Beecher Stowe, and others. Some of these fictional mulattos clearly did uphold racist doctrines of racial degeneration by suffering inevitable tragic ends. However, Hazel Carby's revisionist reading of the mulatto in nineteenth- and twentieth-century African American fiction suggests two more progressive functions for Hopkins's mulatta characters: such characters serve "as a vehicle for an exploration of the relationship between the races and, at the same time, an expression of the relationship between the races. The figure of the mulatto should be understood and analyzed as a narrative device of mediation" (*Reconstructing Womanhood* 89). Claudia Tate also points to the significance of differing historical perspectives on representations of mixed-race characters; while Hopkins and her fellow female writers considered "dark- and white-skinned mulattoes . . . inclusive parts of the African-American population," "twentieth-century readers generally use the term *mulatto* as one of exclusion rather than inclusion; that is, to designate black people who claim or appear to claim privilege as a consequence of light skin color" (80).

The ability of Hopkins's heroine Hagar to pass as white enables her to live the experience of one race in America and then—after her mixed racial identity is revealed—the other: "the one drop of black blood neutralized all [Hagar's] virtues, and she became, from the moment of exposure, an unclean thing. Can anything more unjust be imagined in a republican form of government whose excuse for existence is the upbuilding of mankind!" (62). By embodying both races within one figure—a figure that is ultimately heroic rather than tragic—Hopkins and other African American writers hoped to dramatize the injustice of racism and racist social policies. Writing within the sentimental literary tradition, in which the mulatto figured prominently, and writing against prevalent racist ideologies, which presumed a fundamental qualitative difference between the races, Hopkins presents readers with primary female characters who are indeed creamy-colored women, who both mediate and are forcibly torn between two racial cultures. Hopkins thus subversively portrays an integrated society where none existed.[8] Using racial passing as a plot device, Hopkins shows "the ease with which beautiful half-breeds may enter our best society without detection" (266). Confronting turn-of-the-century racism with visible proof that racial barriers were indeed artificially constructed and imposed, Hopkins uses a strategy that, nearly one hundred years later, ironically leaves her open to charges of elitism and accommodationism.[9]

The Pleasures and Perils of Representation

Writing for a magazine with a predominantly African American audience, Hopkins presents the readers of her serialized novel with several objectified and stereotypical African American characters who are slaves or ex-slaves.[10] Although this initially appears to be a peculiar literary or political strategy, Hopkins enables her readers—in various class positions and reading within different cultural contexts—to find empowerment through these characters. At times, these racially objectified characters act as foils for the novel's mixed-race and free African American characters, who are endowed with subjectivity. Thus, African American readers, measuring the chronological distance between their own literate selves and the "historical" figures of the mammy, buck, and wench (whose dialect alone sets them distinctly apart in the narrative), might feel pleasure at identifying with the representations of contemporary African American subjects that are thrown into such high relief.

At particular moments in the text, Hopkins's minstrel-like figures perform another function. Like the stage minstrel characters so popular among African American and white audiences in the late nineteenth and early twentieth centuries, Hopkins's stereotypical characters sometimes act as tricksters. With their minstrel masks of jollity, stupidity, and sensuality, these characters may be read as operating in disguise in both white and African American, upper- and lower-class social contexts. Depending on the particular scene, then, Hopkins's figures of the mammy, buck, and wench act as foils and tricksters, but their overall effect is to serve yet a third function: with their (southern) exuberance, sensuality, and good humor, the objectified characters emphasize the inhibitions of (northern) bourgeois African Americans and provide a folkloric base for a more diverse and vital African American culture.

Although Hopkins's racial caricatures can thus be read as empowering, they can also be read as demeaning and, in fact, as damaging to the social existence of those who may be misrepresented. Racial caricatures drew strong and often oppositional responses from African American writers, critics, and political leaders in turn-of-the-century

America (as they continue to do today). During a time of increasing violence against African American men—largely based upon spurious charges of raping white women—and continuing sexual harassment or violence against African American women, many African American leaders saw racial representations as crucial to the process of culturally defining their race's sexuality and, in a larger sense, their humanity. According to historian Paula Giddings, the late nineteenth-century black women's club movement was committed to imparting the lesson "that color, class, or the experience of slavery did not nullify the moral strength of true womanhood" (88). A central concern of Hopkins and her contemporary black women's club members was thus the serious and debilitating effects of the sexually licentious "Sapphire" stereotype upon the minds and bodies of African American women.[11]

With the entire race's social and political future seeming to rest on white audiences' interpretations of the African American race's "nature," many black writers and political leaders were unwilling to risk depicting blacks as either comical or radically different from whites. Choosing to spotlight African American achievements in "high," or Western, art forms, many of Hopkins's contemporaries sought to thereby "lift up" their race in accordance with white standards of achievement.[12] Thus, Robert Toll notes that "the Negro press of the nineteenth century, which catered exclusively to the 'black bourgeoisie,' virtually ignored black minstrels even though it went to great lengths to applaud any semblance of cultural or artistic achievement Negroes made in the formal arts" (227).[13] In part, then, debates over racial representations were clearly rooted in class identification, as well as different political ideologies.

In this respect, the ideology of *CAM* was clearly at odds with its contemporary race publications; Hopkins's magazine attempted to encompass a broad range of African American interests and talents, rather than the more narrowly prescribed category of acceptable representations. *CAM* proclaimed its populist editorial policy in its first issue: to publicize "all phases of fact, fiction and tradition of the Negro" (May 1900). In her study of the nineteenth-century African American periodical press, Penelope Bullock reports on one of the consequences of the magazine's stated policy: "The *Colored American Magazine* gave a much broader view of musical activities among Negroes than its contemporary, the *Negro Music Journal*. The *Journal* concentrated on classical music and dismissed popular music. . . . The *Colored American Magazine* carried articles on all types—the grand opera productions of Theodore Drury as well as the vaudeville performances of George Walker and Bert Williams" (214).

As editor and writer, Hopkins strove for a broader based appeal than that of competing periodicals, and, in fact, *CAM* "was the most widely distributed Afro-American periodical before 1909" (Bullock 118). Further insight into Hopkins's authorial motivation can be found in a biographical sketch that informs the magazine's readers that Hopkins's "ambition is to become a writer of fiction, in which the wrongs of her race shall be so handled as to enlist the sympathy of all classes of citizens, in this way reaching those who never read history or biography" (*CAM*, Jan. 1901, 219). In her serialized novel, *Hagar's Daughter*, Hopkins thus seeks to "handle" the volatile material of racial injustice in such a way as to both enlighten and entertain a broad audience with disparate educational and racial backgrounds.

A writer of musical dramas and a musical performer herself, Hopkins sought inspiration from minstrelsy, a popular tradition that links the African American race to both servitude and comic entertainment. Derived from the Latin *ministerialis*, meaning "household officer," "minstrel" describes a hybrid of entertainer and servant. A 1927 article entitled "Black Laughter" graphically describes early (white) audiences' perceptions of the comedy inherent in minstrel performances on film, performances based on those with which Hopkins would have been familiar: "There is something irresistibly contagious about the wide grin of the darkie. Perhaps it is the flash of white teeth against their ebony background that makes it so effective and evokes an immediate answering guffaw. Perhaps it is merely tradition, associated with the many nigger minstrels of one's youth, but black faces and comedy usually go together on the screen. When the darkie is frightened he is apt to roll his eyes and shake like a jelly, and the effect is nearly as funny as when he is pleased" (quoted in Noble 46).

Hopkins depended on her audience's immediate recognition of her characters' vivid minstrel attributes—rolling eyes, head scratching, unrestrained laughter, and heavy dialect, for example—and their comic potential. In drawing upon minstrelsy in *Hagar's Daughter*, which devotes one-quarter of the narrative to plantation culture and three-quarters to post-Reconstruction culture, Hopkins draws upon the double-edged force of the minstrel, who can be read as a figure of ridicule or of irony, and whose effect depends upon readers' (sometimes simultaneous) responses of distancing and/or identification.

In asserting that minstrelsy appealed to both African American and white audiences, I am exploring a topic foreclosed by Tate when she concludes that Hopkins's references to a loyal African American servant as a "buck" suggest a targeted white audience (272). Negotiating the gap between an outside (white) perspective and an inside (African American) perspective on her novel, Hopkins draws upon a form of popular culture that appealed to and even elicited similar responses from both races, yet could signify a range of meanings. This "problem of ambivalence and undecidability," as Kobena Mercer explains in his essay on Robert Mapplethorpe's racial representations, "not only underlines the role of the reader; but also draws attention to the important, and equally undecidable, role of context in determining the range of different readings that can be produced from the same text" (170). African American and white readers of *Hagar's Daughter* undoubtedly read within disparate social and political contexts, but they were surely just as familiar with the same minstrel stereotypes.

The immense popularity of black minstrels (not whites in blackface) with black audiences in the late nineteenth and early twentieth centuries "is difficult to explain," Robert Toll concedes, but may be attributable to the "phenomenon of laughing at the familiar . . . the affirmation of group belonging" (258).[14] Toll's analysis accounts for responses of pleasure from African American readers who may have found Hopkins's racial caricatures both ridiculous and familiar:

> The blacks that attended minstrel shows were basically "from the mass." . . . They were probably not concerned with what impression whites would get from the show or with how well blacks measured up to white standards. It was the difference between the black bourgeoisie with their eyes focused on whites and on middle-class standards and the masses of black people whose perspectives were essentially confined to their group and to Afro-American culture. Certainly, all blacks could recognize that [minstrels] . . . performed caricatures. . . . But they also probably knew people who shared some of these traits. They laughed at the familiar in exaggerated form. At least in part, theirs was in-group laughter of recognition, even of belonging. (258)

The "in-group" reactions of African American audiences to black minstrels, then, can be explained in terms of both self-mockery and self-acceptance. The pleasure of laughing *with* others sharing a similar oppression is clearly distinct from laughing *at* oneself when among a group identified as one's oppressors.[15] Toll also notes that class divisions shape viewers' different responses to minstrel performances, so that the supposedly white-identified black bourgeoisie would dissociate themselves from the caricatures that working-class blacks might embrace. These minstrel characters thus had the potential to tap into readers' reactions of both superiority to and identification with racial caricatures. Reading a century later, readers may continue to find Hopkins's caricatures unfamiliar, offensive, damaging, or even accurate, to the extent that real African Americans were certainly coerced to role play as mammies, bucks, and wenches.

Like minstrelsy, pornography raises troubling questions about representations, questions about the material consequences for those being objectified and the sources of pleasure for their audience. Past and present debates over the interrelationships between race, representation, and social subjects correspond to current feminist debates over sexual representations, which involve questions about whether explicit representations promote violence (against women), reinforce (women's) inequality, and/or lead to a general moral degradation of the viewer.[16] In fact, the leader of the movement to ban pornography through legislation, the law professor Catharine A. MacKinnon, often avails herself of the analogy between legalized sexual pornography and illegal forms of racial discrimination and violence. For example, a recent headline and subtitle of a newspaper article on pornography authored by MacKinnon reads: "An act of violence against women: Akin to lynching, it doesn't deserve legal safeguards" (*San Francisco Examiner,* Nov. 29, 1992, D1). MacKinnon argues that pornographic representations degrade one race or gender as a whole, and, thus, pornography is a civil rights issue. Pornography, she alleges, promotes real violence against real bodies. Another law professor and legal scholar, Patricia Williams, also views certain types of racial representations as pornographic, claiming that, "in racial pornography, whites act and blacks appear" ("Equality's Demise").[17]

Although Williams has not elaborated a theory of "racial pornography," I posit that the *structural* elements of pornography—the objectification of women as sexual "types" and the hierarchical relationship established between viewer and the sexual "object"—are clearly present in racist representations, in which the objectification of African American individuals as types or icons also serves to establish and fix the superiority of the reader, thereby giving him/her pleasure. In referring to Hopkins's representations as racial pornography, I am not claiming that her novel trades in explicit sex nor that the reader's relationship to these representations is sexual. Rather, in Hopkins's novel, those who are objectified fit into narrowly prescribed boundaries of racial "types" (mammy, buck, wench) just as the objects of sexual pornography must fit narrow definitions of sexual types (innocent, nymphomaniac, dominatrix). Pornography, as a form of representation, thus describes both the assignment of object status to one gender, based on their bodily identity as women, and the assignment of object status to one race, based on their bodily identity as (in this case) African Americans.

Though a frequent topic in literary, legal, and aesthetic discourses, pornography remains such a nebulous term that the most widely known and least controversial "definition" may be that provided by U.S. Supreme Court Justice Potter Stewart: "I know it when I see it."[18] Stewart's nondefinition of pornography functions to preserve its taboo aspect; his claim leaves pornography in the visual register and thereby retains its distance from—and perhaps resistance to—the ordering properties of language. Yet, even this nondefinition can be analyzed: pornography is a form of representation, usually visual, and the quality of being pornographic inheres not in the representation itself but in the response it elicits from the viewer or reader. As is the case with the objectification of women, the pleasurable force of racist representations depends upon both the marked status of those who are being objectified and the taboo quality of the visceral response such representations may engender.[19] In racial pornography, the objectification of African Americans is meant to produce pleasure for the audience, pleasure derived *either* from the distance between self and object that is experienced as condescending amusement and/or empowerment *or* from the recognition of sameness between self and object that is experienced as self-deprecating amusement.

In Hopkins's novel, the African American race is effectively split into those with subjectivity and those marked as objects for the reader's gaze, for the reader's pleasure. One source of pleasure for the reader or viewer of pornography is the empowerment gained through "reading" oneself into a position of superiority over those who are objectified in the pornographic representations. Most pornography adheres to rigid binary structures of domination: as Kaja Silverman notes, "within the discourse of pornography one term is always subordinated to the other" (328). Typically, this subordinate term—the object of the reader's or viewer's gaze—is the individual who is marked by and comes to represent either sex (female) or race (African American). Examining Hopkins's caricatures as a form of racial pornography is complicated because we have to acknowledge that the reader's identity and relationship to that object, whether characterized as "difference" or "sameness," will profoundly and differently impact the reader's responses.

While keeping in mind that the reader's identity with respect to race, class, and gender will affect which taboos might be broken through a pleasurable response, we must also acknowledge that, as Lawrence Levine notes, "precisely the same forms of culture can perform markedly distinct functions in different periods or among different groups" (240). For example, while any evocation of the "Sambo" figure today might appear clearly racist and retrograde in its effect, in a turn-of-the-century context that same figure's function and effect on its audience might have been distinctly different. The performer and comedian Dick Gregory, commenting on black comedians who performed in blackface, notes that "what they did, they did well, and it was accepted. You can't take it out of context" (quoted in O'Connor, B4). So long as they remain on film or in print, however, recorded performances and novels, such as *Hagar's Daughter,* which feature minstrel representations, are necessarily interpreted in changing historical contexts. The position of Hopkins's representations within the dual cultural frameworks of minstrelsy and pornography, both of which have begged translation (between and among races, classes, and genders) since their inceptions, necessitates that any critique of the novel take place within "an historicized interpretative model" (Tate 19). Such a model must attend to the ideological and material contexts within which performers and authors choose particular representational strategies at any given historical moment.

The varied and various responses of individual viewers to the minstrel television show *Amos 'n' Andy* (1951–53) illustrate how the taboo quality of racial representations can change over time. "At home, it was very important that we *not* watch *Amos 'n' Andy,*" says Diahann Carroll in the documentary *Color Adjustment.* "It was very important to my mother that I should not see something that was so racist. It was years later that I realized that Amos and Andy are *brilliant.* They were really funny." The passage of time likewise affects Henry Louis Gates's appreciation of minstrelsy: "that marvelous world of warmth and solidarity that makes *Amos 'n' Andy* Christmas show such a rare and poignant memory" ("'Amos'"). The director Marlon Riggs, on the other hand, finds the show's minstrel humor insidious: "I wasn't critical when I watched *Amos 'n' Andy* [as a child]. I mean, what I remember is laughing—like anybody. They were funny. . . . And of course I was totally unaware how that shaped my consciousness and the consciousness of the nation around these issues of race and perceptions of racial difference" (*Color*). Carroll, Gates, and Riggs speak to the critical impact of racial representations on forming public opinion and the conflicting responses one individual can have, depending upon the interpretive framework he or she applies in a given instance. Finding representations of racial difference harmless one moment and dangerous the next, these African American viewers attest that responding with laughter can be an expression of racial solidarity or racial divisiveness. Since the function(s) of racial objectifications change(s) not only over decades but from instance to instance, we must examine each of Hopkins's representations and our responses to it within its particular context in the novel in order to understand how the author is indeed shaping our notions of racial identity and racial difference.

The Buck, the Wench, and the Mammy

In the plantation section of *Hagar's Daughter*, two wealthy, neighboring families are brought together through the marriage of Hagar Sargeant, newly orphaned at the time of her wedding, and Ellis Enson, the eldest son and heir to a large plantation. At this time, Hagar's mammy, Aunt Henny, and Henny's daughter Marthy are both Hagar's inheritance and the remains of her (artificially constructed) family. Shortly after the birth of their first child, Ellis and Hagar's happiness is shattered by the appearance of Walker, a slave-trader who knows Hagar was a "slave child" brought up by the Sargeants as their own daughter (52). In claiming his property rights in Hagar, Walker acts in concert with St. Clair Enson, Ellis's dissolute and greedy brother, who has met the slave-trader after gambling away his own devoted slave, Isaac.[20] After struggling with his racial prejudice, Ellis finally decides to flee with his wife to Europe, but he is found dead before accomplishing this. In March 1862, Walker and St. Clair travel as delegates to a peace congress in Washington and bring a group of slaves, including Hagar, to auction there. In a scene borrowed from William Wells

Brown's *Clotel*, Hagar manages to escape and ends up flinging herself, child in arms, into the Potomac.

In chapter 9, Hopkins shifts the scene from the early days of the Civil War to the post-Reconstruction era, from plantation politics to national politics. Although the names have changed, most of her characters, as will eventually be revealed, are those we have already met in the novel's early chapters. Zenas Bowen, a western senator and self-made millionaire, is introduced as the husband of Estelle and the father of Jewel, whose fiancé, Cuthbert Sumner, serves as private secretary to General Charles Benson, a division chief of the Treasury. By the novel's end, Senator Bowen is revealed to be the man who rescued Jewel from the waters of the Potomac, not her biological father; Estelle is revealed to be not the step-mother but the (biological) mother of Jewel, for Estelle is really Hagar, a "'beautiful half-[breed] . . . [who] is a source of anxiety to the white citizens of our country'" (266). General Benson, who commits both murder and forced abduction in his quest to marry Jewel Bowen and acquire her fortune, is revealed to be St. Clair Enson. His partner in crime, Walker, now using the name of Major Madison, has become an unscrupulous fortune hunter who is using his daughter Aurelia as bait for Cuthbert Sumner. Ellis Enson, Hagar's husband, turns up alive in the person of Henson, chief of the Secret Service and a "celebrated detective" (186) who unravels the mysteries of familial and racial identity (Estelle/Hagar, Jewel, and Aurelia are all revealed to have "black blood") and clears Sumner of the murder committed by St. Clair Enson.[21] Assisting the great detective is Venus (disguised as "Billy"), who is Marthy and Isaac's daughter and Aunt Henny's granddaughter.

Meanwhile, back on the plantation, there are just three characters whose names and racial identities remain constant over the twenty-year span of the novel, thus providing continuity between the two narratives: Aunt Henny, her daughter Marthy, and Isaac. These are the only individuated slave characters in the first narrative, and, in contrast to the second-generation African American characters of Venus and her brother Oliver who are introduced in the second narrative, they speak consistently in a dialect that marks them as African American.[22] Their names, too, mark them as (low) comic rather than (high) dramatic characters: Henny and Marthy are not proper given names but diminutive nicknames, while the Hebrew name Isaac (*Yishaq*) means "he laughs."[23] Based on well-known, commonly circulated racial stereo-

types, Aunt Henny, Marthy, and Isaac are static characters incapable
of development: historical and maternal influences that exert their forces on every other character are irrelevant in the cases of these three.
For Hopkins uses the mammy (Aunt Henny), the wench (Marthy), and
the buck (Isaac) primarily as foils for the other African American and
mixed-race characters. Stuck in a time warp and in plantation culture,
the mammy, wench, and buck are not subjects but objects for the reader's gaze. In objectifying some of her African American characters,
Hopkins presents a sideshow—in this case, a minstrel show—to the
main act.

Yet the system of slavery and the portrayal of plantation culture in
the novel are significant, according to Hopkins, insofar as they make
the inevitable process of amalgamation a tragic one. As a human rem-
nant of the institution of slavery, Isaac is an oppositional character, not
only because of his particular role in the novel's plot but in his very
being. Like the stereotypical "buck" of plantation fiction, Isaac enters
the narrative as St. Clair Enson's property—"his man Isaac"—rather
than his own man. Noting that "master and slave were devoted to each
other," Hopkins indicates that Isaac is a slave not only because of cus-
tom but because of his own slavish nature (22). Post-Emancipation,
Isaac is tragically unable to become a free man. His role in the plot is
to obstruct justice by protecting a murderer, his once-and-always master, and by participating in the kidnapping of Jewel. His daughter Venus recognizes Isaac's fatal flaw: "I'm no fool, Mr. Henson; he's my
daddy, but Isaac Johnson's a bad pill. *He's jus' like a bad white man,
sir,*—he'll do anything for money when he gets hard up" (224, emphasis
added). Isaac, fulfilling the literal definition of a slave, is indeed just
like the unprincipled St. Clair Enson; he has no individual will but lives
to serve his master. His greed is not even original but an imitation of
his "bad white" master. As Hopkins writes near the novel's end, "In
his devotion to his employer's interests, the faithful servant and ex-slave,
Isaac Johnson, knowing no law save the will of his former owner, faithful to the traditions of slavery still, concealed the only witness of the
crime" (263). Unable to make the transition from the feudal system of
slavery to "democratic" post-Reconstruction America, Isaac remains
a static character whose slave status cannot be overcome.

For African American and white readers, Isaac's actions—"a sly roll
of his eye," "chuckl[ing]" (42), speaking "with his mouth full of food"
(43), "scratch[ing] his head in perplexity" (176)—create a clear image

of the good-natured, unrefined, slightly dim-witted Sambo. This buck character would seem a very damaging characterization if the goal, according to *CAM*'s editorial statement, was to "enable a people, to assert their racial rights as men, and demand their privileges as citizens" (May 1900, 60). Hopkins, in particular, believed that fiction was the most effective conduit for racial progress because it would reach the broadest audience. Aside from nostalgic pleasure, what did she hope to achieve through this representation of a Sambo figure?

In his study *Sambo: The Rise and Demise of an American Jester*, Joseph Boskin provides a possible answer to that question when he explains that the minstrel figure Sambo "narrowed the contradiction between slavery and the tenets of democracy, . . . undercut the frightening possibility of the hostile black male, and created a 'bond' of affection and sentimentality" between blacks and whites (63). Representations of friendly master/slave relationships would have us believe that if Sambo is happy, then slavery is not undemocratic, and if Sambo is naturally devoted to his master then there is nothing to fear from the slave. Applying this analysis to the close relationship between this particular slave and his master, however, will not account for the fact that St. Clair Enson is an unprincipled criminal and thus a decidedly unsentimental figure. Like abolitionist writers, Hopkins characterizes the master-slave relationship—even a supposedly intimate one—as mutually degrading rather than mutually beneficial.[24] As Isaac recounts, "Law*se,* de times me an' young massa had t'gedder, bar hunts, an' gamblin' 'bouts, an' shootin' and ridin'. He goin' so fas' I skacely cud keep up tuh him. We bin like brudders. All his clo's fits me *puffick!*" (177). Like two halves of a whole, the master and his slave stay together before, during, and after the Civil War, both unfit to survive as individuals in a society that ostensibly "approved of freedom and qualified equality for the Negro" (265).

Despite his "perfect" reliance on St. Clair, Isaac also exhibits traits of the traditional trickster figure derived from African folklore, a figure with significant subversive potential. When St. Clair loses Isaac in a game of cards, the master is momentarily devastated and demands from his opponent "the right of redeeming that boy, Mr. Johnson. My father gave him to me when I was a lad. I promised never to part with him." At this moment of crisis, Isaac appears unconcerned, responding to his new master with a "Yas, sir," and a "good-natured smile." His deceptive character, though, is revealed by his "long side-glance at

Enson, in which one might have seen the lurking deviltry of a spirit kindred to his master's" (28). Like the traditional trickster figure, Isaac's "deviltry" is apparent only to those who can ("one *might*") interpret the duality of his actions: "The apparent significance of the message ['Yas, sir'] differs from its real significance ['No, sir']" (Gates 291).

The trickster's potential for subversive power is undercut, however, by the attribution of "deviltry" to Isaac's master: Isaac is *like* St. Clair in his unscrupulousness, not a distinct subject able to counter his master's "tricks" with one of his own. In her first novel, *Contending Forces*, Hopkins's narrative voice also points to the distinction between a trickster like Isaac and his criminal master/employer: "We are virtuous or non-virtuous only when we have a *choice* under temptation. We cannot by any means apply the word to a little child. . . . So with the African brought to these shores against his will—the state of morality which implies will-power on his part does not exist, therefore he is not a responsible being" (149–50). In depicting slave characters like Isaac as essentially amoral, not responsible for their actions, Hopkins attempts to demonstrate the inhumanity of the institution of slavery.

In presenting Isaac as a veritable extension of his corrupt master, however, Hopkins objectifies the African American slave as something less than human. This characterization enables readers to take (pornographic) pleasure in their intellectual, social, and moral superiority to this buck figure. His lack of social or moral development renders him an unthreatening character who does not challenge white privilege and is therefore ill-suited to survive in an era when racial equality is at least a nominal national goal. Irresponsible, deceptive, yet dependent, Isaac owes much to the stock characters of both Sambo and the trickster. Though this characterization may now be viewed as an example of racial pornography, in the terms of the novel it also functions to refute a tenet of scientific racism. One of the central arguments about racial difference—that African Americans are degenerate by nature—is voiced near the end of the novel by Cuthbert Sumner: Hagar's positive "characteristics are but an accident of environment, not the true nature of her parent stock. I have always heard that the Negro race excelled in low cunning" (269). Negative stereotypes, such as Sambo, could either attest that nature made African Americans "low" or that nurture was responsible for an immoral character. In the case of Isaac, Hopkins gives proof that the "low cunning" of those in one's environment, particularly the master, affect one much more strongly than the "true nature of [one's] parent stock."

By objectifying Isaac and his wife Marthy as foolish and static figures, Hopkins provides her readers with unfortunate products of a corrupt system. Their roles are largely those of comic relief: laughter based on her readers' sense of superiority to this couple's childlike ways. In her pre-Emancipation incarnation, Marthy is characterized partly as the stereotypical sexually licentious wench and partly as the rather simple and silly "darkey."[25] When Isaac's shadow falls across the doorsill, "Marthy gave a shriek that ended in a giggle" upon seeing him enter the kitchen (41). When her mother threatens her with a whipping if she should gossip about the master's family, "Marthy rolled her eyes in terror," enacting the stereotypical image of a cowardly servant (63). Like Sambo, whom Boskin notes may be either male or female in manifestation, Marthy's character is prone to extravagant physical reactions, like "an overgrown child at heart . . . given to impetuous play, humorous antics, docile energies, and uninhibited expressiveness" (Boskin 13).

Even twenty years after her first appearance, Marthy has "the same frank, fun-loving countenance" she had when she was a plantation slave. In accordance with these descriptions of her simple, childlike nature, post-Reconstruction Marthy also espouses an unenlightened philosophy about racial differences. Calling her son "silly" for his desire to graduate from college and provide for his mother and grandmother, Marthy explains to him: "Colored women wasn't made to take their comfit lak white ladies. They wasn't born fer nuthin' but ter wurk lak hosses or mules" (171). Marthy complacently accepts the racial status quo, but this attitude proves to be as foolish and mired in the past as is her character. For Hopkins shows that Hagar and her daughter Jewel, "colored women" both, are indeed "lak white ladies" in appearance, refinement, and social position. In this way, racial objectification keeps Marthy distant from readers, an object of amusement who must be rejected (along with her regressive beliefs about racial differences) as a poor role model for reading subjects.

As represented by Hopkins, Marthy exhibits no sign of inner conflict about or resistance to her own debased self-image. The author thus guides the reader toward objectifying Marthy rather than responding to her with empathy. In contrast to the one-dimensional character of Marthy, the mulatta character Hagar undergoes the complex process of internalizing racism before the reader's eyes. Upon learning of her own racial heritage, "Hagar suddenly arose, caught [Marthy] by the shoulders and turned her toward the light, minutely examining the black skin, crinkled hair, flat nose and protruding lips. So might her grandmother have looked" (56). Within the aesthetics of the novel, Marthy is objectified in the harshest of physical terms by Hagar. This description conveys what Patricia Williams identifies as "the underlying yet dominant emotion of racism": that blackness is ugly, unaesthetic, and unpleasant (*Alchemy* 117). Williams writes that "the cultural domination of blacks by whites means that the black self is placed at a distance even from itself. . . . So blacks in a white society are conditioned from infancy to see in themselves only what others, who despise them, see" (62).

The image of desirable female beauty is Hopkins's depiction of Hagar before her "fall": "Hagar's face haunted [Ellis]; the pure creamy skin, the curved crimson lips ready to smile,—lips sweet and firm,—the broad, low brow, and great, lustrous, long-lashed eyes of brilliant black—soft as velvet, and full of light with the earnest, cloudless gaze of childhood" (35). The dichotomy between Hagar the beautiful "white" woman and Hagar the ugly "nigger-wench" (70) turns out to be false: they are one and the same woman, of one and the same African American race. In showing the racial kinship of Marthy and Hagar, Hopkins provides a critique of racially based definitions of beauty, but, to do so, she uses the "black" figure of Marthy as a foil for Hagar's mixed-race beauty. Morally, too, Marthy serves as a foil for Hagar, whose racially based self-hatred is clearly a reflection of cultural prejudices rather than individual ignorance. Hagar ultimately evolves from her position "in the dust of utter humiliation" upon learning of her racial heritage (57), to a state of acceptance, which, though marked by "a shade of sadness," is "serene. She was happy—happier than she had ever hoped to be in this life" (273). Significantly, her "happy ending" coincides with accepting her identity as an African American, while Marthy's post-Reconstruction self-definition continues to link race and bondage: "Jes' seems lak we [colored women] mus' wurk 'tell we draps into the grave" (171).

Another explicit contrast Hopkins draws between Hagar and Marthy is their differing sexual natures, which might suggest that Hopkins elevates "white" love while degrading "black" love. Hopkins was necessarily limited in the range of acceptable representations of black female sexuality, writing within a literary tradition that Carby claims was characterized by "the repression of the sensual . . . in response to the long history of the exploitation of black sexuality" (*Reconstructing Womanhood* 174). Obeying the dictates of this tradition, Hopkins portrays Hagar, the mulatta heroine, as sexually passive. When Hagar falls in love with Ellis Enson, she is subject *to* desire rather than a desiring subject:

> The veil was drawn away. She understood—this was the realization of the dreams that had come to her dimly all the tender springtime. Never in all her young life had she felt so happy, so strangely happy. A soft flush mounted to cheek and brow under his caresses. "I don't understand," murmured the girl, trembling with excitement. . . . Hagar had not dreamed that such passion as this existed in the world. It seemed to take the breath of her inner life and leave her powerless, with no separate existence, no distinct mental utterance. . . . [Ellis] bent over the sweet lips that half sought his kiss. (38)

In this passage, desire is displaced so as to reside outside of Hagar; both dreams and "passion" are somehow inflicted upon her. Her happiness is "strange," her knowledge only partial, her reaction indistinct and uncertain.

By contrast, "Marthy was a born coquette" (47). When Isaac "gave a sly roll of his eye in the direction where the girl stood," Marthy is caught "regarding the athletic young Negro with undisguised admiration" (42). Within the novel's late nineteenth-century terms, Marthy's desire is like a man's: based on the opposite sex's physique, not the other's "character."[26] Here is a woman who knows what she wants and recognizes it when she sees it: "Isaac improved the time between the going and coming of Aunt Henny by making fierce love to Marthy, who was willing to meet him more than half way" (44). Placed just six pages apart, the two love scenes are physically opposed: Hagar and Ellis share "one long moment" of physical expression (the half-sought kiss), while Marthy and Isaac mutually and enthusiastically "speak" with their bodies. Yet, these are not representations of "white" and "black" love. In portraying Hagar as a beautiful *and* virtuous woman who will later accept her identity as African American, Hopkins denounces the idea that Hagar's race is a physical or moral taint. In her portrayal of the black woman Marthy, Hopkins thus indicates that it is not racial nature but the racist nurture provided by the institution of slavery that results in Marthy's less virtuous character.

In the characters of Hagar, Jewel, and Venus, Hopkins links the quality of virtue with women of African American ancestry; in her first novel, *Contending Forces,* she presents readers with a virtuous, mixed-race heroine who is also a rape victim. However, the conflicting cultural and political uses of the wench stereotype—to amuse minstrel audiences and to denigrate African American women's morality—are foregrounded by Marthy's character. Uninhibitedly expressing her sexual curiosity and desires, Marthy may satisfy a reader's pornographic interest in the African American woman's body, already culturally coded as available. If considered within the context of the minstrel tradition, however, Marthy's response to Isaac's overtures conveys female sexuality in the form of the (humorous) sexually licentious wench stereotype.

The humor of Marthy's character can be read in terms of its populist appeal, most particularly to African American, probably nonbourgeois, readers.[27] Like both minstrel artists and her literary descendant, Zora Neale Hurston, Hopkins mines African American "folk" culture for its riches. Hurston, writing in 1935, celebrates such "stereotypical" African American characteristics as "Drama," "Will to Adorn," "Dancing," "Imitation," "Absence of the Concept of Privacy," and "Dialect" and claims that "the average Negro glories in his ways. The highly educated Negro the same. The self-despisement lies in a middle class who scorns to do or be anything Negro. . . . He wears drab clothing, sits through a boresome church service, pretends to have no interest in the community, holds beauty contests, and otherwise apes all the mediocrities of the white brother" (231). In some ways, Hagar may be said to "ape" the sentimental love scenes of numerous white fictional sisters, but, in Marthy, Hopkins offers a representation of a woman who is naturally sexual. Writing more than thirty years before Hurston, Hopkins does not offer Marthy as a role model, but this character serves to broaden the range of definitions of what an African American woman looks like and how she acts within the confines of literary traditions of the time.

Hopkins also revises the derogatory wench stereotype and its pornographic potential in a significant way: African American female sexuality is not represented in the novel as unfettered. Marthy expresses desire physically but not indiscriminately: she desires an African American man, whom she marries, and thus, retrospectively, their lovemaking is domesticated in much the same way as Hagar's and Ellis's more chaste moment of passion is domesticated by their ensuing marriage.[28] The sexual availability of the wench is thus contained within the narrative, and its containment within an African American domestic space indicates that Hopkins was more concerned with "what pleases Negroes" than with what would fulfill a white audience's pornographic desires.

Notably, in the novel's second narrative, when Marthy is a wife and the mother of two children, she is no longer represented as sexual but rather as the other available African American female stereotype: the mammy. Her modified attitude toward men ("gittin' jined to a man's a turrible 'spons'bility, 'specially the man") and her expanded figure ("Years have added to her weight. . . . Her tidy calico gown was hidden by an immense blue-and-white-checked apron, and a snowy towel tied turban-fashion hid her soft crinkly hair") both mark Marthy as a mammy rather than a carefree wench (219, 168–69). Thus, Hopkins also displaces female sexuality into the past, corrupt era of slavery, which indicates that, while Marthy's sexual behavior may appear natural, it is also "the [remnant] of an old irresponsible life."[29] As such, this characterization, like that of the buck, has a subversive edge, commenting ironically on (inhibiting) white standards of behavior while concomitantly reinscribing them as the cultural norm.

The distance between past and present, slavery and humanity, objectification and womanhood can perhaps best be measured in Hopkins's representation of Aunt Henny, an older female slave. In the novel's first section, she is a prototypical mammy, "a coal-black Negress of kindly face," who speaks in a heavy dialect and whose identity is rooted in the master-slave relationship (33). "Aunt" Henny's familial title is not based on blood ties to the Sargeant family but is simply a designation of the place she occupies in the range of female roles. As opposed to the identities of mother, daughter, or sister, the aunt stands in indirect relation to the family so that, even if she acts in a maternal capacity, she is distanced from the primary bonds between mother and child. Yet, in accordance with racist fantasies of slaves' so-called family loyalty, Aunt Henny is more protective of her (white) mistress than her own daughter: "See hyar, chile [Marthy], I don' no 'bout tellin' a disrespons'ble gal like you fambly secrets,—an' ef you goes to 'peatin' my words all 'roun' de plantation, I hope Marse Ellis whop yer back" (63). That this characteristic seems *un*natural is relevant to Aunt Henny's function: it is not her *nature* that unfits her for subjectivity and the reader's identification but her *nurture* under the southern system of slavery that overrides "natural" maternality and renders her an object.

In good mammy fashion, Aunt Henny's primary identification is not as a mother to Marthy but as a slave to Hagar: "Her head was held higher, if possible, in honor of the new dignity that had come to *the family* from the union of the houses of Enson and Sergeant. . . . Aunt Henny rolled up her eyes in silent ecstasy" (40, emphasis added). In describing Henny's masters as "the family" Hopkins both naturalizes this unnatural relationship and marks the distance at which the slave stands from *the* (rather than "her") family. In this scene, Aunt Henny also exemplifies what Catharine MacKinnon has dubbed "visual thingi-fication," as she is rendered an object through representation (*Feminism Unmodified* 53). Her rolled-back eyes indicate a deviation from rationality, a lack of control, and her literal inability to see or possess "the gaze" that marks one kind of subject position, while her silence confirms her status as an object for our—the readers'—gaze.

If Aunt Henny the mammy is "thingified" in this racial caricature, it is Hopkins who acts as the objectifier. Many antipornography feminists, who assume that fixed and gendered positions are inherent to pornographic representations, would argue that Hopkins dissociates herself from, or in some sense betrays, her own race and/or gender in authoring this mammy character. According to Suzanne Kappeler, "the pornographic structure of representation [is] . . . the systematic objectification of women in the interest of the exclusive subjectification of men. . . . Writer and reader bond in the exercise of usurping female subjectivity and experience, moving into the whole available space of writing and of reading which thus become activities predicated upon the male gender, yielding the pleasure of the feeling of life at the cost of the death of female subjectivity" (103). Kappeler's formulation effaces the female production of pornographic representations and presumes that the female reader must metaphorically kill (another's) female subjectivity as she reads herself into the position of a male subject. Indeed, to account for female subjectivity Kappeler resorts to the notion of false consciousness: "The fact that women, as individual subjects, . . . have apprenticed to the male viewpoint which surveys women as objects and as products of fine art, is itself one of the most fundamental sources of female alienation: women have integrated in themselves, have internalized, a permanent outpost of the other gender—the male surveyor" (57–58). In proposing a model of transvestism (or is it gender alchemy?)—"she turns surveyor of women and thus 'male,' turning the women she surveys into objects" (45)—Kappeler renders the female objectifier, either as author or reader, oxymoronic.

Yet, to call Hopkins "male" or "white," based on her objectification of Aunt Henny, seems singularly meaningless. Imposing a binary structure (male *or* female, white *or* black) upon the relationship between a black and female author/subject and her black and female character/object is ineffective, in part, because it (re)inscribes a hierarchical boundary between genders and races. In critiquing "the totalizing gestures of feminism," Judith Butler notes, "the effort to identify the enemy as singular in form is a reverse-discourse that uncritically mimics the strategy of the oppressor instead of offering a different set of terms. That the tactic can operate in feminist and antifeminist contexts alike suggests that the colonizing gesture is not primarily or irreducibly masculinist" (13). In representing an objectified black woman for the reader's gaze, Hopkins marks the social and cultural distance she maintains from this mammy figure, but her own subjectivity is not suddenly and radically altered through this transaction. To assume that a shared site of identification, such as race or gender, constitutes an identical social and cultural position is to insist upon the objective truth of these categories, a truth that Hopkins herself refutes through her characterizations of mutable (racial and social) identities in *Hagar's Daughter*.

The mammy figure in this novel is particularly interesting because of the similarities—gender, race, and (in the first of the novel's narratives) age—she bears to her author as well as the clear differences. In her social and political position, Hopkins is clearly no mammy; according to a statement appearing in *The Crisis* eight years after Hopkins lost her editorship of *CAM*, "her attitude was not conciliatory enough. As a white friend said: 'If you are going to take up the wrongs of your race then you must depend for your support absolutely upon your race. . . .' The final result was that the magazine was bought by friends favorable to the conciliatory attitude [i.e., Booker T. Washington's associates]" (quoted in Johnson and Johnson 9). If Hopkins uses the figure of an accommodationist African American woman as a straw man that she and her readers can easily reject—and probably take pleasure in that rejection—she also sets up this mammy character as a lightning rod for the more mutable identities in *Hagar's Daughter*. The novel's white and mixed-race characters appear to need some (novelistic) reality against which to stake their shifting identities, and this function is fulfilled by Aunt Henny, who, in 1882, "was seventy, but save for rheumatism she had not changed since she left the Enson plantation" (175). Without subjectivity, this character could hardly develop, and it is her very physical fixity that defines her role in the narrative.

The scene of Aunt Henny's key testimony in Cuthbert Sumner's murder trial reveals both her objectification and the grounding role she plays within the novel. While employed in her job of cleaning the Treasury offices, Henny hides behind a portière and sees General Benson poison Elise Bradford, but the significance of her evidence rests not on her role as an eyewitness but on her role as a mammy: "He ain't Gin'ral Benson no more'n I'm a white 'ooman. His name's St. Clair Enson; he was born nex' do' to de Sargeant place on the Enson plantation. Ise one ob de fus' ones what held him when he was born. Ise got a scar on me, jedge, where dat imp ob de debbil hit me wid a block ob wood when he warn't but seven years ol'" (256). Unlike Hagar, her daughter Jewel, or Aurelia Madison, Aunt Henny cannot be mistaken for a "white woman"; her appearance alone testifies to her racial identity. Significantly, her proof of the murderer's real identity—a scar inflicted by the young St. Clair Enson—is also based on bodily (rather than verbal) evidence. Aunt Henny performs the crucial act of exposing the moral "passing" of St. Clair Enson as General Benson and thus acts as a limitation on the white man's subjectivity (he cannot become someone he is not); yet she remains an objectified Other.

In this courtroom scene, Aunt Henny appears as a "picture" within the picture (or text) and is thus doubly objectified. Her appearance—skin color, rolled-back eyes, clothing, and accessories—is preeminent and clearly framed by Hopkins for the reader's gaze and amusement: "She *made a weird picture,* her large eyes peering out from behind the silver-bowed glasses, her turbaned head and large, gold-hoop earrings, and a spotless white handkerchief crossed on her breast over the neat gingham dress" (255, emphasis added). Aunt Henny's "weirdness," in relation to others in the courtroom, consists of her peculiar combination of antithetical qualities: her costume is West Indian in flavor, and thus exotic, and impeccably clean and tidy, thus domestic. While obviously foreign to this mainly white courtroom audience, she is so unthreatening that the defense lawyer, ex-Governor Lowe of Massachusetts, addresses her only as "Aunt Henny" or simply "Aunty" (254–56).

In addition to objectifying the mammy through her appearance, Hopkins furthers the reader's identification with the (white male) speaking subjects and dis-identification with Aunt Henny through a brief exchange. Aunt Henny testifies, "'I hearn people talkin' in one ob de rooms—the private office—an' I goes 'cross de entry an' peeks roun' de corner ob de po'ter—' 'The what?' interrupted the judge. 'Po'ter, massa jedge; don' yer kno' what a po'ter am?' 'She means, portière, your honor,' explained Gov. Lowe, with a smile. 'Go on, aunty'" (254). Following the tradition of minstrels who "used heavy dialect to portray Negroes as foolish, stupid, and compulsively musical," Hopkins draws attention to Aunt Henny's "peculiar" language in order to amuse her readers (Toll 67).[30]

This miscommunication is not simply a matter of differing language usage or pronunciation; Governor Lowe's indulgent act of translation effects a two-way conversation between the white men, while Aunt Henny is left in the position of a curiously speaking object whose words require mediation. Readers are thus encouraged to laugh *at* Aunt Henny but at the same time—consistent with minstrel humor—they are also encouraged to laugh at the Governor's grandiloquence: "The perpetual effect of [the minstrel's] presence on stage was the eradication of even the slightest hint of decorum. . . . Minstrelsy . . . consistently deflate[s] the 'highbrow' and thus affirm[s] the image of the common man" (Engle xxvi-viii). Aunt Henny's *presence,* not her subjective commentary, is indeed the medium through which readers find amusement at the expense of the aristocratic character in this scene. By speaking the truth through the voice of the mammy, Hopkins challenges the racism of the prosecuting attorney, who characterizes Aunt Henny's evidence as "the idiotic ramblings of an ignorant *nigger*" (257). Yet this challenge is ultimately based upon readers' acceptance of Aunt Henny as an objectified Other, whose scarred body is the primary evidence for the truth she speaks in the courtroom.

A static character, Aunt Henny upholds, through deed and word, the continuance of master-slave relations but, over the course of her narrative, Hopkins renders the mammy and her attitudes toward racial difference obsolete just as she renders the buck's and wench's racial ideologies obsolete. At the novel's end, Henny predicts that "a gal brung up like [Jewel] has been's gwine break her heart to fin' herself nuthin' but common nigger trash" (281), thereby naming herself and anyone who shares her racial identity as "common nigger trash." In one sense,

Henny speaks the truth, for Jewel does die of a broken heart, but the hatred that destroys her is external rather than the internalized self-hatred of Aunt Henny: Jewel reacts to the revelation of her racial heritage by recognizing "my sin, for it is a sin to hold one set of God's creatures so much inferior to the rest of creation simply because of the color of the skin" (281–82). Finding herself a member of the African American race does not break her heart but allows her to question and ultimately reject her own racist ideology. It is Jewel's northern-born husband Sumner who "was strongly prejudiced" against interracial relations (281) and is punished by Jewel's death and left to question "wherein he had sinned and why he was so severely punished" (283).[31] For Jewel, as for many of Hopkins's female characters, inner change is not enough to yield a happy ending. *Hagar's Daughter* ends on a prophetic note: while Jewel and her husband learn "a lesson of the degradation of slavery," they do so at the cost of personal happiness and even, in Jewel's case, her life (284).

One Uncommon Little Black Girl

Aunt Henny's belief in "common nigger trash" is yet more clearly contradicted by the uncommon subjectivities of her descendants, in particular, Venus, Jewel's maid. The distance between Henny and her granddaughter is marked by their positions vis-à-vis their white "families." As a mammy, Aunt Henny is important as a substitute mother to Hagar but, upon reaching adulthood, Hagar outgrows her need for Henny. In historical terms, the mammy may still hold great cultural resonance after the Civil War, but her social position is no longer naturalized once slavery itself has been delegitimated. Aunt Henny becomes a cleaning woman at the Treasury building, where her "family" is now the U.S. government. Though Venus, like her grandmother, is employed by a white family, she acts as a free agent in assuming a male disguise to assist her employers. She represents herself as "somebody who knows something" and vows that she will challenge her father in the course of her own investigation: "I'll see him out on this case or my name ain't Venus Johnson. I'll see if *this one little black girl* can't get the best of as mean a set of villains as ever was born" (221, emphasis added). In contrast to Aunt Henny, Venus associates pride and power with both her race and gender, even while marking the distance between her social status as a "little black girl" and her own definition of herself as "Venus Johnson." In the character of Venus, Hopkins thus counters Aunt Henny's devaluation of African American womanhood.

Though her parents are objectified within the novel in terms of minstrel caricatures, Venus stands out as an African American woman who can think, speak, and act as a full subject. Claudia Tate claims that, while "the text reveals Venus's integrity, intelligence, and courage, . . . her presence does not disrupt or even challenge the viewpoint that she is not the material of which real heroines are made" (63). However, this claim depends upon one's definition of heroism. Able to take action without being directed, to move in and out of "the Negro vernacular," Venus is represented as "a young colored girl who had an extremely intelligent, wide-awake expression" (224, 223). "She had her own ideas about certain things," Hopkins assures her readers (218). Venus's remarkable powers of disguise and detection result in the rescue of Jewel and the resolution of all the novel's hidden identities; it is her exploits that enable "for [a] time all thoughts of caste [to be] forgotten while the representatives of two races [Venus, Aunt Henny, Hagar, and Jewel] met on the ground of mutual interest and regard" (240). In short, she is a figure who can mediate between the slave characters who cannot survive off the plantation and the mixed-race characters such as Jewel and Aurelia whose unhappy fates attest to persistent racism. Both chronologically and geographically, then, Venus serves as a bridge: between the (slave) ancestors and the (free) descendants, and between the southern and northern cultures where these characters are located.[32]

Yet, the racial stereotypes Hopkins relies on in her representations of slave characters also inflect her portrayals of Venus and her love interest, John Robinson Williams.[33] Though Venus is a "plucky" woman (239), she still retains marks of a degraded past. In her agitation over her mistress's disappearance, "Venus forgot her education . . . and *fell into* the Negro vernacular, talking and crying at the same time" (224, emphasis added); when Chief Henson presents her with the idea of disguising herself in boy's clothing to help in the investigation, "Venus showed her dazzling teeth in a giggle. She ducked her head and writhed her shoulders in suppressed merriment as she replied: '*Cain't* I? well, I reckon'" (227). Here, black dialect is clearly represented as a step below "white" English, which is consistently spoken by all of the mixed-race female characters; likewise, the minstrel-like physical reactions of

Venus are inconceivable in conjunction with Hagar, Jewel, or Aurelia. In the character of Venus, Hopkins thus blends representations of African Americans as simple and childlike with representations of the African American woman as competent and adult in her intellectual and emotional development.

The interpretively slippery Venus Johnson, who exhibits characteristics of both racial stereotypes and unique subjectivity, thus presents readers with some middle ground between the caricatures who inhabit the past and the nearly white, fully bourgeois African American characters who look toward the future. Hopkins objectifies Isaac, Marthy, and Aunt Henny within the novel in order to elicit varied reactions—dissociation, identification, and the recognition of irony, ridicule, and amusement. With Venus Johnson, however, Hopkins embodies both the comic tradition of black minstrelsy and the uncommon (i.e., unrecorded) tradition of black heroism. Though objectified in particular instances, Venus is primarily an African American subject, whose representation remains distinct from those of her ancestors.

Planning how to break in and rescue Jewel from where she is being held (directing agent Smith to cause a distraction while she sneaks up to Jewel's room), Venus shows herself to be confident in her abilities rather than self-deprecating (like Marthy). In outperforming even the official agents assigned by Chief Henson to the case of Jewel's kidnapping, Venus also identifies herself as rational rather than superstitious (like Aunt Henny): "Again and again Venus was called upon to repeat the story of her adventures. . . . 'Well, you know Mis' Bowen, I ain't a bit slow, no'm, if I do say it, an' I jus' thought hard for a minute, an' then *it struck me!*'" (240). Through these distinct representations of three generations of an African American family, Hopkins depicts a significant shift in African Americans'—and specifically African American women's—self-conceptions and their post-Emancipation social opportunities.

While seeking to upbuild her race through representations of virtuous African American women, however, Hopkins also wants to unite African Americans through representations of both enslaved and freeborn African American characters who exhibit the "exquisitely droll humor peculiar to the Negro" (*Contending Forces* 13). This characteristic, Hopkins asserts, is a source of cultural pride, not shame, a part of the African American race that should not go the way of slavery or servility. In her efforts to delineate a "peculiar," or essential, African

American attribute, Hopkins reinscribes racial difference in the midst of a narrative that foregrounds amalgamation and the tragedy of observing racial boundaries in human relationships. Her ambivalence about racial difference thus informs each of her representations, not just those of the mammy, buck, and wench.

To understand and acknowledge Hopkins's ambivalence, and to begin to explore our own, we, as readers, must consider her novel's representations in relation to their past historical context (minstrelsy) and their current cultural context (racial pornography). Rather than simply labeling as "racist" the caricatures in *Hagar's Daughter,* we must bracket the question of "good" or "bad" in order to analyze the role of pleasure in the interaction between subject and object. As Kobena Mercer points out, the question of whether a given image reinscribes fixed beliefs of racist ideology or problematizes them is impossible to answer unequivocally "because the image throws the question back onto the spectator" (177). Hopkins's racial objectifications require readers to engage in a continuous process of repositioning in regard to their own racial, class, and gender identifications—as well as their place in history—if they hope to understand the uses of fiction in a time of historical crisis, both Hopkins's and our own.

NOTES

I would like to express my heartfelt thanks to Simone Davis, Kimberly Drake, Cynthia Franklin, Kate Garrett, John Gruesser, Adam Landsberg, Arthur Riss, and Steven Rubio for their insightful comments on drafts of this essay. For their helpful guidance, I also thank Mitchell Breitwieser, Barbara Christian, and Susan Schweik.

1. According to Cawelti, the characteristic quality of the social melodrama is its synthesis of "melodramatic structure and character with something that passes for a 'realistic' social or historical setting" (261). Susan Gillman and Claudia Tate have convincingly positioned Hopkins's novels within the tradition of the melodrama (see, especially, Tate 3–22).

2. Professional dance and theater companies have recently experimented with revisionary renderings of minstrelsy. See for example, Bill T. Jones/Arnie Zane Dance Company, *Last Supper at Uncle Tom's Cabin/The Promised Land* (1990); the San Francisco Mime Troupe, *I Ain't Yo' Uncle* (1990, 1992); a collaboration between Seattle's Empty Space Theater and Alice B. Theater, *Unkle Tomm's Kabin: A Deconstruction of the Novel by Harriet Beecher Stowe* (1991); and Donald Byrd/The Group, *The Minstrel Show* (1993) (see Tucker,

C4). For an account of dance and theater revisions of Stowe's *Uncle Tom's Cabin* in particular, see Misha Berson. Television commentators analyze black television shows in this context (for a critical view, see Gregory Lewis; for a positive view, see Margo Jefferson). Eric Lott's recent critical work on minstrelsy, *Love and Theft,* provides an important historical account of minstrelsy as a form of cultural production.

3. In conjunction with the novel's woman-centered, maternal focus, it is interesting to note that Hopkins published this work under the name "Sarah A. Allen," her mother's maiden name. In her study of African American women's fiction in the period 1890–1910, Tate identifies Hopkins's novels and those of Frances E. W. Harper, Amelia E. Johnson, Emma Dunham Kelley-Hawkins, and Katherine D. Tillman as "female texts," "in which the dominant discourses and their interpretations arise from woman-centered values, agency, indeed authority that seek distinctly female principles of narrative pleasure" (8).

4. Lest we assume the time for such a protest is past, "Interracial Kiss Back in Children's Play," an article in the *San Francisco Chronicle* (Sept. 18, 1993), reports that a patron objected to a kiss between a black actor and white actress in a play at the Dallas Children's Theater. The director removed said kiss but reinstated it in the wake of other community members' objections.

5. In particular, Yarborough criticizes Hopkins's representation of John Langley in *Contending Forces.* Hopkins writes that Langley is "a descendant of slaves and southern 'crackers.' We might call this a bad mixture—the combination of the worst features of a dominant race with an enslaved race" (90–91). However, Hopkins ultimately maintains that even this dissolute character could have been saved by a more beneficent environment and thus counters a strictly evolutionary reading of character development: "There came dimly to [Langley's] beclouded faculties a realization of the possibilities of a life which might have been his under opposite conditions from those in which he was born. . . . The man was what he was through the faults of others" (334–36).

6. Throughout this essay, I use the term "subjectivity" in two critical senses. First, it denotes the literary critical notion of the "well-rounded" character who conveys individuality and personhood (as opposed to the "flat" character who is devoid of particularity or a sense of personhood). Second, it refers to the feminist theoretical idea that subjectivity is the (classically male) position of having a point of view, acting upon the world, and expressing one's interiority, while the (classically female) position of being objectified entails being acted upon and thus rendered a nonsubject.

7. I use "identification" and "dis-identification" to describe the psychological process of the individual's recognition of a personal or group identity.

8. Although Carby and Tate provide sympathetic readings of Hopkins's fiction, both posit that Hopkins situates this and her other serialized fiction in "a white community" (Carby *Reconstructing Womanhood* 146) or "a white

social sphere" (198). However, in these novels Hopkins portrays communities that are integrated, albeit secretly. This, I would argue, constitutes a challenge both to segregationist policies and to the ideology upholding them, an ideology that maintained that racial identity was obvious and knowable.

9. For another example of this critical treatment, see Bernard Bell, who claims that "Hopkins's bourgeois predilections for accommodationism in the face of political terrorism and social exploitation" are "reprehensible [to] some readers" (14).

10. By 1900, when the literacy rate for African Americans was over 55 percent, "the publishers of the *Colored American Magazine* reported that within two years after its founding 'fully one-third' of the regular readers were white" (Bullock 9, 218). When considering the responses of Hopkins's audience, I am primarily but not exclusively concerned with those of African American readers.

11. The rich, complex topic of black women's political organizations and their concern with the representation of black sexuality and its influence on black citizens is beyond the scope of this essay. Interested readers should turn to Hazel Carby's *Reconstructing Womanhood* and to Paula Giddings's *When and Where I Enter* for further discussion of this issue. Hopkins treated the interconnected issues of rape (of black women by white men) and lynching (of black men for alleged rapes of white women) most prominently in her first novel, *Contending Forces* (1900).

12. I am calling attention here to the designation of Western art forms as "high" and non-Western art as primitive or "low" and the prominent metaphor of "racial uplift" used by African Americans to describe efforts to achieve greater economic and social status. This terminology highlights the problematic tension between African Americans' desires to improve their living conditions and attain their full rights as citizens and the concessions or deformations to white expectations that this could entail.

13. Penelope Bullock notes that, of the twenty-seven general race periodicals published between 1880 and 1909, those published without the support of established black institutions (such as the African Methodist Episcopal Church), rarely lasted more than three years. The exceptions were *CAM*, and the combined *Howard's Negro-American Magazine* and *Howard's American Magazine,* both of which endured for at least ten years; those surviving for at least three years were *McGirt's Magazine, Alexander's Magazine,* the *Voice of the Negro,* and the *Horizon* (70). See Bullock, and Johnson and Johnson for an account of these periodicals' editorial policies and political positions.

14. Richard Waterhouse offers a slightly different explanation for why African American audiences for minstrel performances increased even as northern whites lost interest: "For African-Americans from all regions, black minstrel performances may have served a similar cultural function to that provid-

ed by the ritual of the cakewalk on the ante-bellum plantation. The blacks enjoyed themselves in observing the white images of African-American character and culture, images which the blacks themselves knew to be absurd. Once again the blacks had slipped the yoke by changing the joke and at the same time rendered a vicious white stereotype into something that was less harmful" (56). The folklorist Roger D. Abrahams analyzes "Negroes' ways of typing themselves, both as a group in open contest with whites and as different personality types in contest with each other." He claims that when blacks use stereotypes of blacks, "in most cases the [stock] characters and their actions are not used to publish prejudice but merely to point to social types that exist within the group" (19).

15. The controversy over Ted Danson's blackface routine at the Friar's Club roast held in Whoopi Goldberg's honor on October 8, 1993, clearly illustrates the line between private and public humor based on racial stereotypes. While Goldberg stated that she had, in fact, written Danson's "minstrel" jokes, talk-show host Montel Williams protested that, "If that's what Whoopi and Ted find funny in their bedroom, it's not funny to the outside world" (McShane). In response, Bob Saks, chairman of the Friars Club celebrity luncheons, defended Danson's performance on the basis of its construction as a "private" act: "[Danson and Goldberg] are a couple. Their friends are there. It's a private party."

16. Analyses of pornography, both pro and con, often include analogies to the master/slave relationship or to the relationship between whites and blacks more generally to illustrate the pornographic paradigm. Adrienne Rich claims that "Pornography is about slavery. To oppose pornography requires that we connect culturally glorified violence against women with more traditionally recognized forms of political enslavement," and "all objectification is a prelude to and condition of slavery" (320, 322). Issues of representation—who is the author? who is represented? whose desire is manifested? whose pleasure is served?—are absent from Rich's essay, as is an explanation of the correspondence between image and reality, between the representations and material conditions of slavery. In developing a theory of racial pornography, I seek to engage these critical questions of the politics of representation. Racism and sexism may literally and figuratively look the same, insofar as both are oppressions based on an identity characteristic, but their historical contexts and particular manifestations differ in ways that should be acknowledged.

17. When she made this statement, Williams was referring to John Berger's analysis in Ways of Seeing ("men act and women appear") (47). It is interesting to note that Williams claimed that Berger was describing sexual pornography. In fact, he was analyzing the tradition of European oil paintings of (nude) women, but this mistake (or act of misremembrance) illustrates how subjective and fluid the definition of pornography is.

18. Concurring opinion in 6–3 ruling that overturned a ban on pornographic films (*Jacobellis v. Ohio*, 378 U.S. 184, 197 [1964]).

19. Linda Williams notes that both pornography and sentimental fiction are meant to effect primarily a "visceral appeal to the body," and, due to this position on the body side of the mind/body dichotomy, both have been classified as "low culture" genres by cultural custodians (i.e., critics, historians, educators) (5).

20. The similarities between Hopkins's characterizations and those in Harriet Beecher Stowe's *Uncle Tom's Cabin* (1852) are striking. In an essay for *CAM*, Hopkins praises at length "the great work of Harriet Beecher Stowe" (Feb. 1901, 299). Stage versions of Stowe's melodrama, participating in the minstrel tradition and conveying both abolitionist and pro-slavery positions, were incredibly popular and endured into the twentieth century. Hopkins might well have borrowed the name "St. Clair" from Stowe's kind but misguided white character, Augustine St. Clare. Though ugly slave-traders are, of course, ubiquitous in abolitionist fiction, Hopkins's slave-trader, Walker, might also be indebted to Stowe's characterization of the slave-trader Haley: both are harsh and repulsive in appearance and character.

21. Given the available literary historical evidence, *Hagar's Daughter* appears to be the first novel by an African American to feature African American detectives (both Venus and another male agent). Another detective serial, "The Stress of Impulse," authored by Maitland Leroy Osborne, appeared in *CAM* from Aug. 1900 through Jan. 1901, but there is no narrative indication that the detective is African American. Carby discusses Hopkins's use of the detective figure in her introduction to *The Magazine Novels* (xl) and in *Reconstructing Womanhood* (147–50).

Whether due to a typographical error or to Hopkins's inability to keep all these names straight, Henson appears in the text as both "J. Henson, Detective" (187) and "the sleuth hound E. Henson" (243). I will refer to the character as Henson to avoid unnecessary confusion.

22. Besides Hagar and her daughter Jewel, there are three other African American characters in the novel: Aurelia Madison (Walker), who is a freeborn, tragic quadroon figure, who does not speak in dialect; Cuthbert Sumner's manservant and Venus's suitor, John Robinson Williams, "a New England colored man" (127), also freeborn, who has enlightened northern ideas about racism but who nonetheless speaks in a dialect; and the minor figure of Mr. Henson's agent Smith, whose undercover identity of "Uncle William Henry" necessitates a linguistic disguise, so that we never hear his real voice.

23. In *Reconstructing Womanhood*, Carby analyzes Hopkins's career and her fiction, devoting eight pages to *Hagar's Daughter* (146–53). Carby notes the many biblical references in the novel, most significantly of course the name Hagar (153). Hopkins also uses the name Isaac, the biblical Sarah and Abra-

ham's son, for an oppositional character, if not an outright enemy, of her novel's Hagar and her offspring—notably, a *daughter* in Hopkins's narrative. In
the novel, Isaac also acts against Hagar's best interests later in the plot by
participating in the kidnapping of her daughter.

24. Also like abolitionist writers, Hopkins portrays friendly relations between a kind and moral (if not completely enlightened) master and his servant.
Although not strictly a master-slave relationship, the relationship between
Cuthbert Sumner and his manservant John, for example, is portrayed as mutually beneficial and does not morally degrade John, who says, "'Clare, I'd do
anyting on yearth for Mr. Cuthbert" (182). Although this quotation indicates
John's dialect, his speech is in fact less consistent than that of the slave characters. Like Venus, who can "[forget] her education in her earnestness, and
[fall] into the Negro vernacular," John is bilingual, able to speak with or without a dialect (224).

25. This derogatory term is used by Ellis Enson—"such an afternoon . . . [is]
hot enough to kill a darkey" (37)—to indicate his racism; consequently, when
he later learns his wife Hagar is of African American ancestry, his initial rejection of her does not come as a complete surprise to readers. I use the term
here to signify the racist stereotype I believe Hopkins invokes in her characterization of Marthy.

26. Ellis Enson experiences "enthralment" to the image of Hagar: "Such
beauty as this was a perpetual delight to feast the eyes and charm the senses—aye, to witch a man's heart from him" (35). Despite the more flowery prose
in this passage, the preeminence of the physical qualities of the woman and
Enson's objectification of her for his pleasure echoes the physical force of attraction Marthy feels for Isaac.

27. This interpretation is supported by Hopkins's enthusiastic interest in
and use of other elements of popular fiction to appeal to her readers. Carby
notes that "within the pages of the *Colored American Magazine,* Hopkins made
a decision to incorporate some of the narrative formulas of the sensational
fiction of dime novels and story papers. Consequently, her magazine fiction
shows an increased emphasis on such narrative elements as suspense, action,
adventure, complex plotting, multiple and false identities, and the use of disguise" (Introduction xxxvi).

28. The parallels between Marthy and Hagar extend to the quality of their
marriages. Although Ellis and Hagar end up "happily ever after" in terms of
their own relationship, Ellis initially fails to put love for his wife before prejudice and is thus shown as less than heroic. Likewise, Isaac causes Marthy "a
world of worry" because he is "a ne'er-do-well, working when the notion
pleased him or when actual starvation compelled him to exert himself, at other times swearing, drinking and fighting" (174). Despite the class differences,
Ellis and Isaac both disappoint their wives in some substantial way.

29. Hopkins, *Contending Forces*. This quotation is spoken by Will Smith, who responds to a white southerner's charge that "Negroes are all alike . . . ignorant, thieving, dirty and lazy." Smith replies, "These faults you speak of are but the remnants of an old irresponsible life. The majority of our race has turned aside forever from the old beaten paths of slavery into the undiscovered realms of free thought and free action" (294).

30. Whether readers find amusement through their distance *from* this character and her dialect or their identification *with* her depends upon the particular reader, but African American readers might certainly have had either reaction depending on class position or their conception of the boundaries of African American culture.

31. Although not merely a punishment for her white lover, Jewel's death does carry a significant punitive force. This trope appears frequently in women-authored fiction of the period; for example, Lily Bart's death in Edith Wharton's *The House of Mirth* is meant as a rebuke to those who, in some sense, destroyed her.

32. Although the interactions among Venus, Jewel, and Aurelia take place in Washington, D.C., twenty-year-old Jewel is clearly a northerner, having spent the majority of her life at "the convent of the Sacred Heart at Montreal, where she had remained until she was eighteen" (83). Although rootless, Aurelia Madison is not represented as southern. Her father's hypothetical company is based in Colorado; she attended the same Montreal convent as Jewel; she met Cuthbert Sumner at Cape May (New Jersey); and she "had lived at Monte Carlo two seasons" (92).

33. Hopkins's portrait of John Robinson Williams is much sketchier than that of Venus, but in his court appearance his speech clearly marks him as a comic figure: "During the cross-examination, John got angry and told the Attorney-General that the Sumners were top-crust, sure; and never one of them had been known to show up as underdone dough no half-and-half's, if it wasn't so he'd eat his own head; he didn't object to meeting any man who disputed the 'pint,' in a slugging match, the hardest to 'fend' off" (252). By framing John's speech here as a foreign, or nonstandard, dialect, Hopkins marks the distance between this character and her own narrative voice, as well as between him and others, including Venus, Jewel, and Hagar, who share his racial identity. Yet, like Venus, John is not a slave but a servant, and his character shifts from being comic, as in this scene, to being dramatic, as when he tries to protect and defend his employer in other scenes.

WORKS CITED

Abrahams, Roger D. *Positively Black*. Englewood Cliffs, N.J.: Prentice-Hall, 1970.

Bell, Bernard. *The Afro-American Novel and Its Tradition.* Amherst: University of Massachusetts Press, 1987.

Berger, John. *Ways of Seeing.* London: British Broadcasting Corporation and Penguin, 1977.

Berson, Misha. "Cabin Fever: Stowe's Once-Taboo Anti-Slavery Classic." *American Theatre,* May 1991, 16–23, 71–73.

Boskin, Joseph. *Sambo: The Rise and Demise of an American Jester.* New York: Oxford University Press, 1986.

Bullock, Penelope. *The Afro-American Periodical Press, 1838–1909.* Baton Rouge: Louisiana State University Press, 1981.

Butler, Judith. *Gender Trouble: Feminism and the Subversion of Identity.* New York: Routledge, 1990.

Carby, Hazel V. Introduction. *The Magazine Novels of Pauline Hopkins.* By Pauline Hopkins. New York: Oxford University Press, 1988. xxix–l.

———. *Reconstructing Womanhood: The Emergence of the Afro-American Woman Novelist.* New York: Oxford University Press, 1987.

Cawelti, John G. *Adventure, Mystery, and Romance: Formula Stories as Art and Popular Culture.* Chicago: University of Chicago Press, 1976.

Color Adjustment. Created and directed by Marlon Riggs. PBS/KQED. San Francisco, 1992.

Engle, Gary D. *This Grotesque Essence: Plays from the American Minstrel Stage.* Baton Rouge: Louisiana State University Press, 1978.

Fredrickson, George M. *The Black Image in the White Mind, 1817–1914.* New York: Harper and Row, 1971.

Gates, Henry Louis, Jr. "The Blackness of Blackness: A Critique of the Sign and the Signifying Monkey." In *Black Literature and Literary Theory.* Ed. Henry Louis Gates, Jr. New York: Methuen, 1984. 285–321.

Giddings, Paula. *When and Where I Enter: The Impact of Black Women on Race and Sex in America.* New York: Morrow, 1984.

Gillman, Susan. "The Mulatto, Tragic or Triumphant? The Nineteenth-Century American Race Melodrama." In *The Culture of Sentiment: Race, Gender, and Sentimentality in Nineteenth-Century America.* Ed. Shirley Samuels. New York: Oxford University Press, 1992. 221–43.

Hopkins, Pauline. *Contending Forces: A Romance Illustrative of Negro Life North and South.* 1900. New York: Oxford University Press, 1988.

———. *Hagar's Daughter: A Story of Southern Caste Prejudice.* In *The Magazine Novels of Pauline Hopkins.* New York: Oxford University Press, 1988. 1–284.

Hurston, Zora Neale. "Characteristics of Negro Expression." 1935. In *Voices from the Harlem Renaissance.* Ed. Nathan Irvin Huggins. New York: Oxford University Press, 1976. 224–36.

Jefferson, Margo. "Seducified by a Minstrel Show." *New York Times,* May 22, 1994.

Johnson, Abby Arthur, and Ronald Maberry Johnson. *Propaganda and Aesthetics: The Literary Politics of Afro-American Magazines in the Twentieth Century.* Amherst: University of Massachusetts Press, 1979.

Kappeler, Suzanne. *The Pornography of Representation.* Minneapolis: University of Minnesota Press, 1986.

Levine, Lawrence W. *Highbrow/Lowbrow: The Emergence of Cultural Hierarchy in America.* Cambridge, Mass.: Harvard University Press, 1988.

Lewis, Gregory. "Back to Minstrel TV." *San Francisco Examiner,* March 21, 1993.

Lott, Eric. *Love and Theft: Blackface Minstrelsy and the American Working Class.* New York: Oxford University Press, 1993.

MacKinnon, Catharine A. *Feminism Unmodified: Discourses on Life and Law.* Cambridge, Mass.: Harvard University Press, 1987.

McShane, Larry. "Ted Danson Assailed for Blackface Routine." *San Francisco Examiner,* Oct. 10, 1993.

Mercer, Kobena. "Skin Head Sex Thing: Racial Difference and the Homoerotic Imaginary." In *How Do I Look? Queer Film and Video.* Ed. Bad Object-Choices. Seattle, Wash.: Bay Press, 1991. 169–222.

Noble, Peter. *The Negro in Films.* New York: Arno, 1970.

O'Connor, John J. "A Survey of Black Comedy in America." *New York Times,* Feb. 9, 1993.

Rich, Adrienne. Afterword. *Take Back the Night: Women on Pornography.* Ed. Laura Lederer. New York: Bantam Books, 1980. 315–23.

Silverman, Kaja. "Histoire d'O: The Construction of a Female Subject." In *Pleasure and Danger: Exploring Female Sexuality.* Ed. Carole S. Vance. Boston: Routledge and Kegan Paul, 1984. 320–49.

Tate, Claudia. *Domestic Allegories of Political Desire: The Black Heroine's Text at the Turn of the Century.* New York: Oxford University Press, 1992.

Toll, Robert C. *Blacking Up: The Minstrel Show in Nineteenth-Century America.* New York: Oxford University Press, 1974.

Tucker, Marilyn. "'Minstrel Show': Old Plague, New Spin." *San Francisco Chronicle,* May 21, 1993.

Waterhouse, Richard. *From Minstrel Show to Vaudeville: The Australian Popular Stage, 1788–1914.* Kensington: New South Wales University Press, 1990.

Williams, Linda. *Hard Core: Power, Pleasure, and the "Frenzy of the Visible."* Berkeley: University of California Press, 1989.

Williams, Patricia J. *The Alchemy of Race and Rights: Diary of a Law Professor.* Cambridge, Mass.: Harvard University Press, 1991.

———. "Equality's Demise and the Issue of Identity." Speech, University of California, Berkeley, Feb. 29, 1992.

Yarborough, Richard. Introduction. *Contending Forces.* By Pauline Hopkins. xxvii–xlviii.

SIX

"Fate Has Linked Us Together": Blood, Gender, and the Politics of Representation in Pauline Hopkins's *Of One Blood*

JENNIE A. KASSANOFF

Between the years 1900 and 1904, Pauline Elizabeth Hopkins worked as the editor-in-chief for the newly established *Colored American Magazine* (*CAM*). In addition to an extensive number of laudatory biographical articles describing "famous men and women of the Negro race," Hopkins also published three magazine novels, including *Of One Blood; or, The Hidden Self* which appeared serially in 1902–3. The Editorial and Publishers' Announcements declared the periodical's intent when its first issue left the press in May 1900: "The *Colored American Magazine* proposes to . . . offer the colored people of the United States a medium through which they can demonstrate their ability and tastes, in fiction, poetry, and art, as well as in the arena of historical, social and economical literature" (60). As Hazel Carby has argued, Hopkins and the staff of *CAM* assumed "a hegemonic position as representatives of black people" (*Reconstructing Womanhood* 166), proclaiming themselves, in the words of staff writer R. S. Elliot, "the mouth-piece and inspiration of the Negro race throughout not only this country, but the world" (45).

In 1904, however, the Boston magazine moved its press and offices to New York City and began operating under the editorial and financial leadership of Booker T. Washington and Fred R. Moore. Washington apparently found reason to disagree with Hopkins's political opinions: after the April 1904 issue, her name was summarily dropped from the masthead. As W. E. B. Du Bois later recalled, "It was suggested to the editor, who was then Miss Pauline Hopkins, that her attitude was not conciliatory enough" (quoted in Yarborough xliii). This sequence of events suggests that Hopkins simply did not conform to Washington's image of the "representative" African American woman, an opinion that was corroborated by another contemporary observer, William Stanley Braithwaite. Describing Hopkins as "temperamental," Braithwaite complained that the novelist "regarded herself as a national figure . . . and as such felt free to impose her views and opinions upon her associates in the conduct of . . . the . . . magazine publications" (25). As Carby rather dryly points out, though Braithwaite had nothing but praise for the male editors of the magazine, he "seemed to think that Hopkins should have remained in grateful and silent submission for having had the opportunity to publish in the *Colored American Magazine*" (*Reconstructing Womanhood* 192).[1]

The termination of Hopkins's career with *CAM* highlights a problem central to the discourse on race in the first decade of the twentieth century. What exactly constituted the "representative" African American—and more specifically, the African American woman? How precisely was one to "represent" this person whom the turn-of-the-century black intelligentsia stressed was to be the distinctly "New Negro"?[2] Much of the racial discourse in this period circulates around the body. Indeed, such politically diverse commentators as Washington and Du Bois sought to create the black body entirely anew. As Henry Louis Gates has observed, contemporary intellectuals attempted to "reconstruct" the African American body in a "representative" way, literally re-presenting what they insisted was an emphatically "New Negro," thereby combatting racist stereotypes. In this effort, Frederick Douglass, the escaped slave and manly, self-made intellectual, served as an emblematic hero: he was, in Gates's words, "the race's greatest opportunity to represent itself in the court of racist public opinion. Black Americans sought to re-present their public selves in order to reconstruct their public, reproducible images" ("Trope" 129). Yet as Hopkins's abrupt termination from *CAM* suggests, the politics of representation—the power, that is, to (re)construct the "representative" African American—constituted a hotly contested intellectual terrain. Only one year after the publication of her final magazine novel, *Of One Blood; or, The Hidden Self*—a text which itself interrogates the very construction of the "representative Negro"—Pauline Hopkins was dismissed, ironically, for seeming "unrepresentative." In this essay I suggest that the interconnected corporeal issues of blood and gender that inform Hopkins's novel effectively deconstruct the monolith of the New Negro by questioning its contours and its limitations.

In many ways, the problem of representing the New Negro at the turn of the century was encoded in the very language of *Plessy v. Ferguson* (163 U.S. 537 [1896]), the U.S. Supreme Court decision that legitimated segregation and thus federally sanctioned Jim Crow laws. Walter Benn Michaels has rightly pointed out that *Plessy* established the notion that "distinctions based on color" were not necessarily visible and consequently a matter for the states to decide (189). What requires further attention, however, is the extent to which the Court's decision circulated around a crucial absence. The Court refused to define what precisely constituted a "Negro." Did Homer Plessy's one-eighth Negro blood forbid him from traveling aboard the "whites only" railroad car?

The Court's majority opinion, written by Justice Henry Billings Brown, held that "these are questions to be determined under the laws of each State and are not properly the issue in this case" (163 U.S. at 552). As Eric Sundquist has recently shown in *To Wake the Nations*, *Plessy* merely culminated "the long assault" on the Fourteenth Amendment's guarantee to equal protection, which had begun soon after the Civil War in 1873 when the Court maintained in the *Slaughterhouse Cases* decision that the amendment authorized essentially "dual" citizenships to both state and country. Indeed, the *Plessy* decision so closely circumscribed federal rights protections that national citizenship was rendered, in Sundquist's words, "virtually meaningless": "*Plessy* was a landmark case not because it drastically altered the direction of legislation and judicial thought but because it concluded the process of transfiguring dual *constitutional* citizenship into dual *racial* citizenship" (Sundquist 237–38, 241).

Brown merely extended the *Slaughterhouse* "logic" in the *Plessy* case. State legislatures, he reasoned, when determining the "question of reasonableness" of separate-but-equal laws, were "at liberty to act with reference to the established usages, customs, and traditions of the people" (163 U.S. at 550). He later added, "If one race be inferior to the other socially, the Constitution of the United States cannot put them upon the same plane" (163 U.S. at 552). Moreover, the language of the Court's opinion made it clear that, because there was no specific federal legislation on this matter, the plaintiff's claim that state segregation laws discriminated against him was merely a matter of personal interpretation. If "separation of the two races stamps the colored race with a badge of inferiority," the Court responded, "it is not by reason of anything found in the act, but solely because the colored race chooses to put that construction upon it" (163 U.S. at 551). The circular reasoning of *Plessy* rendered the definition of African American identity a matter of informal private opinion, thereby providing states with a means of vetoing federal protections.[3]

What Gates has called the "culturally willed myth" of the New Negro seems to have been constructed at least partially in response to the emergence of this ambiguous legal interpretive space ("Trope" 132). The hyperbolic language of Booker T. Washington exemplifies the aggressiveness that often characterized the black intellectual tone. "Springing from the darkest depths of slavery and sorrowful ignorance to the heights of manhood and power almost in one bound," Washington wrote in the introduction to *Progress of a Race*, "the Negro furnishes an unparalleled example of possibility" (v). In much of the rhetoric used to describe the New Negro during this period, the African American is presented as a sort of Progressive Era superman— masculine, clean, hardworking, and selfless. Numerous texts devote many pages to the near perfection of these representative black American men, whose female counterparts are similarly possessed of unassailable virtues. Fannie Barrier Williams, herself described as "the famous club woman, author and writer" in an anthology entitled *A New Negro for a New Century* (1900), celebrates African American club women as "plain, beautiful, charming, bright conversationalists, fluent, resourceful in ideas, forceful in education, and women of all sorts of temperament and idiosyncracies and force and delicacy of character. . . . This woman," she continues, "as if by magic, has succeeded in lifting herself completely from the stain and meanness of slavery as if a century had elapsed since the day of her emancipation" (424).[4]

In part, these intellectual efforts to define the New Negro were orchestrated in response to the increasing prevalence of "biological" arguments used to justify the institutionalized racism of Jim Crow laws. In *Race Traits and Tendencies of the American Negro* (1896), for example, Frederick L. Hoffman marshalled the latest "scientific" evidence to support his claim that weakness and depravity were characteristic of Negro blood; racial uplift, he concluded, would ultimately prove futile (Gosset 281–82; Kinney 151–55; Dearborn 152). The *Plessy* decision had clearly left the question of blood open for debate. "What, after all, is this Negro race?" the journalist Ray Stannard Baker asked in 1908. "What is the Negro spirit? Is it in this black African or in this white American with the drop of dark blood?" (157). What proportion of blood constituted race? As Hopkins herself asked in *Of One Blood*, "The slogan of the hour is 'Keep the Negro down!' but who is clear enough in vision to decide who hath black blood and who hath it not? Can any one tell?" (607). An exasperated Booker T. Washington responded by pointing out the inveteracy of the "one-drop rule" in 1900. "It is a fact," he asserted, "that, if a person is known to have one per cent of African blood in his veins, he ceases to be a white man. The ninety-nine per cent of Caucasian blood does not weigh by the side of one per cent of African blood. . . . The person is a Negro every time" (quoted in Mencke 37).

In defining the New Negro, African American intellectuals went to great lengths to reappropriate the otherwise racist discourse of blood. Indeed, the pervasive idea that blood itself had a "color" was taken so seriously that New Negro social engineers felt obligated to respond with painfully detailed counterarguments. Anna Julia Cooper, author of *A Voice from the South* (1892), defended black genealogy on the basis of blood, pointing out that "there are representatives of [the black race] here as elsewhere who were never in bondage at any time to any man,—whose blood is as blue and lineage as noble as any, even that of the white lady of the South" (109). Hopkins developed an elaborate explanation for skin color, proposing that African pigmentation was produced by a combination of red "coloring matter" and the blue blood that, she stressed, was common to all races: "The real color of the African is really purple and nothing else. Purple involves a mixture of red and blue, and implies the existence of blue in the blood. This is true, or whence comes the blue veins of the white race and its blue eyes?" (*Primer* 8).

H. T. Kealing pressed these sanguine arguments even further by attempting to reappropriate the biologism and social Darwinism that stimulated post-Reconstruction racist discourses. Enumerating what he called "the characteristics of the Negro people," Kealing stressed the distinction between "inborn" traits (ineradicable qualities that "belong to the blood") and those which are "inbred" or acquired. "In considering the characteristics of the Negro people," Kealing wrote in 1903, "we must not confuse the constitutional with the removable" (165). This brand of New Negro essentialism lead Kealing and others to conclude that the African American was, by blood, innately religious, imaginative, affectionate, enduring, courageous, and cheerful.

The pitfalls of these attempts to create and define a somewhat static profile of the New Negro were numerous, as early twentieth-century African American writers recognized. In his 1903 essay entitled "Representative American Negroes," Paul Laurence Dunbar questioned the very project of constructing the "representative" African American: "In considering who and what are representative Negroes there are circumstances which compel one to question what is a representative man of the colored race. Some men are born great, some achieve greatness and others lived during the reconstruction period" (189).

Ultimately, Dunbar concluded that "to have achieved something for the betterment of the race rather than for the aggrandizement of himself seems to be a man's best title to be called representative" (189). Nevertheless, Dunbar's thinking continued to accentuate a tension between individual and collective identity, an ambiguity that blurred the status of the "representative Negro." Did one's salience or one's indistinguishability from the race make him or her "representative"? Anna Julia Cooper objected to the practice of Washington and others who took the successful black man as representative of the whole race. Addressing a convocation of African American clergy in 1886, Cooper declared, "Our present record of eminent men, when placed beside the actual status of the race in America to-day, proves that no man can represent the race. Whatever the attainments of the individual may be, unless his home has moved on *pari passu,* he can never be regarded as identical with or representative of the whole" (30). Only those trapped on the lowest rung of the power hierarchy could authentically represent the entire race, Cooper insisted.

In a now famous statement, Cooper forcefully argued that only when African American women had achieved collective power could the race move forward: "Only the Black Woman can say 'when and where I enter, in the quiet, undisputed dignity of my womanhood, without violence and without suing or special patronage, then and there the whole *Negro race enters with me'*" (31). A series of variables—in this case, gender—again disrupts the act of representation. If the New Negro movement signaled an intellectual effort to create what Gates has called the "black end-of-the-century dream of an unbroken, unhabituated, neological self," then certain corporeal factors problematized the construction of this monolithic self ("Trope" 132).

Indeed, I would suggest that a number of contemporary critics have mistakenly drained the crucial element of blood out of this discourse altogether. Walter Benn Michaels, for example, has persuasively argued that the "technology of racism" in the twentieth century assured the rewriting of biology as ideology. Racial identity, as the "invisible empire" of the Ku Klux Klan so graphically illustrates, transcends mere visibility and speaks instead to the content of the "soul." A new "racism of ideas" has replaced the more antiquated semiotics of skin color (191). This adept replacement of the body with the soul, however, while it might explain notions of whiteness, does not equally inform early twentieth-century conceptions of blackness. Entitling his essay "The Souls of White Folk," Michaels alludes, of course, to Du Bois's celebrated work, *The Souls of Black Folk* (1903). Yet Du Bois himself differs significantly from Michaels as to the definition of African American "race." Du Bois argues that the history of the "American Negro" is characterized by the effort to reconcile precisely these two conflicting terms—"American" and "Negro": "In this merging [the American Negro] wishes neither of the older selves to be lost. He would not Africanize America, for America has too much to teach the world and Africa. He would not bleach his Negro soul in a flood of white Americanism, for he knows that Negro blood has a message for the world. He simply wishes to make it possible for a man to be both a Negro and an American, without being cursed and spit upon by his fellows, without having the door of Opportunity closed roughly in his face" (215). In contrast to Americanness which Du Bois figures as whiteness,[5] the "Negro soul" is equated with "Negro blood." The slippage is significant: whereas white Americanism can be taught, blackness seems to circulate in the veins. The body, it would seem, cannot be easily eliminated from the discourse of race.

This all-but-effacement of the body, and the semiotics of blood in particular, seems problematic in Gates's work as well. In the foreword to the Schomburg Library of Nineteenth-Century Black Women Writers series, Gates seeks to define a critical methodology that will help delineate the "Afro-American literary tradition." More importantly, he seems intent on eschewing essentialism by excising biology altogether in the name of literary formalism: "Literary works configure into a tradition not because of some mystical collective unconscious determined by the biology of race or gender, but because writers read other writers and *ground* their representations of experience in models of language provided largely by other writers to whom they feel akin" (Foreword xviii). Within this context, "kinship" becomes what Gates calls a "formal bonding," distinct from the genealogical logic of biology and blood. In the process of describing the "new racial self" of the New Negro, Gates maintains that "this black and racial self, as we define it here, does not exist as an entity or group of entities but 'only' as a coded system of signs, complete with masks and mythology" ("Trope" 133–35). To eliminate the body completely from the New Negro movement, however, is to assume that the construct itself is a monolithic one.[6] Although I would agree with Gates that African American intellectuals were responding to the racist biological essentialism of the Jim Crow period, I would equally contend that the New Negro served as the locus of a heated debate over the body, particularly the roles of blood and gender in the constitution of African American identity.[7]

As Hopkins's title *Of One Blood; or, The Hidden Self* suggests, blood functioned as a crucial signifier in the emerging struggle to represent the twentieth-century African American. Moreover, the semiotics of blood played out in the text manifests four competing discourses subsumed in the palimpsest of the New Negro. First, "blood," in Hopkins's vocabulary, can justify amalgamation by referring to the monogenist doctrine of racial origins: all people, according to this theory, spring from a common racial ancestry and therefore can intermarry with impunity. Second, however, "blood" also marks a pure African heritage that requires vigilant protection from further dilution. Taken in this sense, the novel manifests a nascent black nationalism, a quest for the recolonization of Africa, and an urge toward total racial separatism. Third, "blood" metonymically signifies the bonds of kinship and thus indicates the threatening possibility of incest. As such, the novel functions as a quest for genealogical origins while simultaneously indicting the sexually violent heritage of slavery in this country. Finally, "blood" serves as a marker for gender difference: because women are the reproductive source of future African American bloodlines, the black maternal body becomes a central focus in the sexual politics of the New Negro movement. In order to begin unraveling Pauline Hopkins's complicated critique of New Negro identity, I would like to examine each of these interpretations of "blood" separately.

* * *

A summary of the byzantine plot of Hopkins's final magazine novel is in order. *Of One Blood* traces the interconnected fates of three characters. Reuel Briggs, a brilliant medical student who is hiding his mixed-race heritage, mesmerically revives a beautiful gospel singer, Dianthe Lusk, from a death-like trance, and marries her, despite her lingering amnesia. Meanwhile, the novel's villain, Aubrey Livingston, a "white" friend, guesses Reuel's racial identity and secretly sabotages the young doctor's employment efforts. Unaware of his friend's duplicity, Reuel follows Aubrey's ill-intentioned advice and departs as a medical advisor with his friend Charlie Vance on an archaeological expedition to Ethiopia without having comsummated his marriage. With Reuel out of the way, Aubrey promptly drowns his white fiancée, Charlie's sister Molly, and mesmerically forces the light-skinned Dianthe to marry him. While all of this is happening, Reuel manages to avoid Aubrey's covert death plot and discovers the hidden city of Telassar where, based on a lotus-shaped birthmark, he is declared King Ergamenes, the long-lost heir to the Ethiopian throne.

Before marrying Queen Candace and assuming his royal duties, Reuel returns to America with the Ethiopian high priest, Ai, to confirm his own supernatural vision of Dianthe's death. He comes home to discover both that Aubrey has poisoned Dianthe and that the three are "of one blood" in two senses: they are not only siblings but, as the African American children of the visionary slave woman Mira and her white master Aubrey Livingston, Sr., they also share the blood of the African race. Her incestuous fears confirmed, Dianthe quickly dies, and Aubrey Jr., guilty of murder, is punished according to the traditions of his Ethiopian royal lineage: he must follow Ai's hypnotic, "mysterious command" and commit suicide. His body is later found floating in the Charles River "at the very point where poor Molly Vance had floated in the tangled lily-bed" (620). Reuel, accompanied by his newly discovered grandmother, a hoodoo expert named Aunt Hannah, is now free to return to his Ethiopian kingdom.

At least from one perspective, Hopkins located her novel at the center of a fierce anthropological debate over the origins of race. Unlike the polygenists who, throughout the nineteenth century, argued that each race constituted a distinct species with unique genetic origins, the monogenists insisted on the original unity of humankind and on the singularity of creation (Mencke 41–42). As early as 1861, Harriet Jacobs had challenged not only the biological determinism but also the hypocrisy that sprang from polygenetic claims to discrete racial bloodlines: "What a libel upon the heavenly Father, who 'made of one blood all nations of men!'" she wrote in *Incidents in the Life of a Slave Girl.* "And then who *are* Africans? Who can measure the amount of Anglo-Saxon blood coursing in the veins of American slaves?" (69).

Pauline Hopkins subscribed to her own elaborately wrought brand of monogenist creationism. In a 1905 tract entitled *A Primer of Facts,* she theorized that "until the entry of Noah's family into the ark, all people were of the one race and complexion." For Hopkins, the case of Noah and his wife, who produced three sons, each of a different race, was ample proof of her point: "Can all races have sprung from the same parent stock? The answer to this question solves the mystery of the brotherhood of man, showing it is possible for persons of three distinct complexions, as was the case in Noah's family—Yellow, Black and White—to be born of the same father and mother of one race and color. It is an easily understood law of God's all-wise providence" (5, 7).

Blood, in *Of One Blood,* at least partially adheres to this monogenist logic. Ai, the high priest of Telassar, castigates Charlie Vance, a white member of Reuel's expedition, for his American racism: "And yet, ye are all of one blood; descended from one common father. Is there ever a flock or herd without its black member?" (585). Recognizing "the truth in the [biblical] words, 'Of one blood have I made all races of men,'" Charlie ruefully reflects, "Where was the color line now?" (590). Later in the novel, the omniscient narrator bursts forth with the revelation that in God's own "mysterious way . . . He has united the white race and the black race in this new continent. By the transgression of the law He proves His own infallibility: 'Of one blood have I made all nations of men to dwell upon the whole face of the earth.' . . . No man can draw the dividing line between the two races for they are both of one blood!" (607). This insistence on shared blood, on the "brotherhood of man," can rationalize both assimilation and amalgamation.[8]

Hopkins's narrative in fact hinges on this blurring of the color line. All three of the light-skinned central characters embody the intermixing of white and black blood which, the narrator insists, bears out the monogenist interpretation of the Bible. In a passage entitled "Of One Blood" in their 1897 work, *Progress of a Race,* H. F. Kletzing, a biblical scholar, and W. H. Crogman, president of Clark College, confidently proclaimed, "To-day the universal belief is that God 'Created of one blood all nations of man to dwell on the face of the earth.' The unity of the race is demonstrated with emphasis in the possible and actual assimilation of all the races in the one man" (24).

Yet even this history of racial origins and amalgamation carries its own set of ambiguities in Hopkins's novel. All three of the novel's central characters "pass" as white—either knowingly or unwittingly. With skin "white, but of a tint suggesting olive" (444), Reuel deliberately hides his racial identity, a scheme later foiled by Aubrey, who betrays his colleague's secret to potential hospital employers. Eventually, Reuel repents his deception: he bows his head in shame before Ai, the Ethiopian high priest, confessing that in America, "'It is a deep disgrace to have within the veins even one drop of the blood you seem so proud of possessing.' . . . He felt keenly now the fact that he had played the coward's part in hiding his origin" (560). In contrast, the amnesiac Dianthe who is as "fair as the fairest woman . . . with wavy bands of chestnut hair" (453) only passes as a white woman because Reuel refuses to inform her of her African American lineage. Although Dianthe remembers her identity midway through the novel, she is forced to conceal her heritage a second time when Aubrey falsely threatens her with Reuel's abandonment.[9]

The dilemma of passing is brought into sharpest focus, however, in the case of Aubrey, whose self-description rings with irony: "I . . . am a Southerner, born and bred, or as the vulgar have it, 'dyed in the wool'" (449). Yet it is precisely the distinction between being "born" and "bred," and indeed the inconsequence of actual skin color (Aubrey is only "dyed" white), upon which the novel subtly insists. In one way or another, the brothers and sister all suffer the consequences of "passing" by variously enduring shame, amnesia, and suicide. Moreover, because they are unaware of or humiliated by their African blood, they cannot reap its royal benefits. Implicitly, the novel urges the return to the purity of "Negro blood"—indeed to Telassar, the civilization that recognizes Reuel as a "pure-blooded Ethiopian" (556).

* * *

Based on this second meaning of the term "blood," Hopkins's novel can be read as a forceful protest against miscegenation and as an example of black eugenics. The mulatto, as Joel Williamson has observed, visibly embodied the sexual violence of slavery: the mulatto "was the walking, talking, breathing indictment of the world the white men made. . . . It was apparent in his very person that white and black had interpenetrated in a graphic and appalling way" (95). As the embodied emblem of racial amalgamation, the mulatto served as a touchstone for racist hysteria throughout the nineteenth and early twentieth centuries. In the words of pro-slavery sociologist Henry Hughes, "Hybridism is heinous. Impurity of the races is against the law of nature. Mulattoes are monsters" (239–40).

From an entirely different perspective, but in a similar mode, much of the rhetoric of the New Negro reifies a certain primal story of miscegenation. T. Thomas Fortune perhaps articulated this narrative best: the inequitable foundations of American society, he argued in a 1903 publication entitled *The Negro Problem,* were based on "the reckless and brutal prostitution of black women by white men in the days of slavery, from which a vast army of mulattoes were produced" (226). Alexander Crummell offered a similar account, insisting that "the gross and violent intermingling of the blood of the southern white man cannot be taken as an index of the future of the black race" (45). Indeed, responding to what she saw as southern white historical revisionism, Hopkins herself incisively charged that "chivalrous Southern men desecrated the purity of the Southern home, and, incidentally, opened this question of racial purity" (*Primer* 28). Thus, it was in a vocabulary saturated with the ironies of purportedly "pure" American blood that H. T. Kealing urged white citizens to "train the Negro to accept and carry responsibility by putting it upon him." As a result, Kealing argued, "America will have enriched her blood" (184–85).

The movement in *Of One Blood* follows the shift from an unknown, assimilated American identity to the recovery (and recolonization) of at least one possible "hidden self," an untainted African heritage.[10] As King Ergamenes, Reuel marries Queen Candace, a perfect dark-skinned woman who is said to look like "a statue of Venus worked in bronze" (567).[11] Pointing out the virgin queen's "warm bronze complexion; thick eyebrows, [and] great black eyes" (568), Claudia Tate has observed that "pigment becomes a positive physical attribute measured in terms of feminine beauty more than sixty years prior to the coinage of the slogan 'Black is Beautiful'" ("Hopkins" 65). By uniting his mixed blood with Candace's racial perfection, Reuel is symbolically reincorporated into Ethiopian royal bloodlines. In this sense, Hopkins's novel can be said to follow in the black eugenicist tradition of Crummell and Fortune. An aggressive Pan-Africanist, Crummell predicted not only that African Americans would resist amalgamation but that they would (re)constitute the race as "a compact, homogenous population of one blood, ancestry, and lineage" (48).

Of One Blood suggests that Hopkins at least partially shared Crummell's Pan-African ambition: she took his racial purity argument to its logical endpoint, visualizing both a return to Africa and a reunification of blood (Crummell 431–53).[12] It was Fortune, however, whose black eugenicist arguments were most compelling. Fortune blamed the oppressed status of the turn-of-the-century African American on the "vitiation of blood" by the white man. It is worthwhile to cite Fortune at length on this point:

> The blood of all ethnic types that go to make up American citizenship flows in the veins of the Afro-American people, so that of the ten million of them in this country, accounted for by the Federal census, not more than four million are of pure negroid descent, while some four million of them, not accounted for by the Federal census, have escaped into the ranks of the white race, and are re-enforced very largely by such escapements each year. The vitiation of blood has operated irresistibly to weaken that pride of ancestry, which is the foundation-stone of pride of race; so that the Afro-American people have been held together rather by the segregation decreed by law and public opinion than by ties of consanguinity since their manumission and enfranchisement. (214–15)

Fortune deplored the impurity of African American bloodlines: only the "ties of consanguinity," he insisted, could preserve the "pride of race." Less ambivalent than Hopkins, Fortune urged the consolidation of blood and a return to the African motherland. In the United States, he predicted, the African American of "pure negroid descent" would disappear, for there was no place in the republic for "the integrality and growth of a distinct race type" (226).

The fear of lost racial identity is the central focus of the incest theme in Hopkins's novel. As the self-proclaimed slavery "perpetualist" Henry Hughes warned in 1854, because members of the "sub-sovereign" black race were "affamiliated" with their white paternalistic masters, miscegenation amounted to the sin of interbreeding: "The same law which forbids consanguineous amalgamation forbids ethnical amalgamation. Both are incestuous. Amalgamation is incest" (240).

To a certain extent, a variation of this logic is at work in Hopkins's novel. Because of the nonconsensual miscegenation practiced under slavery, neither Reuel, Aubrey, nor Dianthe can properly trace their own genealogies and, as a result, they incestuously intermarry. As Hazel Carby points out, "Hopkins developed in *Of One Blood* a unique variation of the Afro-American convention of the search for and discovery of family" (*Reconstructing Womanhood* 157). The dangers posed by unknown ancestry are here dramatically and rather gothically brought to the fore. After Aunt Hannah has informed Dianthe that her husbands are also her brothers—"Yes, honey; all of one blood!" (607)—the narrative is disrupted by a didactic refrain:

> "The laws of changeless justice bind
>   Oppressor and oppressed;
> And close as sin and suffering joined,
>   We march to Fate abreast." (607)

Here, the monogenist "kinship" of all people engenders an incestuous nightmare. The shared blood of oppressor and oppressed breeds a generation of mulatto children who cannot recognize their siblings and thus, as Mary Dearborn observes, always risk violating the incest taboo. "It is not surprising," she remarks, "that the mulatto who passed for white raised such profound anxiety in the white—and black—mind" (138). Although *Of One Blood* explicitly argues for a brotherhood of man, subtexts of incestuous blood (fraternalism run amok) and black eugenics (brothers biologically united against a perceived contaminant) dispute this claim.[13]

* * *

Hopkins pushed this critique of the New Negro's representation one step further by examining and exploiting the disruptive association between the image of blood and the issue of gender. As Hopkins recognized, women in many ways are the locus of "blood" in the discourse of the New Negro. Anna Julia Cooper contended that it was "absurd" to point out the number of "colored men" who had succeeded in becoming doctors, lawyers, and professors "while the source from which the life-blood of the race is to flow is subject to taint and corruption in the enemy's camp" (25). Black women, in Cooper's view, embodied nothing less than the very origin of African American "life-blood." It was thus with some urgency that she beseeched black men to defend their women from "the lower classes of white men": "Oh, save them, help them, shield, train, develop, teach, inspire them!" she wrote; for on "a staunch, helpful, regenerating womanhood . . . rests the foundation stones of our future as a race" (25).

Following this logic, Hopkins identified the genesis of the revived Ethiopian royalty with a woman's blood. Pygmalion-like, Queen Candace is described as "an animated statue, in which one saw the blood circulate, and from which life flowed" (568). Despite the glowing darkness of Candace's skin, her blood is made pointedly visible, emphasizing its metonymic association with the life-producing capacity of women. As Hopkins doubtless knew from her historical research for this novel, though only one ruler named Ergamenes had governed Ethiopia, a long succession of Candaces had populated the Ethiopian royal lineage (Gruesser). Because Candace's name was synonymous with racial continuity, Reuel's union with the Ethiopian queen promises to "give the world a dynasty of dark-skinned rulers, whose destiny should be to restore the prestige of an ancient people" (570).

It is not surprising then that the black maternal body functioned as the site of significant New Negro intervention. As Fortune and others argued, miscegenation had historically been perpetuated by white men upon the unwilling bodies of African American women. New Negro intellectuals consequently sought to exercise a new control over the reproductive capacities of those bodies. Cooper framed her 1886 appeal on behalf of African American women with the explicit assumption that these women represented the generational future of the race: "A stream cannot rise higher than its source. The atmosphere of homes is no rarer and purer and sweeter than are the mothers in those homes. A race," she concluded "is but a total of families" (29). The preservation of racial integrity, Cooper insisted, depended on a commitment to improve the status of black women and thus, as a result, the African American home. Only a strong home life would prevent amalgamation, which Cooper called simply "an unthinkable thought." "Whatever the fluctuations along the ragged edge between the races," she wrote, "the home instinct is sufficiently strong in each to hold the great mass true to its attractions" (221–22).

Alexander Crummell agreed with Cooper's premise that African American mothers embodied the future of racial unity. Arguing that "any movement which passes by the female sex is an emphemeral thing," he proudly reported in 1888 that the end of amalgamation was in sight: "Since emancipation the black woman has gained possession of her own person, and . . . the base process of intermixture has had a wide and sudden decline" (79, 45). Similarly, in 1897, Kletzing and Crogman proclaimed the singular importance of women to the progress of the race: "The work of the mothers of our race is grandly constructive. It is for [them] to build about the wreck and ruin of the past more stately temples of thought and action" (221–22).

Given the New Negro investment in the preservation of African American bloodlines (bloodlines pointedly identified with the bodies of black women), it is curious that *Of One Blood* circulates so persistently around the tragically passive female form. As the eroticized object upon whom Reuel and Aubrey practice their unethical feats of mesmerism, Dianthe Lusk represents a fundamental problem in the text. When Reuel mystically reanimates her lifeless body, Dianthe, in an amnesiac trance, pleads with him to "give me the benefit of your powerful will" (475). Aroused by this spectacle, Aubrey later takes sinister advantage of its effects by forcing Dianthe into marriage. The "numbing influence of the man's presence" again renders her body utterly inert: "In desperation she tried to defy him, but she knew that she had lost her will-power and was but a puppet in the hands of this false friend" (504). Like his slave-owning father before him, Aubrey apparently derives a sadistic pleasure from his erotic machinations: he captures Reuel's wife and obsessively monitors her every move. Although Dianthe, whose "mind [had been] weakened by hypnotic experiments" (601), struggles to resist her new husband's will, she cannot fend off "the power of a fiend in human shape" (579). Reuel's own loving tyranny, however, proves little better than Aubrey's vicious domination. Only by taking advantage of Dianthe's amnesia can Reuel deceive her into thinking that she is white and thus (ironically) a suitable spouse for him. "I'm not unselfish," he admits to Aubrey. "I don't pretend to be. There is no sin in taking her out of the sphere where she was born. God and science helping me, I will give her life and love and wifehood and maternity and perfect health" (479). Like Westervelt, the malevolent mesmerist in Hawthorne's *Blithedale Romance,* both Reuel and Aubrey seek to reconstruct the heroine's subjectivity and to appropriate her body.[14] Dianthe is unable to exert any agency of her own and falls into complete submission to masculine mandates. Hopkins implies that because Dianthe is unable to retrieve her original identity, she is compelled to accept the passive subjectivity forced upon her by the novel's men.

Apparently unsatisfied with this conclusion, however, Hopkins offers an alternative to this male colonization of the female body in the form of an empowering matrilineage. Like her daughter Dianthe, Mira, the enslaved mother, had once fallen prey to the spiritualist manipulations of her white master. While under the influence of one such trance, she had been transformed from "a serious, rather sad Negress, very mild to everyone" into "a gay, noisy, restless woman, full of irony and sharp jesting" (486). One night, before an audience of Livingston dinner guests, Mira had mystically and graphically predicted the Civil War and its destructive "trail of blood" (487). Enraged by this performance, Aubrey Sr. had subsequently sold his former paramour.

If Dianthe represents a seemingly blank text upon which the novel's male characters can inscribe a submissive identity, then Mira articulates an alternative possibility. Hypnosis summons a subversive identity from the mother: Mira becomes "noisy, restless . . . full of irony and sharp jesting." She terrifies the senior Livingston's white guests and, true to her name ("Mira," the imperative form of the Latin verb "to look"), she sees into the future, prophesying the destruction wrought by the forthcoming war. It is little wonder, then, that Mira is the locus of discovery in the novel: not only does she magically "visit" Reuel in Africa and inform him of Aubrey's plot, but she also appears to Dianthe in a succession of ghostly visions, walking across the room, opening the Bible, and writing. Dianthe later examines the volume and discovers part of the twelfth chapter of Luke heavily underlined: "For there is nothing covered that shall not be revealed." At the end of the passage she finds that "on the margin, at the end of this passage was written in a fine female hand, the single word, 'Mira'" (506).

What is striking here is that the woman's hand—and specifically the *mother's* hand—inscribes itself into the *margins* of the text. Hopkins implies that the text, quite literally, cannot contain the renegade mother, whose utterances destabilize the social order. Mira stands outside of cultural norms: she is at once the voice of the partisan separatism (civil war) and the voice of incestuous unity. The mother, then, bespeaks blood violently spilled and blood overly consolidated, thus threatening the entire fabric of society by marking sibling warfare and sibling endogamy. Her ghostly articulations evidence what Julia Kristeva has called "poetic language," or "the semiotic," a maternal discourse that disrupts the patriarchal symbolic order. In a revision of Claude Lévi-Strauss's famous pronouncement that the incest taboo necessitates and legislates the cultural exchange of both language and women, Kristeva aligns the mother with the pre-oedipal, the incestuous, the nonexchangeable, and the no-longer proscribed. "Poetic language," she suggests, "appropriates to itself this archaic, instinctual, and maternal territory; thus it simultaneously prevents the word from becoming mere sign and the mother from being an object like any other—forbidden" (136).

The mother tongue, according to Kristeva, encodes a revolutionary rupture. If Mira, as a female slave, epitomizes the woman-as-exchangeable-object, her maternal voice subversively critiques this system by invoking not only the resulting violence and incest but, perhaps more importantly, the disruptive impact of a continued relation to the mother. By revealing her identity to her children, Mira reappropriates her own maternal body and thereby deconstructs all of the previously accepted genealogical structures in the novel. Through her spectral presence, Mira's children discover that they are of one culturally discordant, maternal blood. From a Kristevan perspective, this finding marks each of them with revolutionary potential: they are incestuous and thus culturally taboo; they are the racial emblems of civil war—in Hopkins's words, the "representatives of the people for whom God had sent the terrible scourge of blood upon the land to free from bondage" (452)—and finally, they are royal heirs to an African civilization that, in radical defiance of the Western historical canon, purports to be the cradle of civilization.[15]

To reinforce the insurgent potential of the mother, Hopkins goes a step further by locating Mira herself in a matrilineage. Like her daughter, Aunt Hannah is identified with a liminal, dream-like, magical realm. Dianthe discovers her grandmother, "the most noted 'voodoo' doctor or witch in the country" (603), in a "spot [that] was wild and unfamiliar" (602). Aunt Hannah represents an alternative embodiment of maternal identity, one Dianthe associates with a verse description of an African princess:

> "I knew a princess; she was old,
>   Crisp-haired, flat-featured, with a look
> Such as no dainty pen of gold
>   Would write of in a fairy book.
>
> "Her face was like a Sphinx's face, to me,
>   Touched with vast patience, desert grace,
> And lonesome, brooding mystery." (604)

The mother is once again affiliated with the extra-textual. Aunt Hannah's representation as an image that exceeds the conventional inscriptions written by a "dainty pen of gold" in a "fairy book" corresponds to Mira's marginalia. Moreover, Aunt Hannah embodies mythic revisionism. Unlike Oedipus the King, Dianthe's princess-grandmother is at once sovereign and Sphinx: she is located both "inside" as the descendant of a royal lineage and "outside" as the guardian of a disruptive secret. This duality aligns Aunt Hannah with the semiotic: the old woman, to borrow Kristeva's terms, embodies "a disposition that is definitely heterogeneous to meaning but always in sight of it or in either a negative or surplus relationship to it" (133). Like her grandson Reuel, Aunt Hannah is a doctor but with a notable difference: as a revolutionary "voodoo" doctor, Aunt Hannah administers the healing antidote of narrative—of decoded genealogies, descriptive histories, and the violent promise of maternal retribution. The old woman's promise to her dying granddaughter haunts the text: "Vengeance is mine; I will repay" (613).[16]

* * *

Shortly after publishing her final serialized novel, Pauline Hopkins departed from the *Colored American Magazine,* leaving behind a pointed critique of the New Negro's appropriation of the female body. If the African American woman were to fall victim to this new form of control, Hopkins indicates in *Of One Blood,* then she would suffer the fate of Dianthe Lusk and become a passive object of exchange. If, however, she could discover alternative ways to articulate herself and her people—through, for example, Mira's powerful mysticism, Aunt Hannah's healing hoodoo, or most potently, through the authority of African American women's writing itself—then she might alter and diversify the quest for the "representative" African American. Like Mira the rebellious mother, Pauline Hopkins subtly—even deviously—inscribed her own complicated text into the margins of the New Negro debate, questioning and challenging the contours of what African American identity would be in the twentieth century.

NOTES

I wish to thank Lora Romero for her thoughtful reading of an earlier draft of this essay.

1. After leaving *CAM,* Hopkins briefly published her work in the more radical *Voice of the Negro.*

2. Though the term "New Negro" reached its widest audience with the publication of Alain Locke's 1925 anthology of the Harlem Renaissance, the phrase itself dates back to the eighteenth century. As Henry Louis Gates has recently noted, the term "New Negro," as "a paradoxical metaphor that combined a concern with history and cultural antecedents with a deep concern for an articulated racial heritage," was in fact most self-consciously defined in the years *preceding* the Harlem Renaissance, between 1895 and 1925. For a history of the creation, usage, and political content of New Negro, see Gates, "The Face and Voice of Blackness" (xxviii–xlvi).

3. Lora Romero has suggested that the *Plessy* decision marked the Court's attempt to depoliticize the issue of racial discrimination by relegating it from a federal "political" matter to a local question of "taste." The Court's refusal to legislate race, she proposes, might have signaled an attempt to avoid transforming race into a "political construction." By localizing and "naturalizing" the issue, the Court implied that something nonpolitical determined it (personal correspondence, July 1990).

4. Equally invested in extolling the attributes of black club women, Hopkins, in her initial capacity as Women's Department editor at *CAM,* frequently reported on the increasingly popular club movement.

5. Michaels makes the same connection, arguing that in the early twentieth century, American identity and white racial identity became synonymous: "One might say that the very idea of American citizenship is a racial and even racist idea, racist not because it embodies a (more or less concealed) preference for white skins but because it confers on national identity something like the ontology of race" (192).

6. Hazel Carby has argued that prior to World War I, the black northern intellectual elite saw the country's African American population, the majority of whom lived in the rural South, as an homogeneous whole. She cites as evidence the *Colored American Magazine,* which "unashamedly asserted that it could speak for and represent the unique historical experience of 'black people' and addressed them in these all-encompassing terms" (*Reconstructing Womanhood* 164). As I suggest in the remainder of this essay, however, at least one member of the magazine's editorial staff, namely Pauline Hopkins, had a far more complicated understanding of early twentieth-century African American identity.

7. Interestingly, Gates's critique of this period in African American history has largely gone unchallenged. Indeed, it has been particularly influential within recent Hopkins criticism. Thomas J. Otten, whose 1992 article on Hopkins credits Gates for his analysis of the New Negro, follows the Harvard scholar in arguing that the black intelligentsia tried to ignore racial difference (233). I

maintain, on the contrary, that an ongoing discussion of the corporeality of race was both critical and central to New Negro discourse.

8. In her *A Primer of Facts,* Hopkins proposes her own utopian theory of amalgamated eugenics in which an entirely new race of geniuses comes to re-populate the earth: "Who is to say that the type of the future American will not be represented by the descendants of men whose cosmopolitan genius makes them the property of all mankind? The offspring of Samuel Coleridge Taylor, or of Henry Tanner, will, in all probability, unite with some one of their social set in the countries of their adoption" (28). "Anglo-Saxon blood," Hopkins adds, "is already hopelessly perverted, with that of other races, and in most cases to its great gain" (29).

9. Unlike her brothers, Dianthe suffers disproportionately for passing. As I argue more fully at the end of this essay, Hopkins could only envision a dim future for the New Negro woman who had dangerously lost authority and control over her own body.

10. As Cynthia D. Schrager points out (in this volume), Hopkins derived the term "hidden self" from William James's analysis of submerged or multi-ple selves within the hysterical subject. Schrager argues, rightly I believe, that the "hidden self" functioned for Hopkins as a metaphor not only for "pass-ing" but also for the overall oppressed social condition of African Americans in the post-Reconstruction era.

11. See *CAM,* "Venus and Apollo Modelled from Ethiopians" (May/June 1903, 465). There is strong evidence to suggest that Hopkins wrote this un-signed article while *Of One Blood* was running simultaneously in the same issue (Carby, *Reconstructing Womanhood* 159).

12. A qualification is necessary here. Despite her obvious fascination with the possibility of the African American recolonization of Ethiopia, Hopkins stated pointedly that wholesale emigration was not necessary: "Are we obliged to emigrate to Africa [in order to restore Ethiopia to its former glory]?—No. Friendly intercourse and mutual aid and comfort are all that are necessary at the present time. The future is in God's hands and will take care of itself" (*Primer* 20).

13. Carby has suggested that the mulatto figure allowed Hopkins to explore the deconstruction of the racial dichotomy, black versus white. "Hopkins' particular use of such figuration," she argues, "is intended, in part, to demy-thologize concepts of 'pure blood' and 'pure race'" ("'On the Threshold'" 313; see also Dearborn 139). In the case of *Of One Blood,* however, I find Carby's analysis somewhat limited. As I suggest here, the movement in Hopkins's final magazine novel increasingly valorizes, from at least one perspective, a more distilled version of African blood that will (re)create racial purity and thus preserve African American bloodlines.

14. The fact that Reuel and Aubrey appear to be white might have been

significant to Hopkins's strategy in the novel. If the novel itself contains an implicit critique of the patriarchal underpinnings of the New Negro movement, it is possible that Hopkins felt reluctant to "break ranks" openly with her African American colleagues. Perhaps some of the confusion in the novel over who is "really" white and who is "really" black is Hopkins's way of *disguising* her critique of black male writers like Washington and Du Bois. I am grateful to Lora Romero for discussions that suggested this idea to me.

15. "Of this we are sure," Professor Stone tells Reuel, "all records of history, sacred and profane, unite in placing the Ethiopian as the primal race" (521).

16. Without attention to the powerfully subversive maternal roles of Mira and Aunt Hannah, the novel does indeed seem "to have silenced the discourse of female agency," as Claudia Tate has recently argued (*Domestic Allegories* 204–8). Tate's thesis that *Of One Blood* ultimately represents a retreat from "racial optimism" into what she terms the "hibernation" of political desire, however, obligates her to disregard the crucial role played by mothers in the novel's insurgent feminist politics.

WORKS CITED

Baker, Ray Stannard. *Following the Color Line: American Negro Citizenship in the Progressive Era*. 1908. New York: Harper and Row, 1964.

Braithwaite, William Stanley. "Negro America's First Magazine." *Negro Digest* 6.2 (1947): 21–26.

Carby, Hazel. "'On the Threshold of Woman's Era': Lynching, Empire, and Sexuality in Black Feminist Theory." In *"Race," Writing, and Difference*. Ed. Henry Louis Gates, Jr. Chicago: University of Chicago Press, 1985. 301–16.

———. *Reconstructing Womanhood: The Emergence of the Afro-American Woman Novelist*. New York: Oxford University Press, 1987.

Cooper, Anna Julia. *A Voice from the South*. 1892. New York: Oxford University Press, 1988.

Crummell, Alexander. *Africa and America; Addresses and Discourses*. 1891. Miami, Fla.: Mnemosyne, 1969.

Dearborn, Mary V. *Pocahontas's Daughters: Gender and Ethnicity in American Culture*. New York: Oxford University Press, 1986.

Du Bois, W. E. B. *The Souls of Black Folk*. 1903. In *The Three Negro Classics*. New York: Avon, 1965. 207–389.

Dunbar, Paul Laurence. "Representative American Negroes." In *The Negro Problem*. By Washington et al. 187–209.

Elliot, R. S. "The Story of Our Magazine." *Colored American Magazine*, May 1901, 43–77.

Fortune, T. Thomas. "The Negro's Place in American Life at the Present Day." In *The Negro Problem*. By Washington et al. 211–34.

Gates, Henry Louis, Jr. "The Face and Voice of Blackness." In *Facing History: The Black Image in American Art, 1710–1940*. Ed. Guy C. McElroy. San Francisco: Bedford Arts, 1990. xxviii–lvi.

———. Foreword. *The Magazine Novels of Pauline Hopkins*. By Pauline Hopkins. New York: Oxford University Press, 1988. vii–xxii.

———. "The Trope of the New Negro and the Reconstruction of the Image of the Black." *Representations* 24 (Fall 1988): 129–55.

Gosset, Thomas R. *Race: The History of an Idea in America*. Dallas, Tex.: Southern Methodist University Press, 1963.

Gruesser, John. "Pauline Hopkins' *Of One Blood*: Creating an Afrocentric Fantasy for a Black Middle-Class Audience." In *Modes of the Fantastic*. Ed. Robert A. Collins and Robert A. Latham. Westport, Conn.: Greenwood, 1995. 74–83.

Hopkins, Pauline Elizabeth. *Of One Blood; or, The Hidden Self*. 1902–3. *The Magazine Novels of Pauline Hopkins*. New York: Oxford University Press, 1988. 439–621.

———. *A Primer of Facts Pertaining to the Early Greatness of the African Race and the Possibility of Restoration by Its Descendants—with Epilogue*. Cambridge, Mass.: P. E. Hopkins, 1905.

Hughes, Henry. *Treatise on Sociology, Theoretical and Practical*. Philadelphia, Pa.: Lippincott, Grambo, 1854.

Jacobs, Harriet. *Incidents in the Life of a Slave Girl, Written by Herself*. 1861. New York: Oxford University Press, 1988.

Kealing, H. T. "The Characteristics of the Negro People." In *The Negro Problem*. By Washington et al. 161–85.

Kinney, James. *Amalgamation! Race, Sex, and Rhetoric in the Nineteenth-Century American Novel*. Westport, Conn.: Greenwood, 1985.

Kletzing, H. F., and W. H. Crogman. *Progress of a Race . . . or . . . The Remarkable Advancement of the Afro-American from the Bondage of Slavery, Ignorance, and Poverty to the Freedom of Citizenship, Intelligence, Affluence, Honor, and Trust*. 1897. New York: Negro Universities Press, 1969.

Kristeva, Julia. *Desire in Language: A Semiotic Approach to Literature and Art*. Ed. Leon S. Roudiez. Trans. Thomas Gora, Alice Jardine, and Leon S. Roudiez. New York: Columbia University Press, 1980.

Mencke, John G. *Mulattoes and Race Mixture: American Attitudes and Images, 1865–1918*. Ann Arbor, Mich.: UMI Press, 1970.

Michaels, Walter Benn. "The Souls of White Folk." In *Literature and the Body: Essays on Population and Persons*. Ed. Elaine Scarry. Baltimore, Md.: Johns Hopkins University Press, 1988. 185–209.

Otten, Thomas J. "Pauline Hopkins and the Hidden Self of Race." *ELH* 59 (1992): 227–56.

Plessy v. Ferguson. 163 U.S. 537. U.S. Sup. Ct. 1896.

Sundquist, Eric J. *To Wake the Nations: Race in the Making of American Literature.* Cambridge, Mass.: Harvard University Press, 1993.

Tate, Claudia. *Domestic Allegories of Political Desire: The Black Heroine's Text at the Turn of the Century.* New York: Oxford University Press, 1992.

———. "Pauline Hopkins: Our Literary Foremother." In *Conjuring: Black Women, Fiction, and Literary Tradition.* Ed. Marjorie Pryse and Hortense J. Spillers. Bloomington: Indiana University Press, 1985. 53–66.

Washington, Booker T. Introduction. *Progress of a Race.* By Kletzing and Crogman. v-vii.

———. *Up from Slavery.* 1901. In *Three Negro Classics.* New York: Avon, 1965. xxiii–205.

Washington, Booker T., et al. *The Negro Problem: A Series of Articles by Representative American Negroes of To-Day.* 1903. Miami, Fla.: Mnemosyne, 1969.

Williams, Fannie Barrier. "The Club Movement among Colored Women of America." In *A New Negro for a New Century.* By Booker T. Washington, N. B. Wood, and Fannie Barrier Williams. 1900. New York: Arno Press, 1969. 379–405.

Williamson, Joel. *New People: Miscegenation and Mulattoes in the United States.* New York: Free Press, 1980.

Yarborough, Richard. Introduction. *Contending Forces: A Romance Illustrative of Negro Life North and South.* By Pauline Hopkins. 1900. New York: Oxford University Press, 1988. xxvii–xlviii.

SEVEN

Pauline Hopkins and William James:
The New Psychology and the Politics of Race

CYNTHIA D. SCHRAGER

In her diary entry of October 26, 1890, Alice James, the invalid sister of Henry and William, wrote of her noted psychologist brother: "William uses an excellent expression when he says in his paper on the 'Hidden Self' that the nervous victim 'abandons' certain portions of his consciousness.... It is just the right [word] ... altho' I have never unfortunately been able to abandon my consciousness and get five minutes' rest" (148–49). As a "nervous victim" herself, Alice undoubtedly felt well-qualified to make this characteristically ironic comment on William's article "The Hidden Self," a discussion of French research into multiple personalities in hysterical subjects, which he had published in *Scribner's Magazine* earlier the same year. Reviewing pioneering new discoveries about the unconscious then emerging from Jean-Martin Charcot's work at the Salpêtrière Hospital in Paris, James discusses the work of two Charcot disciples, Pierre Janet and Alfred Binet, with Janet's *L'Automatisme Psychologique* (1889) the primary focus of his comments. James reports with considerable interest and admiration on a number of case studies of hysterical women in whom traumatic shock resulted in a splitting off of some parts of the personality from the main personality, and on the use of hypnosis or trance-states to resurface these "submerged selves." He concludes: "This simultaneous coexistence of the different personages into which one human being may be split is the *great* thesis of M. Janet's book" (368).

The "new psychology," as it was dubbed, generated considerable interest at the turn of the century not only in academic circles but also among literate middle-class Americans of the sort who composed *Scribner's* audience.[1] Boston was a geographical center both for academic psychology (of which James, in his position on the Harvard faculty, was one of the early American pioneers) and for the various popular psychologies (from mesmerism and spiritualism to mind-cure and New Thought) that were faddish in nineteenth-century middle- and upper-class culture. In another diary entry, Alice James recounts with some delight an unsuccessful encounter with a mind-curist, who found her "too much barricaded" by her "intellectual friends" to receive the cure (153). Whereas Alice was suspicious of any kind of "self-abandonment" of her rational faculty and was reportedly pleased when her lifelong illness was discovered to have an organic rather than a psychological cause (Yeazell 2), William embraced increasingly radical notions about the nature of the unconscious beginning with his article "The Hidden Self."

Intrigued by passive experiences of consciousness such as spiritistic possession (the turn-of-the-century analog to "channeling"), he maintained a receptivity to the irrational and nonmaterial that set him apart from many of his most famous contemporaries.[2] As a founding member of the American branch of the Society for Psychical Research, James entertained a belief in the possibility of a supernatural realm open to scientific investigation and sought to overcome what he saw as the unfortunate antipathy between the "scientific-academic mind" and the "feminine-mystical mind" (362). Although "The Hidden Self" is full of admiration for the work of Janet, James also criticizes the French psychologist for not going far enough in his characterization of the unconscious. Janet's more conservative view was that the subpersonalities he uncovered were limited by the boundaries of the individual ego; James, on the other hand, was receptive to the possibility that the unconscious might open onto the transpersonal realm and provide an avenue of communication with the spirit world. In "The Hidden Self," James states his less conventional belief "well aware," as he puts it, "of all the liabilities to which this statement exposes me" (373).

Such views would eventually marginalize James from the mainstream of his profession. In search of "scientific-academic" recognition, the discipline dissociated itself from the "feminine-mystical" realm of faith healers and spiritistic mediums and rejected James's blend of science and religion. The future belonged to Freud and his work, as James himself reportedly remarked at the famous 1909 psychological congress at Clark University in Worcester, just one year before his death.[3] In the two decades before the conference, however, James's views, along with those of even more radical proponents of psychical research such as

Richard Hodgson and Frederic W. H. Myers, were still within the
mainstream of scientific debate. In his concluding remarks in "The
Hidden Self," James optimistically calls for a *comparative study of
trances and sub-conscious states*," including psychical or supernatural
phenomena: "Anyone who may be induced by this article to follow the
path of study in which [Janet's book] is so brilliant a pioneer will reap
a rich reward" (373).

   This call by the Anglo American psychologist William James found
a sympathetic response in a work by a fellow Bostonian, the African
American novelist and *Colored American Magazine* editor Pauline
Elizabeth Hopkins. In her last novel, *Of One Blood; or, The Hidden
Self,* Hopkins turned to the new discoveries in psychology for thematic material and, more specifically, used James's essay "The Hidden Self"
as an intertext, although she deliberately disguised her source.[4] Unlike
Alice James, who maintained a lifelong skepticism toward the various
psychological discourses that vied to explain, heal, or otherwise admin-
ister to her subjectivity, Hopkins embraced notions about the unconscious emerging from work with hysterical women as a means to explore a subject closer to her own heart—the political situation and
subjectivity of African Americans in the post-Reconstruction period.
Like W. E. B. Du Bois, whose notion of "double-consciousness" was
also profoundly influenced by both James and the new psychology,
Hopkins was deeply engaged by the new discourses about the self
emerging at the turn of the century. Her ideas about this subject appear in her first short story, "The Mystery within Us," and receive their
most sustained treatment in her last complete novel, in which she
fictionally reworks James's essay in order to represent the complexity
of racial subjectivity in post-Reconstruction America.[5]

   In contradictory movements, her novel both exploits the new psychology to theorize about the indeterminacy of racial subjectivity and figures
racial identity in terms of a more deterministic discourse of blood. Authorized both by James's theory of the self and by traditional occult practices that are associated with the figure of the African mother, Hopkins
explores the transpersonal dimensions of consciousness in the context
of a transnational "black Atlantic" geography that is linked, in the novel's ultimate vision, to a pan-Africanist political agenda.[6]

                                * * *

"The Mystery within Us" appeared in May 1900 in the premiere issue
of the *Colored American Magazine* (CAM), a journal dedicated to serv-

ing the interests of American citizens of color and promoting African American art and literature (Carby 122–27). Interestingly, Hopkins's first contribution to the magazine and first published work of short fiction does not explicitly thematize or address issues of race. The short story's narrator relates a story told by his friend Tom Underwood, a successful and wealthy physician who, five years earlier, had been driven to the brink of suicide by desperate financial circumstances. Declaring his belief in "spiritualistic phenomena and the existence of guardian angels" (21), Underwood relates to his friend the following "psychological experience" (24). Late one night, just as he is about to drink a bottle of poison, Underwood is visited by the spirit of a deceased physician, Dr. Thorn, whose work he had greatly admired. The spiritistic "presence" of Dr. Thorn uses his mesmeric power to prevent the suicide, condemning Underwood's rash act and informing him that God's will is that he continue the deceased physician's life work. The next morning Underwood finds on his bedside table the manuscript for the book that makes him rich and famous. Disclaiming any rational explanation for his experience, Underwood concludes his narration of this strange tale by citing a well-known quotation from *Hamlet* that appears frequently in turn-of-the-century discourses on spiritualism and psychical research: "There are more things in heaven and earth than are dreamt of in our philosophy" (26).

Hopkins's depiction of the problem of suicidal despair and it solutions reflects the widespread interest in this subject among turn-of-the-century Americans. Neurasthenia—that peculiarly American "nervousness" that George M. Beard made famous in 1881—was epidemic among middle- and upper-class "brain-workers." Linked to the "over-civilization" of modern life, it affected, to greater or lesser extent, almost all of the period's notable cultural producers—including William James (Lutz, esp. chap 2; Feinstein, chap. 12). James's 1895 address to the Young Men's Christian Association of Harvard University, entitled "Is Life Worth Living?," reflects both his own neurasthenic inclinations as well as those of his social class. His opening remarks included this melancholy sentiment, echoed strikingly in the title of Hopkins's supernatural tale: "In the deepest heart of all of us there is a corner in which the ultimate mystery of things works sadly" (1). Following conventional turn-of-the-century wisdom on the relationship between the life of the mind and neurasthenic illness, James attributed suicidal despair to the pessimism "which reflection breeds" and proposed "religious faith" as the answer (6).

In its use of neurasthenic discourse, "The Mystery within Us" intriguingly combines the secular rags-to-riches narrative with a version of its religious antecedent—the spiritual autobiography of sin and redemption. Softening the Calvinist emphasis on sin typical of Puritan conversion narratives to produce a more ecumenical representation of spiritual despair, Hopkins addresses contemporary anxieties about the loss of faith in a post-Darwinian world. Underwood's material success—the rags-to-riches story—is presented as the result of a passive religious experience that leads him to spiritual redemption, rather than as the result of the more familiar Franklinesque narrative of autonomous self-making. In representing the protagonist as an instrument of the divine will whose life is devoted to the service of the larger community, "The Mystery within Us" presents material success as a dividend in the more important business of spiritual uplift. Moreover, it substitutes a spiritual and collectivist ethos for the values of materialism and individualism typically associated with dominant American culture.

The opening chapter of *Of One Blood; or, The Hidden Self* incorporates a number of the thematic elements Hopkins had already treated in "The Mystery within Us": the poor struggling physician protagonist, the depiction of suicidal despair, and the spiritistic visitation that will lead, in the course of the novel, to the redemption of the protagonist and his dedication to a larger, altruistic endeavor.[7] The novel's opening scene finds the protagonist Reuel Briggs, a poor Harvard medical student of ambiguous ethnic ancestry, deep in morbid thoughts of suicide. Hamlet-like, Reuel wonders whether or not to "rend the veil" separating this life from the next and thus obtain a solution not only to his poverty and loneliness but also to the questions of the nature of consciousness and immortality that haunt him (442).

A student of mysticism and psychology as well as medicine, Hopkins's protagonist spends his days and nights pouring over esoteric scientific treatises. When the reader first meets Reuel, he is obsessed by certain passages of a book he has been reading entitled "The Unclassified Residuum" by "M. Binet." In fact, all of the quoted passages attributed to Binet are taken verbatim from William James's essay "The Hidden Self," whose opening line provides Hopkins with her invented title: "'The great field for new discoveries,' said a scientific friend to me the other day, 'is always the Unclassified Residuum'. . . a sort of dust-cloud of exceptional occurrences . . . which it always proves less easy to attend to than to ignore" (361). The passages that obsess Reuel and that Hopkins quotes at some length are those that particularly concern James's ideas about the supernatural aspects of the unconscious. Like James, Reuel believes that the "unclassified residuum" of mystical and supernatural phenomena, generally dismissed by the scientific community as "the effects of the imagination," should be included within the realm of respected scientific pursuit (442). As Reuel contemplates these various thoughts, his beliefs are confirmed by a vision of a lovely woman whose appearance temporarily diverts him from his morbid despair.

As in "The Mystery within Us," *Of One Blood*'s thematization of psychology and mysticism initially appears to be disengaged from the sociological and political treatment of the race question that characterizes the majority of Hopkins's fictional and nonfictional work. Reuel's ambiguous desire to "go farther than M. Binet in unveiling the vast scheme of compensation and retribution carried about in . . . the human soul" (448) seems but a faint echo of the question of "compensation and retribution" for the wrongs perpetrated against African Americans under slavery that Hopkins had explored in the more realistic mode of her first novel *Contending Forces*.[8]

Indeed, as the opening chapter concludes, Reuel's friend Aubrey Livingston calls attention to precisely this disjunction between Reuel's esoteric preoccupations and the burning political questions of the day when he interrupts Reuel's ruminations with an invitation to attend a concert of the Fisk University Jubilee Singers: "Coming down to the practical, Reuel, what do you think of the Negro problem? . . . I believe it is the only burning question in the whole category of live issues and ologies about which you are silent." Reuel enigmatically replies: "I have a horror of discussing the woes of unfortunates, tramps, stray dogs and cats and Negroes—probably because I am an unfortunate myself" (449).[9] As this brief conversation makes clear, far from representing another thematic departure for Hopkins, *Of One Blood* grafts the political issue of post-Reconstruction racial justice onto the supernatural and psychological themes that had fascinated her in "The Mystery within Us." The question of race—made overt in this first chapter's exchange between Reuel and Aubrey—has in fact been a subtext throughout the opening scene. Reuel's "horror" at the so-called "Negro problem" and his characterization of himself as an "unfortunate" link his morbid psychological state to his social condition as a black man passing as white.

As in the case of Tom Underwood, Reuel's nervous despair might initially be read within a conventional discourse of neurasthenia. His "morbid self-consciousness" marks him as a "brain-worker" and member of the new professional classes; it marks him, at first glance, as white. In keeping with the scientific racism of the period, neurasthenia was thought to affect only individuals of the so-called "advanced" races and religious persuasions, that is white Anglo-Saxon Protestants. As such, the class and race associations of the disease reflected and reinforced the prejudices of the dominant Anglo American culture (Lutz 6–7).[10] By rewriting neurasthenic discourse along the axis of race, Hopkins complicates and revises the racial meanings of the disease. Reuel's neurasthenic despair can be read as both the sign of his professional status, however marginal, and the price of the sacrifice of his black identity that even such a tentative status exacts. If the blues was a name for neurasthenia before it was a name for the African American musical form (Lutz 273), then Reuel's "blues" must here be understood as race specific.

Reuel's fascination with "the hidden self lying quiescent in every human soul" (448) can be seen, then, as a trope for the situation of the African American who is "passing." Both his morbid self-consciousness and interest in esoteric psychology are embedded in a particular historical experience of African American subjectivity. Hopkins's skillful synthesis of new psychological discourses about the nature of the unconscious with the turn-of-the-century intellectual debate over the race question was not, of course, entirely idiosyncratic. In an essay called "Strivings of the Negro People" published in the *Atlantic Monthly* in 1897 and best known in slightly altered form as the opening chapter of *The Souls of Black Folk* (1903), W. E. B. Du Bois describes African American subjectivity as an experience of "double-consciousness": "One ever feels his twoness,—an American, a Negro; two souls, two thoughts, two unreconciled strivings; two warring ideals in one dark body, whose dogged strength alone keeps it from being torn asunder" (194).[11]

Several critics have noted Du Bois's intellectual debt both to William James, with whom he studied at Harvard University, and to the new psychology. In formulating the notion of "double-consciousness," Du Bois borrowed a term that already had wide currency in the late nineteenth century as a name for the phenomenon of multiple personality.[12] Du Bois's powerful rhetorical image of two souls in one body simultaneously evoked a traditional religious discourse of spiritual possession (with both African and Calvinist resonances) as well as the emerging secular/scientific discourse on multiple personality that was rapidly supplanting it.[13] This use of spiritistic discourse also extended to Du Bois's figurative use of the "veil"—identified by Arnold Rampersad as the central organizing metaphor of *Souls*—to describe the barrier dividing African Americans and Anglo Americans. The veil metaphor figures the physical separation that divided nineteenth-century Americans along the color line; at the same time, it suggests the "other-worldliness" of the African American who is "born with a veil, and gifted with second-sight in this American world" (45). Du Bois's trope places African American culture closer to the spirit world, contrasting it powerfully with the materialism of Anglo American culture.[14]

The degree to which Hopkins was influenced by Du Bois's rhetorical use of psychological and spiritistic discourses is difficult to know; it is certainly possible, even likely, that she had read his 1897 essay "Strivings of the Negro People."[15] In any event, given the evidence of her knowledge and use of James's "The Hidden Self," she was unquestionably influenced directly by accounts of the new psychology through public lectures and in the popular press. The distance between academic and popular psychologies in American culture has always been relatively small, and the new psychology was reported widely in the popular press at the turn of the century. One survey of popular magazines of the period reveals widespread interest in such subjects as mental healing, hypnosis, and multiple personality, beginning in 1890 and remaining strong into the first decade of the twentieth century (Hale 229–230). James's 1896 Lowell Lectures on Exceptional Mental States, covering such subjects as dreams, hypnotism, multiple personality, and demoniacal possession, were delivered to a general audience and reported widely in such newspapers as the *Boston Transcript* and *Boston Globe* (Taylor).

The strikingly similar confluence of the discourses on the "new psychology" and the "race problem" in the writings of Du Bois and Hopkins is not entirely surprising. For both writers, the various scientific and lay discourses in circulation on psychological and psychical phenomena offered a ready language with which to attempt a representation of African American subjectivity. Both writers borrowed new psychological and psychical research discourses to represent the doubleness of African American consciousness, the experience of being psychically split. Further, both drew on spiritistic discourse to contrast the spirituality of African American culture to the materialism and exploitation of Anglo American culture.

Hopkins and Du Bois thus bring together a remarkably similar network of discourses on race and psyche in their work. Yet Hopkins's use of a surface-depth model of selfhood, which represents a surface consciousness in hierarchical relation to a hidden or submerged (un)consciousness, is quite distinct from Du Bois's notion of "doubleness." Critics have praised Du Bois's model, suggesting that it allows for a "sense of distinctiveness that [does] not imply inferiority" (Bruce, "W. E. B. Du Bois" 305) and contrasting it favorably to the "popular hierarchical doubleness of moral surfaces and depths" (Lutz 246). In using the more hierarchical model, Hopkins is able to achieve both more and less than Du Bois. Whereas Du Bois's model of "double-consciousness" represents the distinctiveness of African American subjectivity, Hopkins, as we shall see, extends the "hidden self" to explore more generally the nature of racial identity for whites as well as blacks in the post-Reconstruction period. At the same time, however, the surface-depth model of the self all too easily lends itself to appropriation within a hierarchical racist discourse of white superiority and black inferiority. It may be precisely this danger that leads Hopkins away from the notion of the "hidden self" toward a more deterministic notion of racial identity by the end of the novel.

* * *

Before turning to these dangers and to Hopkins's more deterministic deployment of a discourse of blood, however, I want to detail her multiple representations of the hidden self, which depend upon an understanding of the history of slavery inscribed into the family history of her main characters. In the course of the novel, Reuel is revealed to be the son of a slave named Mira and her master Aubrey Livingston, Sr. Significantly, Hopkins also implies that Reuel is the product of an incestuous relationship, since his grandmother Aunt Hannah, Mira's mother, reveals that she too was kept as the mistress of Aubrey Sr.'s father, referred to simply as "old massa": "As soon as I was growed up, my mistress changed in her treatment of me, for she soon knowed of my relations with massa. . . . Mira was de onlies' child of ten that my massa lef' me for my comfort; all de res' were sold away" (604–5). By implying that Reuel's mother and father are half-siblings, Hopkins suggests that the pattern of white patriarchal abuse of slave women is multigenerational and incestuous, resulting in widespread miscegenation. Incest is recognized as a condition of the slave institution. As Aunt Hannah puts it: "Dese things jes' got to happen in slavery" (605). The incestuous relationships among the characters are further intensified in the next generation. Reuel falls in love with and unknowingly marries his sister, Dianthe Lusk, a Fisk Jubilee singer who, in the opening chapter, first appears to him in a vision, and whom Reuel later brings back to life using his mesmeric powers. Dianthe has lost all memory of her past life, and Reuel gives her a white identity in order to take her "out of the sphere where she was born" and make her his wife (479). Aubrey Jr., the apparent half-brother of both Reuel and Dianthe, also falls in love with Dianthe. Unaware of the incestuousness of his love, Aubrey uses his knowledge of Reuel's race to sabotage Reuel's attempts to find work in the United States; he then arranges for Reuel to obtain a medical position as part of an archaeological expedition to Ethiopia. With Reuel safely out of the way, Aubrey kills his own fiancée, Molly Vance, and uses his mesmeric influence to force Dianthe to marry him.

Within this complex plot, the metaphor of the hidden self functions in relation to all three of the major characters—Reuel, Dianthe, and Aubrey. Most obviously, the hidden self refers to Reuel's situation as a black man deliberately passing as white and to his complex relationship to his suppressed black identity. Dianthe, too, has a hidden self but, unlike Reuel, Dianthe's relation to it is passive rather than active, volitionless rather than willed. The narrative elements of Dianthe's story—her employment by a traveling magnetic physician, her seeming death and subsequent reanimation by Reuel, her loss of memory, as well as the creation of her double identity—follow conventions that borrow from two quite different but nevertheless related genres: the medical case study and the literary romance.[16]

Reuel reads Dianthe as an exceptional case study, an unusual instance of "dual mesmeric trance": "Binet speaks at length of this possibility in his treatise. We have stumbled upon an extraordinary case." Indeed, the narrator tells us, "The scientific journals of the next month contained wonderful and *wondering* [?] accounts of the now celebrated case,—re-animation after seeming death. Reuel's lucky star was in the ascendant; fame and fortune awaited him; he had but to grasp them" (472). Molly Vance (Aubrey's fiancée), in contrast, sees Dianthe's story not as a brilliant scientific advancement but as an incredible piece of fiction: "Who would believe . . . that at this stage of the world's progress one's identity could be so easily lost and one still be living. It is like a page from an exciting novel" (489). But whether marvel of science or marvelous fiction, as these two passages would variously have it, the narrative of dual personality clearly offered Hopkins a discourse for representing the complexities of racial identity.[17]

Dianthe's suppressed African American identity survives, despite her loss of memory and the creation of her new white identity as "Felice Adams," and dramatically resurfaces at a social gathering among Boston white society. Possessed by a "weird contralto, veiled as it were," Dianthe is moved unconsciously to sing "Go Down, Moses"—the same spiritual that she had performed as a soloist for the Fisk Jubilee Singers. The other guests are horrified, and the host of the party whispers to his daughter Molly: "Do you not hear another voice beside Mrs. Briggs'?" (502). In this striking image of Dianthe's double-voicedness and the reemergence of her African American identity from "behind the veil," Hopkins powerfully matches Du Bois's more famous conceptualization of African American consciousness and gives it a female form.

Dianthe's susceptibility to mesmeric trance-states and her dual consciousness link her to her mother, Mira, and to the history of black women in slavery. Similarly, Reuel and Aubrey are linked by profession to their father Aubrey Sr., a noted physician who had authored some books on the subject of mesmeric phenomena "referred to even at this advanced stage of discovery, as marvellous in some of their data" (486). Aubrey recalls his father's habit of hypnotizing Mira for the entertainment of his houseguests: "My father made the necessary passes and from a serious, rather sad Negress, very mild with everyone, Mira changed to a gay, noisy, restless woman, full of irony and sharp jesting. In this case this peculiar metamorphosis always occurred" (486–87).[18] On one level, the mesmeric bond represented here can be read as figuring the slave institution itself, in which the slaveowner exercises complete control over the will of the slave; at the same time, however, under the neutralizing guise of "entertainment," Mira's subversive secondary personality gives vent to those qualities that are unacceptable within her conventional role as the subservient slave, allowing her to exercise powers of clairvoyance that go well beyond her master's control. When Mira foretells the defeat of the South in the Civil War and her master's death as a Yankee prisoner of war, she is sold away from the plantation; her prophecy is borne out, nevertheless, suggesting that her subversive spiritual gifts cannot be fully controlled by the economic arrangements of slavery.

Whereas Mira is allowed some degree of subversive subjectivity, Hopkins's treatment of Dianthe's mesmeric trances conforms to a more conventional representation of passive femininity.[19] When the unconscious Dianthe is first hospitalized, Reuel administers to her lifeless, prone body while an assembly of doctors looks on. In its juxtaposition of passive femininity with active male spectatorship, the scene recalls the well-known tableau of Charcot demonstrating a case of hysteria to a lecture hall of male doctors as his assistant holds the patient's fainting body (Ellenberger, between 330–31; Auerbach 129). Later, when Dianthe has recovered consciousness, she trusts Reuel implicitly "like a child" (470). In the weeks that follow, Reuel continues his treatment of her by hypnosis, and she in turn asks him to "give me the benefit of your powerful will" to bring about her healing (475).

But Hopkins's introduction of race into conventional representations of mesmerized women (both medical and fictional) complicates contemporary feminist debates that focus on the question of the patient/ heroine's agency solely in relation to gendered power relations (e.g., Auerbach). Hopkins deliberately disrupts conventional gender representations of the seductive bond between mesmerist and trance-maiden; Dianthe's "poor, violated mind" was destroyed by the "heartless usage" (489) of a *female* mesmeric physician whose services Dianthe entered "for a large salary" (473–74). Although Dianthe is well compensated for her services, Hopkins's choice of language—"violated mind," "heartless usage"—distinctly implies sexual exploitation that is more typically associated with male mesmerist/seducer figures. Hopkins does not specify the race of the female magnetic physician, but given the fact that the novel is set entirely within white society, the omission of racial indicators suggests strongly that she is white. The double meaning of the phrase "heartless usage," implying exploitation of Dianthe's labor as well as her sexuality, reinforces the unmistakable analogies between the mesmeric bond, which entails the subjugation of one individual's will to another, and the institution of slavery. For black women in slavery, "heartless usage" often meant exploitation of both sexual and nonsexual labor. In this case, Hopkins's choice of gender might be read as an indictment of white women's collusion with the abuses of the slave institution and, by analogy, with the widespread, interlocking practices of lynching and rape of African American men and women in the post-Reconstruction era as an equally heinous form of social control.

In contrast, Hopkins carefully distinguishes Reuel from conventional representations of the physician/mesmerist as seducer: "Absolutely free from the vices which beset most young men of his age and profession, his daily life was a white, unsullied page" (473). The telepathic/mesmeric connection between Reuel and Dianthe is represented in a register that is benign, almost utopian. Reuel's spiritual connection to Dianthe enables him to exercise his own will over her, but his mesmeric powers are presented as life-giving and genuinely loving. Moreover, Reuel's departure for Africa directly after the wedding ceremony prevents their spiritual connection from being physically embodied, thus keeping the threat of actual incest from occurring. Finally, Reuel is equally as susceptible as Dianthe to states of passive consciousness. Reuel is visited spiritistically on several occasions both by Dianthe and by his deceased mother Mira. Dianthe's visitation first rouses Reuel from his initial neurasthenic despair, and her supernatural connection to him results in his professional success, leading Elizabeth Ammons to characterize their relationship as one of "mutual revitalization" (82).[20] Reuel himself credits his success with the case to a supernatural source, rejecting the classic American success narrative of autonomous self-making: "I am an instrument—how I know not—a child of circumstances" (471). Like his fictional prototype Tom Underwood in "The Mystery within Us," Reuel often occupies the "feminine" position in the classic opposition between an active male mesmerist and a passive female trance-maiden, subverting the traditional gendering of these positions.

Hopkins sharply contrasts Aubrey's prurient interest in Dianthe's case to Reuel's exceptionally pure motivations: "Enthused by its scientific aspect, he vied with Reuel in close attention to the medical side of the case, and being more worldly did not neglect the material side" (473). Aubrey's interest in the "material side" of the case exploits the familiar convention of the evil mesmerist who uses his powers to compromise sexually the female heroine. The relationship between Dianthe and Aubrey is conveyed in the highly charged language of the seduction novel: "In vain the girl sought to throw off the numbing influence of the man's presence. In desperation she tried to defy him, but she knew that she had lost her will-power and was but a puppet in the hands of this false friend" (504). Hopkins appropriates the conventions of the seduction narrative to represent black women's sexual exploitation in a white patriarchal culture. Aubrey's coercive control over Dianthe continues uninterrupted the multigenerational pattern of sexual appropriation of black women by white men that had been exercised under slavery in the previous two generations of their family history. While Reuel's marriage to Dianthe is never consummated, Dianthe is sexually compromised, exploited, and coerced into taking her own life by Aubrey.

The text's characteristically Gothic doubling of the male protagonist creates two contrasting heterosexual bonds—one between a black man and woman, the other between a white man and black woman—each of which plays out alternative gendered power configurations that are differentiated along the axis of race. Aubrey's mesmeric influence over Dianthe represents white patriarchal power and its exploitative result; in contrast, the telepathic/mesmeric connection between Reuel and Dianthe suggests the utopian possibility of a mutual heterosexual relationship between black men and women.[21] As a social allegory then, at this point in the narrative, the novel might read like this: the betrayal of the black brother Reuel by the white brother Aubrey takes place via the "theft" of the black woman Dianthe.[22] Although this interpretation may seem troubling in its emphasis on the black woman as a passive site of contestation in a struggle between black and white men, it is clearly one level on which the text asks to be read.

Yet this allegorical narrative of black-white relations as the betrayal of black brother by white brother via the figure of the black woman is destabilized in two ways. Most obviously, any attempt to represent a utopian black heterosexual union between Reuel and Dianthe is undercut by Reuel's betrayal, not only of his own black identity, but also of Dianthe's. By withholding from Dianthe the knowledge of her black ancestry and colluding with Aubrey in assigning her a fictitious white identity, Reuel directly enables Aubrey to exploit and blackmail her. But Hopkins also destabilizes the allegorical narrative of black-white relations that she has constructed in another, more fundamental way, revealing in the process yet a third instance of the existence of a "hidden self." In the novel's denouement, Aunt Hannah reveals Aubrey's actual identity and the true Livingston family history: when Aubrey Sr.'s legitimate heir died at birth, Aunt Hannah switched Mira's illegitimate baby for the legitimate Livingston heir. Aubrey, Reuel, and Dianthe share not only the same father, but also the same mother; they are "of one blood."

Through the manipulation of Aubrey's racial identity, the category of "whiteness" is destabilized, as is the possibility of conclusively fixing racial identity. At a time of increased legal and scientific attempts to police the color line, Hopkins's representation of the interchangeability of "black" and "white" babies exposes the absurdity of such attempts.[23] In her representation of the complex history of miscegenation in the Livingston family tree and, moreover, in her final revelation of Aubrey's status as a mulatto, Hopkins insists on the presence of intermixed blood in the southern white aristocracy as a historical fact of oppressive social relations under slavery. As Hazel Carby has argued persuasively, Hopkins's "use of mulatto figures engaged with the discourse of social Darwinism, undermining the tenets of 'pure blood' and 'pure race' as mythological, and implicitly exposed the absurdity of theories of the total separation of the races" (140). In mobilizing the trope of the hidden self in relation to Reuel and Dianthe, Hopkins uses the figure of the mulatto to dramatically represent the split consciousness of the African American subject; in the figure of Aubrey, she goes further, exposing the hidden self at the foundation of Anglo American subjectivity and the suppression of the truth of miscegenation upon which the color line depends.

Despite the authority granted Aunt Hannah to reveal the characters' true family histories, the extraordinarily implausible lack of knowledge that Hopkins's characters exhibit with regard to both their own identities and family relationships is never entirely accounted for. Even this implausibility takes on a kind of narrative logic, however, when we recall the "singular forgetfulness" of the hysterical subjects in "The Hidden Self" whose situations captured Hopkins's imagination (364). Describing this amnesia, James wrote: "In certain persons . . . the total possible consciousness may be split into parts which coexist, but mutually ignore each other" (369). Like these hysterical subjects whose multiple personalities are mutually ignorant of one another, Hopkins's characters are divided by the color line and mutually estranged, although they are "of one blood"—part of a single family rather than a single self. Hopkins's remarkable imaginative achievement is her translation of the notion of a hidden self from the intrapsychic field that Janet and Binet investigated to the social field.

The hidden self becomes a metaphor for the suppressed history of oppressive social and familial relations under the institution of slavery, the collective legacy of abusive power relations, rather than simply the residue of repressed individual trauma. The African self is the "submerged self" that must be reclaimed not only by the black man Reuel, who is "passing," but also by the "white" man Aubrey, whose African blood has been suppressed and denied. Hopkins's use of the surface-depth model of selfhood enables her to counter a racist determinist notion of racial identity with a more indeterminate and destabilizing model. By embedding her multiple representations of the hidden self within the larger collective history of black-white social relations, Hopkins exploits the political possibilities of the surface-depth model of selfhood—its usefulness as a way of talking about racial identity as a socially constructed phenomenon.

Yet this achievement, although considerable, is not the sole endpoint of *Of One Blood*. Whereas in *Contending Forces,* the revelation of the characters' true family histories and identities results in restitution and compensation for the wrongs perpetrated against African Americans under slavery, in *Of One Blood,* the revelation of the characters' hidden selves does not result in social justice. Rather, the sequence of events set in the United States ends in a vision of social chaos marked by incest, bigamy, murder, and suicide, suggesting Hopkins's pessimism about the possibility of transformative political change on American ground. The politicization of the figure of the hidden self (described above), offers a powerful allegorical representation of the tragedy of American race relations but not a political solution.

Reuel's participation in a British archaeological expedition to Ethiopia both shifts the plot from an American to a "black Atlantic" geography and translates the metaphor of the hidden self to that of the "hidden city of Telassar," the legendary royal seat of the ancient Ethiopian civilization, which the expedition hopes to discover and excavate. The excavation of the hidden city will enable the expedition's British leader, Professor Stone, to prove his theory that Ethiopia antedated Egypt as the source of Western civilization. Stone's theory of "the Ethiopian as the primal race" (521) challenges racist Darwinian narratives of the period, which posited the inferiority of the African race, with a positive Afrocentric narrative of origins that celebrates Africans as "the most ancient source of all that [Anglo-Saxons] value in modern life" (520).

The deliberateness of this shift from psychology to archaeology, from hidden self to hidden city, is reinforced in the pivotal scene where Reuel's descent down a ruined staircase that will lead him to the hidden city is accompanied by a simultaneous descent into unconsciousness. In its metaphorical association of the uncovering of the mysteries of the unconscious with the work of archaeological excavation, this scene anticipates Freud's often cited analogy between his psychological insights into the pre-oedipus phase in girls and the archaeological discovery of the Minoan-Mycenean civilization behind the civilization of Greece (40). Reuel's descent into unconsciousness and the hidden city leads to the revelation of his hidden self, his true African identity, and to the discovery of the submerged but still vibrant city of Telassar. The lotus lily birthmark on his breast, the biological mark of race that apparently cannot disappear through miscegenation, identifies Reuel to the inhabitants of Telassar as King Ergamenes, their long-awaited royal heir "who shall restore to the Ethiopian race its ancient glory" (547). United in marriage to Queen Candace, a dark-skinned incarnation of Dianthe, he will "give to the world a dynasty of dark-skinned rulers, whose destiny should be to restore the prestige of an ancient people" (570).[24]

In this (literally) crowning disclosure of Reuel's hidden self, Hopkins metaphorically associates the work of what we might call "self-recovery" with the work of cultural and political reconstruction. By linking Reuel's discovery of his hidden African identity to the recovery of a long-buried Ethiopian civilization, Hopkins represents the African origins of Western civilization and establishes the basis for a contemporary reconstructed Pan-African political community. But if the African portion of the narrative symbolically joins the therapeutic project of self-recovery to the political project of cultural reconstruction, it does so by substituting a model of racial identity rooted in a discourse of blood for the indeterminate model that is suggested by the figure of the hidden self. This deployment of an "identity politics" that is in tension with a notion of race as socially constructed has political and strategic motivations. Although, as I have argued, the surface-depth model afforded by the figure of the hidden self enables inroads against the determinism of turn-of-the-century racial constructions of self, such a model also presents dangers: it risks reinscribing African Americans in the position of the "repressed unconscious" or "secret self" of Anglo America, a construction of selfhood that invokes racist connotations of Africans as "inferior," "primitive," "irrational," or "uncivilized."

Hopkins's allegorical narrative symbolically refutes racist polygenesist views that blacks and whites were separate species, not "of one blood." By the late nineteenth century, however, Darwinian theory had already discredited polygenesists by asserting a common origin for all the races. Instead, social Darwinists had appropriated racist polygenesist arguments about black inferiority into a racist monogenesist argument: blacks and whites had a shared origin but blacks had over time evolved into an inferior species.[25] The surface-depth model of selfhood lends itself in troubling ways to appropriation by the inferior/superior paradigm of social Darwinism. Although positioning blackness as the suppressed figure in this binary surface-depth opposition offers a powerful representation of American racism in the post-Reconstruction period, Hopkins may have been increasingly dissatisfied with the possibilities the hidden self model afforded for envisioning a more empowering political future for African Americans. Whereas *Contending Forces* and *Hagar's Daughter* both foreground mulatto characters and the reconstitution of families arbitrarily sundered by the color line, *Of One Blood* turns increasingly away from representations of mulatto characters and their deployment as figures of racial indeterminacy and increasingly toward a discourse of blood that reconstructs family and community based on an essential notion of race. In shifting her narrative from America to Africa, Hopkins abandons the Gothic figure of the hidden self and the narrative of familial incest, miscegenation, and degeneration as a political allegory for failed race policies in the United States. Instead, she embraces a symbolics of blood that seeks to reconstruct an African bloodline that will form the basis of a reconstructed Pan-African political community.[26]

* * *

These two contrasting models of racial identity coexist in her novel, much like two contradictory or "split" personalities might inhabit a single body, a "double-consciousness" that is present in the duality of the very title *Of One Blood; or, The Hidden Self*. In Hopkins's earlier novels, *Contending Forces: A Romance Illustrative of Negro Life North and South*, *Hagar's Daughter: A Story of Southern Caste Prejudice*, and *Winona: A Tale of Negro Life in the South and Southwest*, the subtitle glosses the main title. In *Of One Blood; or, The Hidden Self*, the main and subtitles compete with rather than complement one another. Joined by the conjunction that both yokes them together and signifies their oppositional relationship, they name the very doubleness of the text's representation of racial identity, a split that is never satisfactorily reconciled, so that the critic is continually forced to confront its contradictions. On the one hand, the novel's secondary title, *The Hidden Self*, suggests a model of racial identity that is fluid, indeterminate, and socially constructed; on the other hand, the novel's primary title *Of One Blood* invokes an essentialist notion of racial identity.

The novel's resolution—which includes not only Reuel's repatriation but also that of his grandmother, the former slave Aunt Hannah—introduces a notion of "home" that is secured through a discourse of blood. Both models of racial identity, albeit contradictory, have important strategic uses for Hopkins. By showing "whiteness" to be a fiction, Hopkins can launch a crucial challenge to the legal separation of the races upon which Jim Crow depends. By reintroducing a notion of "home" and "blood," she can reestablish a network of kinship ties to family and ancestors that at least potentially may enable the formation of a Pan-African community capable of collective resistance and change.

Hopkins's increasing reliance on a politically enabling discourse of blood, then, places fundamental limits on the notion of a hidden self as a figure of racial indeterminacy. But Hopkins also recuperates one important aspect of James's notion of the hidden self within her deployment of the discourse of blood. In attributing his mystical powers to his mother Mira, Reuel demonstrates his belief in a transpersonal or psychical dimension of the unconscious and links it to his African blood: "He remembered his mother well. From her he had inherited his mysticism and his occult powers. The nature of the mystic within him was, then, but a dreamlike devotion to the spirit that had swayed his ancestors; it was the shadow of Ethiopia's power" (558). This passage establishes a genealogy that links Reuel's psychical power not to his Anglo-Saxon father, with his scientific medical training and the authority he still derives posthumously for the publication of mesmeric studies, but to his African mother's "second sight" and the magical power of what Toni Morrison calls black people's "discredited knowledge" (342). Unlike Aubrey, who has inherited only his white father's exploitative "scientific-academic" mind, Reuel is connected to his maternal African heritage: to his clairvoyant mother, his conjure woman grandmother, and the "feminine-mystical" whose denigration James decried in "The Hidden Self."

Recasting James's "unclassified residuum" as the legitimate epistemological domain of Western science's racial and sexual Other, *Of One Blood* reclaims this "discredited knowledge"—of Africa, of the maternal—as an antidote to the psychic and spiritual alienation of dominant American culture. It is not surprising, then, that in this novel, as in "The Mystery within Us," Hopkins gives her protagonist the occupation of a healer. In the earlier short story, she presents a neurasthenic physician, who is both healed through a spiritistic experience and rededicated to the service of healing a larger community; in *Of One Blood*, Hopkins adds an explicitly racial dimension to this narrative. Depicting Reuel's spiritual reclamation from the devastating isolation and neurasthenic despair of "passing" to a reconnection with a Pan-African community and collective purpose, she refigures the healer as a political leader whose own spiritual recovery prefigures the possibility of political reconstruction. In her representations of passive experiences of selfhood, Hopkins's critique of the dominant American model of autonomous individualism is both successful and profound.

Spiritistically joining the self to ancestor and community, Hopkins both affirms and politicizes the supernatural realm in ways that anticipate the work of so many contemporary African American women writers: Toni Morrison's desire to "blend acceptance of the supernatural and a profound rootedness in the real world" (342) and Toni Cade Bambara's attempts to fuse the "split between the spiritual, psychic, and political forces in my community" (165).[27] While twentieth-century American culture has largely preserved the division between the material and the spiritual that James tried unsuccessfully to bridge at the turn of the century, many contemporary African American women writers have questioned this opposition, politicizing the split itself. Deliberately traversing the boundaries between science and "pseudo-science," the natural and supernatural, realism and the fantastic, the sociopolitical and the psychological, *Of One Blood* is Hopkins's considerable contribution to that project.

NOTES

Shorter versions of this essay were presented at the American Women Writers of Color Conference in Ocean City, Md., May 1992, and at the MELUS Conference at the University of California, Berkeley, May 1993. I am grateful to everyone who has read and commented on this essay. I especially wish to thank John Gruesser and Helene Moglen for their generous suggestions.

1. John Dewey and G. Stanley Hall each published articles entitled "The New Psychology" in 1884 and 1885, respectively (Cotkin 32–35). For a discussion of popular interest in the new psychology, see Hale's chapter 9, "Mind Cures and the Mystical Wave: Popular Preparation for Psychoanalysis, 1904–1910." Ellenberger provides the most exhaustive general history of the field of psychology. On the emergence of the new psychology in an American context, see Fuller, *Americans and the Unconscious,* and *Mesmerism;* and Kenny, *The Passion of Ansel Bourne.*

2. James's writings on psychical phenomena have been collected in a volume of *The Works of William James* entitled *Essays in Psychical Research.* See also Eugene Taylor's reconstruction of James's Lowell lectures on this subject; and Barzun, *A Stroll with William James* (227–261). For a general history of spiritualism and psychical research in the United States, see Moore, *In Search of White Crows.*

3. Ernest Jones recounts this anecdote about James's reception of Freud's American lectures: "William James, who knew German well, followed the lectures with great interest. He was very friendly to us, and I shall never forget his parting words, said with his arm around my shoulder: 'The future belongs to your work'" (57). Michael G. Kenny cites the Worcester Conference as the moment when "psychoanalysis effectively displaced the older psychical research tradition and made the study of psychopathology and the unconscious a thing of this world only" (93).

4. This essay was completed before Thomas J. Otten's essay on the intertextuality of Hopkins and James came to my attention. Otten's article shares my concern with Hopkins's appropriations of new psychological discourse to explore questions of racial identity, and my argument bears a coincidental resemblance to his on several points. My approach differs significantly, however, in its attention to the crucial intersection of race and gender. For another recent discussion of Hopkins's use of James's essay in the larger context of turn-of-the-century Pan-Africanist discourse, see Sundquist, *To Wake the Nations* (569–73). Claudia Tate also discusses a James connection, without specifically identifying Hopkins's use of "The Hidden Self" (204–8).

5. Hopkins's interest in the new psychology also manifests itself in the two installments of her last work of serial fiction, "Topsy Templeton." The uncompleted work appeared in the *New Era Magazine,* which Hopkins edited for its two issues (Feb. 1916, 11–20, 48; Mar. 1916, 75–84). I am grateful to John Gruesser for calling these fictional pieces to my attention.

6. I take the phrase "black Atlantic" from Paul Gilroy's brilliant reading of the transatlantic cultural exchanges shaping African American cultural production. In its representation of a transpersonal theory of consciousness that is intimately linked to a transnational subject, Hopkins's novel figures a psychical version of transatlantic travel, one that is extremely suggestive in rela-

tionship to contemporary postcolonial critical debates. In an essay published in *Cultures of United States Imperialism,* Kevin Gaines has emphasized the conservatism underlying Hopkins's attempts to "refute racism by adopting a 'scientific' Western ethnological persona," condemning the failure of this strategy to counter effectively racist imperialism at the turn of the century (434). In what follows, I argue that her appropriations of scientific psychological discourse have a far more radical potential as a location of cultural critique.

7. Hazel Carby has observed Hopkins's reworking of the spiritistic and supernatural themes of "The Mystery within Us" in *Of One Blood,* but she focuses primarily on the novel's Pan-African political perspective and establishment of an African genealogy (155–62). This essay extends Carby's reading by exploring the interrelationship between Hopkins's use of psychological and spiritistic themes and her Pan-Africanist politics.

8. In *Contending Forces,* members of the black middle-class Smith family are financially restituted for the estate that was wrongfully stolen from their ancestors because of their imputed black blood; the descendant of the man responsible for the initial wrong is punished.

9. Reuel's equation of "stray dogs and cats and Negroes" links him to the Harvard-educated white northerner Cuthbert Sumner in *Hagar's Daughter* who "gave large sums to Negro colleges and on the same princpal [*sic*] gave liberally to the Society for the Prevention of Cruelty to Animals, and endowed a refuge for homeless cats. Horses, dogs, cats, and Negroes were classed together in his mind as of the brute creation whose sufferings it was his duty to help alleviate" (265–66). By linking Reuel rhetorically to the hypocritical racism of the New England liberal philanthropic tradition, Hopkins immediately establishes the moral bankruptcy of his conscious choice to "pass."

10. Although the racial and class associations of neurasthenia are clear, the gender coding is more ambiguous. George M. Beard found neurasthenia to be more prevalent in men than in women; S. Weir Mitchell, however, preferred the diagnosis of "neurasthenia" to the more common "hysteria" for his mostly female clientele (Drinka 184–209). For a related discussion of the gendering of the disease, see Lutz, *American Nervousness* (31–37).

11. The identical passage appears in *The Souls of Black Folk* (45). For the publication history of the essays collected in *Souls,* see Rampersad, *The Art and Imagination* (303–4*n*9).

12. Dickson D. Bruce, Jr., links Du Bois's use of the term "double-consciousness" both to medical accounts of split personality and to Emersonian transcendentalism ("W. E. B. Du Bois"). On Du Bois's relation to the new psychology, see also Lutz, *American Nervousnous* (244–46, 261–75) and Rampersad, *The Art and Imagination* (74). In his autobiography, Du Bois refers to James as "my friend and guide to clear thinking" (143).

13. For a fascinating account of the transition from a religious to a psycho-

logical explanatory framework for multiple personality, see Kenny, *The Passion of Ansel Bourne*. Kenny's discussion of the case of Mary Reynolds, the first recorded case of "double consciousness" (1816), also suggests an intriguing line of inquiry. In her letters and diary, Reynolds consistently associated her two personalities with the imagery of darkness and light that reflected the Calvinist dualism of her upbringing. While Kenny does not pursue this imagery, it suggests strongly how thoroughly the discourse on race may already have been embedded into the discourse on multiple personality well before 1900. Similarly, in one of the more famous case studies of multiple personality in our own century, popularized as *The Three Faces of Eve,* Corbett H. Thigpen and Hervey Cleckley gave their patient the pseudonym "Eve White" and referred to her alter-personality as "Eve Black."

14. The "veil" was also used in white middle-class psychical research circles at the turn of the century to designate the separation between this world and the world beyond the grave. For an example of that discourse, see Anne Banning Robbins's 1909 memoir, *Both Sides of the Veil.* William Dean Howells, another dabbler in psychical research, offers a more skeptical representation of the turn-of-the-century white middle-class interest in the occult in his 1903 short story collection, *Questionable Shapes*. In the larger project from which this essay is taken, I explore more fully the relationship between Du Bois's rhetorical use of the "veil" and the discourses mentioned above, an inquiry that also complicates the simple racialized opposition between the spiritual and the material.

15. In *Contending Forces,* Hopkins presents fictional characters modeled after both Du Bois and Booker T. Washington, using the novel in part as a forum to debate the various positions of the leading black intellectuals of her day. Hopkins's own attitudes on the race issue were much more closely aligned ideologically with those of Du Bois than of Booker T. Washington.

16. In designating a train accident as the cause of Dianthe's loss of memory, Hopkins associated her heroine with a traumatic condition known as "railway spine" or "railway brain" that was a widespread and medically recognized diagnosis in the late nineteenth century (Drinka 108–22). At the same time, she places Dianthe in a literary tradition of mesmerized heroines that includes Hawthorne's Priscilla, James's Verena Tarrant, and du Maurier's Trilby.

17. A number of critics and historians have noted the twin beginnings of psychology and romanticism in the late eighteenth century and the close association between scientific and literary representations of dual personality, particularly in the last two decades of the nineteenth century. See for example, Miller, *Doubles* (49–51, 209–44, 329–48). For a compelling feminist reading of the "rich, covert collaboration between documents of romance and the romance of science" in the 1890s, see Auerbach, "Magi and Maidens" (111). As Claudia Tate observes, Hopkins's choice of the Gothic romance genre (Tate refers spe-

cifically to the "psychological ghost story") complements her fascination with the new psychology and discursively links *Of One Blood* not only to the psychological writings of William James but also to his brother Henry's fiction as well (205). The relationship between Hopkins's participation in and revisions of the Gothic tradition and the kinds of appropriations of scientific-psychological discourses I explore in this essay is beyond the scope of my inquiry. I want to emphasize, however, the mutual interconnectedness of the discourses of scientific psychology and literary romance, conventional disciplinary boundaries notwithstanding, as well as the ways in which these two discourses of "hidden selves" are deeply implicated in a discourse of race (see also note 21).

18. Hopkins apparently borrowed this description of Mira's dual personality from Janet's case study of "Leonie," which is quoted extensively in James's "The Hidden Self." In her "normal state," Leonie was "a serious and rather sad person . . . very mild with everyone." Under hypnosis, she became "gay, noisy, restless" with a "tendency to irony and sharp jesting" (366). This type of contrast is typical of medical accounts of white female multiple personalities from Mary Reynolds to "Eve White."

19. Claudia Tate convincingly observes that "Hopkins's serial novels decenter the heroine's prominence," arguing that she "silenced the discourse of female agency, which was a very important feature of [black women's] 1890s domestic novels." My conclusions differ significantly from Tate's characterization of the novel's vision as one of "chronic racial despair" (208).

20. For a more sinister representation of a telepathic heterosexual bond in a white middle-class marriage, see Howells's short story "Though One Rose from the Dead," in *Questionable Shapes*.

21. Taylor Stoehr's discussion, apropos of Hawthorne, of the close generic relationship between the Gothic novel, featuring an evil mesmerist/pseudoscientist, and the utopian novel, featuring an idealistic social scientist/reformer, seems to me especially germane to an analysis of Hopkins's revisions of the Gothic mode. Taking *The House of the Seven Gables* as an instance of the culmination of the high Gothic novel and *The Blithedale Romance* as an example of the reemergence of the utopian novel, Stoehr reads Hawthorne's work as a case study of the former genre bleeding into the latter (251–75). I would argue that *Of One Blood* can be usefully read as a hybrid of the two genres, combining an American Gothic plot that features an evil (white) mesmerist with an African utopian plot that features an idealistic (black) social scientist. Through her explicit engagement with a discourse of race, Hopkins crucially revises the genre, reversing and critiquing the racism implicit in the traditional figure of the Gothic double.

22. Elizabeth Ammons similarly reads the novel as an allegory about racism, focusing primarily on Dianthe as an allegorical figure for the plight of the black woman artist (81–85).

23. For an excellent collection of essays on another text of the period that uses the narrative device of black and white babies switched at birth to explore the nature of racial identity, see Gillman and Robinson, *Mark Twain's Pudd'nhead Wilson*. On the period's legal and scientific policing of the color line, see esp. Sundquist, "Mark Twain," and Rogin, "Francis Galton."

24. The "Ethiopian prophecy," which predicted the rise of Africa and the decline of the West, is thematized in the work of many black intellectuals at the turn of the century, including W. E. B. Du Bois, Frances E. W. Harper, and Paul Laurence Dunbar (Moses). For a discussion of Ethiopianism that situates Hopkins's novel in relationship to a larger discourse on Pan-Africanism, especially in the work of Du Bois, see Sundquist, *To Wake the Nations* (551–81). For a discussion of the representation of Egypt and Ethiopia in the work of turn-of-the-century African American historians, see Bruce, "Ancient Africa."

25. On the pre-Darwinian debate over monogenesis versus polygenesis, see Frederickson, *The Black Image* (71–76), and Gould, *The Mismeasure of Man* (chap. 2). On the marriage of polygenesist ethnology and Darwinism, see Frederickson (chap. 8).

26. On the discourse of "blood," see Foucault, *The History of Sexuality* (124–25). Foucault notes a shift in the late eighteenth century from an aristocratic concern with genealogy to the emerging bourgeois preoccupation with heredity. Whereas the aristocracy had asserted itself through a symbolics of blood and a concern with ancestry, the middle class looked to the health of its progeny. One might turn to a text like Kate Chopin's short story "Desiree's Baby" (1892) for one (tragic) inscription of the bourgeois preoccupation with racially pure offspring. In contrast, *Of One Blood* might be read as a return to an older discourse of aristocratic legitimation to counter emergent white racist discourse on "pure blood."

27. Despite his gender, Reuel arguably prefigures such female healers as Baby Suggs in Morrison's *Beloved* and Minnie Ransom in Bambara's *The Salt Eaters*. His positioning within a feminine African lineage partially destabilizes the undeniably patriarchal bias of Hopkins's Pan-Africanist political vision.

WORKS CITED

Ammons, Elizabeth. *Conflicting Stories: American Women Writers at the Turn into the Twentieth Century.* New York: Oxford University Press, 1991.

Auerbach, Nina. "Magi and Maidens: The Romance of the Victorian Freud." In *Writing and Sexual Difference.* Ed. Elizabeth Abel. Chicago: University of Chicago Press, 1982. 111–30.

Bambara, Toni Cade. "What It Is I Think I'm Doing Anyhow." In *The Writer on Her Work.* Ed. Janet Sternberg. New York: Norton, 1980. 153–68.

Barzun, Jacques. *A Stroll with William James.* New York: Harper, 1983.

Bruce, Dickson D., Jr. "Ancient Africa and the Early Black American Historians, 1883–1915." *American Quarterly* 36 (1984): 684–99.

———. "W. E. B. Du Bois and the Idea of Double Consciousness." *American Literature* 64 (1992): 299–309.

Carby, Hazel. *Reconstructing Womanhood: The Emergence of the Afro-American Woman Novelist*. New York: Oxford University Press, 1987.

Cotkin, George. *Reluctant Modernism: American Thought and Culture, 1880–1900*. New York: Twayne, 1992.

Drinka, George Frederick. *The Birth of Neurosis: Myth, Malady, and the Victorians*. New York: Simon and Schuster, 1984.

Du Bois, W. E. B. *The Autobiography of W. E. B. Du Bois: A Soliloquy on Viewing My Life from the Last Decade of Its First Century*. Ed. Herbert Aptheker. New York: International, 1968.

———. *The Souls of Black Folk*. 1903. New York: New American Library, 1969.

———. "Strivings of the Negro People." *Atlantic Monthly*, August 1897, 194–98.

Ellenberger, Henri F. *The Discovery of the Unconscious: The History and Evolution of Dynamic Psychiatry*. New York: Basic, 1970.

Feinstein, Howard M. *Becoming William James*. Ithaca, N.Y.: Cornell University Press, 1984.

Foucault, Michel. *The History of Sexuality*. Vol. 1. *An Introduction*. 1976. Trans. Robert Hurley. New York: Vintage, 1980.

Frederickson, George M. *The Black Image in the White Mind: The Debate on Afro-American Character and Destiny, 1817–1914*. New York: Harper and Row, 1971.

Freud, Sigmund. "Female Sexuality." 1931. In *Women and Analysis: Dialogues on Psychoanalytic Views of Femininity*. 1974. Ed. Jean Strouse. Boston: G. K. Hall, 1985. 39–56.

Fuller, Robert C. *Americans and the Unconscious*. New York: Oxford University Press, 1986.

———. *Mesmerism and the American Cure of Souls*. Philadelphia: University of Pennsylvania Press, 1982.

Gaines, Kevin. "Black Americans' Racial Uplift Ideology as 'Civilizing Mission': Pauline E. Hopkins on Race and Imperialism." In *Cultures of United States Imperialism*. Ed. Amy Kaplan and Donald Pease. Durham, N.C.: Duke University Press, 1993. 433–55.

Gillman, Susan, and Forrest G. Robinson, eds. *Mark Twain's Pudd'nhead Wilson: Race, Conflict, and Culture*. Durham, N.C.: Duke University Press, 1990.

Gilroy, Paul. *The Black Atlantic: Modernity and Double Consciousness*. Cambridge, Mass.: Harvard University Press, 1993.

Gould, Stephen Jay. *The Mismeasure of Man*. New York: Norton, 1981.

Hale, Nathan G., Jr. *Freud and the Americans: The Beginnings of Psychoanalysis in the United States, 1876–1917*. New York: Oxford University Press, 1971.

Hopkins, Pauline. *Contending Forces: A Romance Illustrative of Negro Life North and South*. 1900. New York: Oxford University Press, 1988.

———. "The Mystery within Us." *Colored American Magazine*, May 1900, 14–18. Reprinted in *Short Fiction by Black Women, 1900–1920*. Ed. Elizabeth Ammons. New York: Oxford University Press, 1991. 21–26.

———. *Of One Blood; or, The Hidden Self*. 1902–3. In *The Magazine Novels of Pauline Hopkins*. New York: Oxford University Press, 1988. 441–621.

Howells, William Dean. *Questionable Shapes*. New York: Harper, 1903.

James, Alice. *The Diary of Alice James*. 1894. Ed. Leon Edel. New York: Penguin, 1987.

James, William. "The Hidden Self." *Scribner's Magazine* 7 (1890): 361–73.

———. "Is Life Worth Living?" *International Journal of Ethics* 6 (1895): 1–24.

———. *The Works of William James*. Vol. 16. *Essays in Psychical Research*. Ed. Robert E. McDermott. Cambridge, Mass.: Harvard University Press, 1986.

Jones, Ernest. *The Life and Work of Sigmund Freud*. Vol 2. New York: Basic, 1955.

Kenny, Michael G. *The Passion of Ansel Bourne: Multiple Personality in American Culture*. Washington, D.C.: Smithsonian Institution Press, 1986.

Lutz, Tom. *American Nervousness, 1903: An Anecdotal History*. Ithaca, N.Y.: Cornell University Press, 1991.

Miller, Karl. *Doubles: Studies in Literary History*. New York: Oxford University Press, 1985.

Moore, R. Laurence. *In Search of White Crows: Spiritualism, Parapsychology, and American Culture*. New York: Oxford University Press, 1977.

Morrison, Toni. "Rootedness: The Ancestor as Foundation." In *Black Women Writers (1950–1980): A Critical Evaluation*. Ed. Mari Evans. Garden City, N.Y.: Anchor-Doubleday, 1984. 339–45.

Moses, Wilson J. "The Poetics of Ethiopianism: W. E. B. Du Bois and Literary Black Nationalism." *American Literature* 47 (1975): 411–26.

Otten, Thomas J. "Pauline Hopkins and the Hidden Self of Race." *ELH* 59 (1992): 227–56.

Rampersad, Arnold. *The Art and Imagination of W. E. B. Du Bois*. Cambridge, Mass.: Harvard University Press, 1976.

Robbins, Anne Banning. *Both Sides of the Veil: A Personal Experience*. Boston, Mass.: Sherman, 1909.

Rogin, Michael. "Francis Galton and Mark Twain: The Natal Autograph in

Pudd'nhead Wilson." In *Mark Twain's Pudd'nhead Wilson*. Ed. Gillman and Robinson. 73–85.

Stoehr, Taylor. *Hawthorne's Mad Scientists: Pseudoscience and Social Science in Nineteenth-Century Life and Letters*. Hamden, Conn.: Archon Books–Shoe String Press, 1978.

Sundquist, Eric J. "Mark Twain and Homer Plessy." *Representations* 24 (Fall 1988): 102–28.

———. *To Wake the Nations: Race in the Making of American Literature*. Cambridge, Mass.: Harvard University Press, 1993.

Tate, Claudia. *Domestic Allegories of Political Desire: The Black Heroine's Text at the Turn of the Century*. New York: Oxford University Press, 1992.

Taylor, Eugene. *William James on Exceptional Mental States: The 1896 Lowell Lectures*. New York: Scribner's, 1983.

Thigpen, Corbett H., and Hervey Cleckley. "A Case of Multiple Personality." *Journal of Abnormal and Social Psychology* 49.1 (1954): 135–51.

Yeazell, Ruth Bernard, ed. *The Death and Letters of Alice James*. Berkeley: University of California Press, 1981.

AFTERWORD

Winona, Bakhtin, and Hopkins in the Twenty-first Century

ELIZABETH AMMONS

The essays in this volume identify Hopkins as a major, complex, serious American writer. With dazzling variety, they present her as a literary figure whose work and career repay close, sophisticated study. My goal is to organize one perspective on these essays into an overt case for Hopkins as a radical experimenter whose work will be read in the next century as a model of early modernist innovation and revolution in the United States. My point is that the disruliness of her performance as an artist, in particular the formal outrageousness of her long fiction—its refusal to conform to inherited well-made novel dicta—attacks the idea of rules itself. As we can now understand, Hopkins insistently defied the power structure—racial, sexual, intellectual, economic—that sought to contain and discipline her. Her rebellion against mastery was both subject and medium for her art.

The early twentieth-century theorist Mikhail Bakhtin, who wrote during Hopkins's lifetime, argued that the novel contradicts the basic premise of traditional elite Western literary form. It differs fundamentally from the epic or the sonnet, for example, either of which refers to literary expression that inhabits a clearly prescribed, predetermined structure. The novel, in contrast, rebels. By definition unregulated, even anarchic, it is, as its name suggests, new—novel—in not obeying the rules of elite literary production, including those which say that literary form must obey rules. In "Epic and Novel," Bakhtin considers three Western historical periods that have much in common with the era in which Hopkins wrote, "the Greek classical period, the Golden Age of Roman literature, [and] the neoclassical period." These periods were, like the United States at the turn of the century, extraordinary periods of empire building. He observes, "All genres in 'high' literature (that is, the literature of ruling social groups) harmoniously reinforce each other to a significant extent; the whole of literature, conceived as a totality of genres, becomes an organic unity of the highest order. But it is characteristic of the novel that it never enters into this whole, it does not participate in any harmony of the genres. In these eras the novel has an unofficial existence, outside 'high' literature" (4). Reflecting on the novel's outsider status in early periods, Bakhtin says of prestigious literature that "only already completed genres, with fully formed and well-defined generic contours, can enter into such a literature as a hierarchically organized, organic whole" (4). This analysis of the relationship between the novel and elite literary tradition is very suggestive for thinking about the neglect of Hopkins's work for the past ninety years on the grounds that her writing was allegedly not "good" (i.e., smooth, integrated, coherent, harmonious). If Bakhtin is right, the very roughness and *un*harmoniousness of Hopkins's work speak to its integrity and vitality in the kind of new, inclusive, ever-changing literary history we are now able to envision.

The essays in this volume emphasize the diversity and profoundly experimental nature of Hopkins's writing. She wrote within *and* sabotaged the sentimental novel, invented black detective fiction, fictionalized African American history, assumed the role of race historian, entered contemporary scientific and spiritistic discourses, shadow-wrote lost maternal texts in the margins of her own narratives, and attempted to negotiate the extremely difficult formal terrain that one critic identifies as "racial pornography." The essays' multiplicity of focus, the way they go in so many directions, perfectly reflects the principles animating Hopkins's work: her venturesomeness, defiance of categories, resistance to received tradition, and determination to articulate new forms not to *contain* stories but to *release* new possibilities and paradigms. Kristina Brooks argues a brilliant theory of "racial pornography" as a form of representation, like sexual pornography, that assigns and fixes object status to one group and dominance to another. C. K. Doreski explicitly states that Hopkins's construction of history "challenges conventional generic distinctions." Kate McCullough and Lois Brown disagree on Hopkins's relation to the sentimental novel and particularly the representation, in Brown's phrase, of "the traumatized mixed-blood woman," while Jennie Kassanoff examines the issue of the body in light of the emerging trope of the New Negro at the turn of the century and the eruption into the textual margin of the mother's "hand." John Gruesser finds multiple significance in Hopkins's alteration of an historical name, and Cynthia D. Schrager offers a fascinating analysis of Hopkins's manipulation of the psychological and psychical research discourses of her day, especially that of William James.

I rehearse this partial perspective on the essays (they in fact do much more than my summaries suggest) to make concrete my point about Hopkins's complex shape-changing. Formally and substantively she does not stay fixed. She constantly borrows, innovates, invents, enjambs, and switches—which means we must do likewise.

Discussing Bakhtin, Michael Holquist labels the novel a "militantly protean" form (xxvii). He explains that if the novel as a structure is not about binary opposition but, rather, about the expression of many voices, even "languages," then it follows that (as we repeatedly see in Hopkins's work) "literary language is not represented in the novel as a unitary, completely finished off, indubitably adequate language—it is represented precisely as a living mix of varied and opposing voices" (xxviii). As a result, and as Bakhtin's writings maintain, novels are "defined by their proclivity to display different languages interpenetrating each other"; and the structure of the form itself "constantly experiments with new shapes" (xxix). Explaining that "it is the nature of novels to resist" clear, tidy, "organizing categories," Holquist also emphasizes Bakhtin's belief that the novel "dramatizes the gaps that always exist between what is told and the telling of it, constantly experimenting with social, discursive and narrative asymmetries" (xxviii).

Pauline Hopkins's employment of the novel registers precisely the radical instability of form—the "militantly protean" character of the genre—that, writing half a world away and in exile in his own country, Bakhtin argued was by definition what makes a novel a novel. Herself also in many ways an exile within her own country—and certainly about to be exiled from the publishing world that was her life's blood, the *Colored American Magazine*—Hopkins wrote novels that almost uncannily correspond in practice to key ideas articulated by Bakhtin, especially the concept of the novel's being barely controlled or contained, if at all, by its form. Critics routinely remark on how unsummarizable Hopkins's plots are, how bizarre her mixture of literary genres and expectations, how contradictory and often irreconcilable her themes and symbolic implications, and how unconventional and chaotic her narrative structures. The thesis that strikes me is that Hopkins, far from being minor, flawed, or artistically incompetent, is

actually one of the United States's important great experimental novelists. As we work toward a new national literary history that includes
both the full range of American writers and the complexities raised by
contemporary literary theory, I think that the diversity of Hopkins's
literary production and in particular the volatile, unstable, long fiction
that she wrote as a consciously political, marginalized, experimental
author stand as crucially important paradigms.

Although seldom discussed, *Winona: A Tale of Negro Life in the
South and Southwest* is an excellent example. The multivocality of the
text is immediately obvious—and by no means totally under control.
Generically the novel combines the western, fugitive slave narrative,
romance, potboiler/soap opera, political novel, and traditional allegory to tell the story of the paradisiacal possibility but real life destruction of a truly mixed-race North American family. The book opens in
an idealized natural space, literally an island in the Niagara River that
belongs to no nation (thus anticipating Gloria Naylor's narrative geography in *Mama Day* decades later); representing both past and future, but not the present, this isolated, "primal," green place poised between Canada and the United States denies racial categories. As
Hopkins announces, "Many strange tales of romantic happenings in
this mixed community of Anglo-Saxons, Indians and Negroes might
be told similar to the one I am about to relate, and the world stand
aghast and try in vain to find the dividing line supposed to be a natural barrier between the whites and the dark-skinned race" (287). It is
quite significant that the dramatic action begins with the violent inva-
sion of this world by two white men whose first language is gunfire,
not words.

Hopkins's mixed-race family in *Winona* consists of a white father
who has chosen to live as an Indian, "White Eagle"; a fair-skinned, well-
educated, ex-slave, African American mother, who is dead by the time
the story opens; an African American son, Judah, born to another ex-
slave who died while fleeing slavery and was adopted by White Eagle
and his (now deceased) wife; a daughter, Winona, born to White Eagle and his wife; and an Indian "squaw" Nikomis who lives with the
motherless family as housekeeper and caregiver. White, black, red, the
family is very deliberately socially constructed. It stands as a trope for
what could be the human family in North America: multicultural,
multiracial, anti-imperialist, unnational, antimaterialistic, environmentally attuned. The composition of this family brilliantly introduces a

Bakhtinian mix or contestation of voices and cultural perspectives that remains pronounced throughout the novel as Hopkins introduces more characters and cultures, some of them entirely imagined and some historically inspired, such as the well-known figure John Brown and his outlaw society of militant abolitionists.

This idealized family unit also, however, presents major problems. With its dead black mother, fake Indian father, and silenced "real" Indian housekeeper, it simply reiterates empire's script. Even as Hopkins seeks to deconstruct racism and colonialism, she reinscribes them. Imagining a new North America while writing within the old proves as difficult for her as it has been for other American writers.

One source of the problem is *Winona*'s debt to the western. Drawing heavily on this genre, Hopkins claims for African American literary tradition the revered U.S. stereotype of the frontiersman, represented in this narrative by the heroine's Indianized father White Eagle, the rough-hewn hotelkeeper Ebenezer Maybee, the backwoods abolitionist preacher Parson Steward, and John Brown. The way to come to terms with the white man, this novel suggests, is through the border character, in particular the antiracist outlaw. That figure, along with the novel's British aristocrat, Warren Maxwell, occupies a position on the edge or even outside of mainstream white middle-class American values and therefore provides a way of identifying white male allies even as one lives and writes within a system dominated and controlled by a white racist patriarchal power structure. Yet the use of these figures, the American frontier outlaw and the British aristocrat, creates huge contradictions. From James Fenimore Cooper to Gary Cooper, the white frontier outlaw by definition configures an imperialist agenda, as does the British aristocrat. They are both conquerors, invaders—as the presence of appropriated Indianness in *Winona* (White Eagle) makes inescapable. The primary Native American in Hopkins's book is not native but nativeness taken over by a white man. The "good guys" in *Winona* consist of gentry from England, men who live off the spoils of empire, which is not investigated, and frontier trappers, settlers, and preachers, who represent the first line in white imperial aggression against indigenous people on the North American continent, a fact that likewise is unquestioned.

It may be that *Winona* has received less attention than Hopkins's other long fiction because the dominant culture form it most obviously employs—the western—cannot be reconciled with the slave narra-

tive or the racialized protest novel, the two other genres most important to Hopkins in *Winona*. The western's imperial plot of valorizing
white men, especially outlaws, is only the popular culture, bad-boy
version of the high culture, imperial, national script of white territori-
al and cultural expansion and dominance. Right down to featuring an
incredibly virtuous but almost invisible heroine, a staple in the western, *Winona,* we could argue, is trapped into profound self-contradic-
tion by its generic participation in the western. The book's effort to
recuperate right-minded white men, including the abolitionist John
Brown, and thus write into its own revolutionary plot representatives
of the power structure who have denounced that structure, radically
conflicts with its reliance on the western, by definition an imperialist
form (see, for example, Tompkins).

At the same time, Hopkins's affirmation in *Winona* of alliance between Native American and African American cultures *does* successfully articulate a revolutionary vision. Writing at a time of intensified
U.S. genocidal policy against Native Americans, most vividly obvious
in the massacre of Sioux at Wounded Knee in 1890, as well as a period of escalating atrocities against African Americans, evident particularly in lynchings, which were both terrorist and genocidal (Drinnon;
Gossett), Hopkins stages in *Winona* a new origins myth for North
America that renounces European cultural values in favor of Indian and
African American ones. Winona's father chooses for himself and his
children a life that is Indian and African American, not European-de-
rived. The white father, in other words, chooses not to be the white
father. *Winona* radically rewrites the primary, romantic, American myth
of our great (white) "founding fathers," making their representative
in this fiction an opponent of white authority.

But the fact that Indianness in *Winona* is stereotyped and phony
demands attention. We barely see the only "real" Indian, Nikomis. Her
knowledge is praised (292), yet she has no agency; she is given a minis-
cule role and is for the most part talked about, rather than speaking
and acting for herself. Furthermore, the Indianness we do see is stock.
Winona and Judah glide around in canoes or move noiselessly through
the woods; stoicism and material frugality are emphasized; intimate
knowledge of plants and animals gets invoked. Counterbalancing this
cliché of the "noble savage" are some standard, negative stereotypes.
The narrator, speaking of Judah, refers at one point to "scenes that
rivalled in cruelty the ferocity of the savage tribes among whom he had

passed his boyhood" (320). At another point, John Brown, affectionately presented by the narrator, casually calls Winona a "pretty squaw" (375). Drawing on stereotypes, positive and negative, Hopkins's novel is not about Indians. It is about Hopkins's fantasy of non-Western cultural affinity and solidarity among people of color on the North American continent. She uses Indians, or more accurately what Phillip Round calls the "sign of the native," to communicate her own cultural vision and desire. Her text's relation to actual people who were/are Indian is as problematic as, for example, that of many white authors who include representations of blacks.

Yet there is an important difference between Hopkins's relation to racial stereotyping and that of white authors. White writers' racial stereotypes a priori reinscribe the power structure from a position of privilege (even if the author tries to disclaim it). In contrast, Hopkins's stereotypes do so from an analogous subject position, or laterally, so to speak; and they operate within a context overtly committed to deconstructing racial stereotypes, a situation that may or may not obtain in white texts, depending on the work. The complexity of this confusion and inconsistency is what makes *Winona* and Hopkins's work in general so compelling. As others have argued in this volume with regard to her treatment of gender, African American identity, the body, the genre of the sentimental novel, and any number of other concerns, it is precisely this issue of contradictoriness, itself inseparable from the fantastic contradictions that Hopkins had to experience daily as a single, ambitious, black, American woman writer at the turn of the century, that makes her life and work so illustrative.

There are many questions at this point in Hopkins scholarship. For example, who *is* Winona? Present throughout the narrative yet still, somehow, almost invisible, she is white (her paternal heritage), black (her maternal heritage), Indian (her upbringing), female (her usual identity), and male (her assumed identity). In drag as a boy late in the novel, Winona calls herself Allen Pinks and secretly kisses the sleeping Warren, whom she is nursing back to health (387). The scene is constructed so that we suspect but do not know that Allen is "really" Winona, the boy is "really" a girl; we have a hunch that gender is straight (pun intended), but we cannot know. The text only permits us to see same-sex attraction, a man tenderly caring for and kissing another man. Complicating the scene even more, the name Hopkins gives Winona in drag, Allen, is the same name she gave herself when she

wanted to publish anonymously in the *Colored American Magazine,*
Sarah Allen—her mother's name. How do we read this dense network
of signs? We know so little about Hopkins's biography that we can say
almost nothing about her sexual orientation. At the same time, this
scene, so carefully but obviously coded (and therefore inviting decod-
ing), forces us to think broadly rather than narrowly about Hopkins's
sexuality. At the very least, the entire hazy characterization of Winona—
sharing an assumed name with her author as she does—in combination with Sappho in *Contending Forces* and Dianthe in *Of One Blood,*
the former named for the earliest known lesbian poet and the latter for
the virgin goddess of the hunt, must caution us against mindless heterosexual assumptions as we continue reading and thinking about
Hopkins's work (on Sappho and Dianthe, see Ammons).

The questions Hopkins's work raises about race, gender, sexuality,
multiculturalism, nationalism, history, empire, the politics of representation, the limits of genre, and the construction of literary history are
questions we all—students, teachers, readers of many sorts—confront
as we enter the twenty-first century. As the essays in this volume attest, Hopkins's rich complexity, her dense polyvocality, to recall Bakhtin, makes answers difficult. But that is precisely why Hopkins will be
more, not less, studied as we enter the next century. As Barbara Johnson
has wisely observed, "Unification and simplification are fantasies of
domination, not understanding" (170; see also Oakes). Pauline Hopkins's work may tempt us toward simplification but, like the conjure
often found in the world of her fiction, it's a trick.

WORKS CITED

Ammons, Elizabeth. *Conflicting Stories: American Women Writers at the Turn
    into the Twentieth Century.* New York: Oxford University Press, 1991.
Bakhtin, Mikhail. *The Dialogic Imagination: Four Essays.* Ed. Michael
    Holquist. Trans. Michael Holquist and Caryl Emerson. Austin: University
    of Texas Press, 1981.
Drinnon, Richard. *Facing West: The Metaphysics of Indian-Hating and Em-
    pire-Building.* Minneapolis: University of Minnesota Press, 1980.
Gossett, Thomas F. *Race: The History of an Idea in America.* Dallas, Tex.:
    Southern Methodist University Press, 1963.
Holquist, Michael. Introduction. *The Dialogic Imagination.* By Mikhail Bakh-
    tin. xv–xxxiv.
Hopkins, Pauline. *Winona: A Tale of Negro Life in the South and Southwest.*

In *The Magazine Novels of Pauline Hopkins*. New York: Oxford University Press, 1988.

Johnson, Barbara. *A World of Difference*. Baltimore, Md.: Johns Hopkins University Press, 1988.

Oakes, Karen. "Reading Trickster; or, Theoretical Reservations and a Seneca Tale." In *Tricksterism in Turn-of-the-Century American Literature*. Ed. Elizabeth Ammons and Annette White-Parks. Hanover, N.H.: University Press of New England. 1994.

Round, Phillip. "'The Posture That We Give the Dead': Freneau's 'Indian Burying Ground' in Ethnohistorical Context." *Arizona Quarterly* 50 (Autumn 1994): 1–30.

Tompkins, Jane. *West of Everything: The Inner Life of Westerns*. New York: Oxford University Press, 1992.

WORKS
BY AND ABOUT PAULINE HOPKINS

MALIN LAVON WALTHER

Works by Hopkins

BOOKS

Contending Forces: A Romance Illustrative of Negro Life North and South. Boston: Colored Co-operative Publishing Company, 1900; Rpt. Miami: Mnemosyne, 1969. Rpt. with an afterword by Gwendolyn Brooks. Carbondale: Southern Illinois University Press, 1978. Rpt. with an introduction by Richard Yarborough. New York: Oxford University Press, 1988.

The Magazine Novels of Pauline Hopkins. 1901–3. With an introduction by Hazel Carby. New York: Oxford University Press, 1988.

A Primer of Facts Pertaining to the Early Greatness of the African Race and the Possibility of Restoration by Its Descendants—with Epilogue. Cambridge, Mass.: P. E. Hopkins, 1905.

PLAYS

Peculiar Sam; or, The Underground Railroad. 1879. In *The Roots of African American Drama.* Ed. Leo Hamalian and James V. Hatch. Detroit, Mich.: Wayne State University Press, 1991. 100–123. Words and music also in *African American Theater: Out of Bondage (1876) and Peculiar Sam; or, The Underground Railroad (1879).* Ed. Eileen Southern. New York: Garland, 1994. 117–205.

PERIODICAL PUBLICATIONS[1]

"As the Lord Lives, He Is One of Our Mother's Children." *Colored American Magazine,* Nov. 1903, 795–801. Rpt. in *Short Fiction.* Ed. Ammons. 276–86. Rpt. in *Invented Lives.* Ed. Washington. 130–46.

"Bro'r Abr'm Jimson's Wedding: A Christmas Story." *CAM,* Dec. 1901, 103–12. Rpt. in *Short Fiction.* Ed. Ammons. 107–25.

"Converting Fanny." *New Era Magazine,* Feb. 1916, 33–34. Published under the name Sarah A. Allen.

"The Dark Races of the Twentieth Century." *Voice of the Negro,* Feb. 1905, 108–15; Mar. 1905, 187–91; May 1905, 330–34; June 1905, 415–18; July 1905, 459–63.

"A Dash for Liberty." *CAM,* Aug. 1901, 243–47. Rpt. in *Short Fiction.* Ed. Ammons. 89–98.

"Echoes from the Annual Convention of Northeastern Federation of Colored Women's Clubs." *CAM,* Oct. 1903, 709–13.

"Elijah William Smith: A Colored Poet of Early Days." *CAM,* Dec. 1902, 96–100.

"Famous Men of the Negro Race." A series published in the *Colored American Magazine:* "Toussaint L'Overture," Nov. 1900, 9–24; "Hon. Frederick Douglass," Dec. 1900, 121–32; "William Wells Brown," Jan. 1901, 232–36; "Robert Browne Elliott," Feb. 1901, 294–301; "Edwin Garrison Walker," Mar. 1901, 358–66; "Lewis Hayden," Apr. 1901, 473–77; "Charles Lenox Remond," May 1901, 34–39; "Sargeant Wm. H. Carney," June 1901, 84–89; "Hon. John Mercer Langston," July 1901, 177–84; "Senator Blanche K. Bruce," Aug. 1901, 257–61; "Robert Morris," Sept. 1901, 337–42; "Booker T. Washington," Oct. 1901, 436–41.

"Famous Women of the Negro Race." A series published in the *Colored American Magazine:* "Phenomenal Vocalists," Nov. 1901, 45–53; "Sojourner Truth," Dec. 1901, 124–32; "Harriet Tubman," Jan./Feb. 1902, 210–23; "Some Literary Workers," Mar. 1902, 276–80; "Literary Workers," Apr. 1902, 366–71; "Educators," May 1902, 41–46; "Educators (Continued)," June 1902, 125–30; "Educators (Concluded)," July 1902, 206–13; "Club Life among Colored Women," Aug. 1902, 273–77; "Artists," Sept. 1902, 362–67; "Higher Education of Colored Women in White Schools and Colleges," Oct. 1902, 445–50.

"George Washington: A Christmas Story." *CAM,* Dec. 1900, 95–104. Rpt. in *Short Fiction.* Ed. Ammons. 69–82.

Hagar's Daughter: A Story of Southern Caste Prejudice. A serialized novel in *CAM,* Mar. 1901, 337–52; Apr. 1901, 431–45; May 1901, 24–34; June 1901, 117–28; July 1901, 185–95; Aug. 1901, 262–72; Sept. 1901, 343–53; Oct. 1901, 425–35; Nov. 1901, 23–33; Dec. 1901, 113–24; Jan./Feb. 1902, 188–200; Mar. 1902, 281–91. Published under the name Sarah A. Allen. Rpt. in *The Magazine Novels.* 1–284.

"Heroes and Heroines in Black: I. Neil Johnson, American Woodfolk, et al." *CAM*, Jan 1903, 206–11.

"How a New York Newspaper Man Entertained a Number of Colored Ladies and Gentlemen at Dinner in the Revere House, Boston, and How the Colored American League Was Started." *CAM*, Jan. 1904, 151–60.

"Josephine St. Pierre Ruffin at Milwaukee, 1900." *CAM*, July 1902, 210–13.

"Latest Phases of the Race Problem in America." *CAM*, Feb. 1903, 244–51. Published under the name Sarah A. Allen.

"Men of Vision: I. Mark Rene Demortie." *New Era Magazine*, Feb. 1916, 35–39.

"Men of Vision: II. Rev. Leonard A. Grimes." *New Era Magazine*, Mar. 1916, 99–105.

"Mr. Alan Kirkland Soga." *CAM*, Feb. 1904, 114–16. Published under the name Sarah A. Allen.

"Mr. M. Hamilton Hodges." *CAM*, Mar. 1904, 167–69. Published under the name Sarah A. Allen.

"Munroe Rodgers." *CAM*, Nov. 1902, 20–26.

"The Mystery within Us." *CAM*, May 1900, 14–18. Rpt. in *Short Fiction*. Ed. Ammons. 21–26.

"A New Profession: The First Colored Graduate of the Y.M.C.A. Training School, Springfield, Mass." *CAM*, Sept. 1903, 661–63. Published under the name Sarah A. Allen.

"The New York Subway." *Voice of the Negro*, Dec. 1904, 605, 608–12.

Of One Blood; or, The Hidden Self. A serialized novel in *CAM*, Nov. 1902, 29–40; Dec. 1902, 102–13; Jan. 1903, 191–200; Feb. 1903, 264–72; Mar. 1903, 339–48; May/June 1903, 423–32; July 1903, 492–501; Aug. 1903, 580–86; Sept. 1903, 643–47; Oct. 1903, 726–31; Nov. 1903, 802–7. Rpt. in *The Magazine Novels*. 439–621.

"Reminiscences of the Life and Times of Lydia Maria Child." *CAM*, Feb. 1903, 279–84; Mar. 1903, 353–57; May/June 1903, 454–59.

Reply to Letter to the Editor. *CAM*, Mar. 1903, 399–400.

"A Retrospect of the Past [excerpt from *Contending Forces*]." *CAM*, Nov. 1900, 64–72.

"Talma Gordon." *CAM*, Oct. 1900, 271–90. Rpt. in *Short Fiction*. Ed. Ammons. 49–68.

"The Test of Manhood." *CAM*, Dec. 1902, 113–19. Published under the name Sarah A. Allen. Rpt. in *Short Fiction*. Ed. Ammons. 205–17.

"Topsy Templeton." *New Era Magazine,* Feb. 1916, 11–20, 48; Mar. 1916, 75–84.

"Whittier, Friend of the Negro." *CAM,* Sept. 1901, 324–30.

Winona: A Tale of Negro Life in the South and Southwest. A serialized novel in *CAM,* May 1902, 29–41; June 1902, 97–110; July 1902, 177–87; Aug. 1902, 257–68; Sept. 1902, 348–58; Oct. 1902, 422–31. Rpt. in *The Magazine Novels*. 285–437.

PAPERS

Pauline E. Hopkins Papers, Negro Collection, Fisk University Library. Nashville, Tenn. Includes: original ms. for "The Evils of Intemperance and Their Remedy," Hopkins's first essay; original ms. for *One Scene from the Drama of Early Days,* a play; original ms. for *Peculiar Sam; or, The Underground Railroad,* a musical drama dated 1879; a notebook in Hopkins's handwriting of the story of Peculiar Sam, with the variant title "The Slaves' Escape; or, The Underground Railroad"; a scrapbook inscribed by Hopkins containing clippings, poems, and quotations; original ms. of an untitled play.

Works on Hopkins

GENERAL COMMENTARY

Ammons, Elizabeth. *Conflicting Stories: American Women Writers at the Turn into the Twentieth Century.* New York: Oxford University Press, 1991. Esp. 77–85.

———. Introduction. *Short Fiction by Black Women, 1900–1920.* Ed. Elizabeth Ammons. New York: Oxford University Press, 1991. 3–20.

Baker, Houston A., Jr. *Workings of the Spirit: The Poetics of Afro-American Women's Writing.* Chicago: University of Chicago Press, 1991. Esp. 23–35.

Bell, Bernard W. *The Afro-American Novel and Its Tradition.* Amherst: University of Massachusetts Press, 1987.

———. "Literary Sources of the Early Afro-American Novel." *CLA Journal* 18 (1974): 29–43.

Berzon, Judith R. *Neither White nor Black: The Mulatto Character in*

American Fiction. New York: New York University Press, 1978. Esp. 190–217.

Bone, Robert A. *The Negro Novel in America*. New Haven, Conn.: Yale University Press, 1958.

Brooks, Gwendolyn. Afterword. *Contending Forces: A Romance Illustrative of Negro Life North and South*. 1900. Carbondale: Southern Illinois University Press, 1978. 403–9.

Brown, Martha Hursey. "Literary Portrayals of Black Women as Moral Reformers: Novels by Harper, Henry, and Hopkins." In *Transactions of the Conference Group for Social and Administrative History*. Vol. 6. Oshkosh, Wis.: State Historical Society, 1976. 75–90.

Bruce, Dickson D., Jr. *Black American Writing from the Nadir: The Evolution of a Literary Tradition, 1877–1951*. Baton Rouge: Louisiana State University Press, 1989. Esp. 136–89.

Byrd, James W. "Stereotypes of White Characters in Early Negro Novels." *CLA Journal* 1 (1957): 28–35.

Campbell, Jane. "Hopkins, Pauline Elizabeth (1859–1930)." In *Black Women in America: An Historical Encyclopedia*. Vol. 1. Ed. Darlene Clark Hine et al. Brooklyn: Carlson, 1993. 577–79.

———. *Mythic Black Fiction: The Transformation of History*. Knoxville: University of Tennessee Press, 1986. Esp. 18–41.

———. "Pauline Elizabeth Hopkins." In *Dictionary of Literary Biography*. Vol. 50. *Afro-American Writers before the Harlem Renaissance*. Ed. Trudier Harris and Thadius M. Davis. Detroit, Mich.: Bruccoli-Clark, 1986. 182–89.

Carby, Hazel. *Reconstructing Womanhood: The Emergence of the Afro-American Woman Novelist*. New York: Oxford University Press, 1987. Esp. 121–61.

———. Introduction. *The Magazine Novels of Pauline Hopkins*. By Pauline Hopkins. New York: Oxford University Press, 1988. xxix–l.

Clark, Edward. *Black Writers in New England*. Boston, Mass.: National Park Service, 1985.

———. "Boston Black and White." *Black American Literature Forum* 19 (Summer 1985): 83–89.

Dearborn, Mary V. *Pocahontas's Daughters: Gender and Ethnicity in American Culture*. New York: Oxford University Press, 1986.

Dramatic Compositions Copyrighted in the United States, 1870–1916. Vol. 1. Washington, D.C.: Government Printing Office, 1918.

duCille, Ann. *The Coupling Convention: Sex, Text, and Tradition in*

Black Women's Fiction. New York: Oxford University Press, 1993. Esp. 30–47.

Gaines, Kevin. "Black American Racial Uplift Ideology as 'Civilizing Mission': Pauline E. Hopkins on Race and Imperialism." In *Cultures of United States Imperialism.* Ed. Amy Kaplan and Donald Pease. Durham, N.C.: Duke University Press, 1993. 433–55.

Giddings, Paula. *When and Where I Enter: The Impact of Black Women on Race and Sex in America.* New York: Morrow, 1984.

Gillman, Susan. "The Mulatto, Tragic or Triumphant? The Nineteenth-Century American Race Melodrama." In *The Culture of Sentiment: Race, Gender, and Sentimentality in Nineteenth-Century America.* Ed. Shirley Samuels. New York: Oxford University Press, 1992. 221–43.

Gloster, Hugh M. *Negro Voices in American Fiction.* 1948. New York: Russell and Russell, 1965.

Gruesser, John. "Pauline Hopkins' *Of One Blood:* Creating an Afrocentric Fantasy for a Black Middle-Class Audience." In *Modes of the Fantastic.* Ed. Robert A. Collins and Robert A. Latham. Westport, Conn.: Greenwood, 1995. 74–83.

Hamalian, Leo, and James V. Hatch. "Pauline Elizabeth Hopkins." In *The Roots of African American Drama: A Collection of Early Plays, 1858–1938.* Ed. Leo Hamalian and James V. Hatch. Detroit, Mich.: Wayne State University Press, 1991. 96–99.

Hayden, Robert C. *African Americans in Boston: More than 350 Years.* Boston, Mass.: Boston Public Library, 1992.

Lamping, Marilyn. "Pauline Elizabeth Hopkins." In *American Women Writers: A Critical Reference Guide from Colonial Times to the Present.* Vol. 2. Ed. Lina Mainiero. New York: Frederick Ungar, 1980. 325–27.

Loggins, Vernon. *The Negro Author: His Development in America to 1900.* New York: Columbia University Press, 1931.

Moses, Wilson Jeremiah. *The Golden Age of Black Nationalism, 1850–1925.* 1978. New York: Oxford University Press, 1988.

[Notice regarding *Contending Forces.*] *Woman's Journal,* Nov. 25, 1899. N.p.

[Obituary.] "Aged Writer Dies of Painful Burns." *Chicago Defender,* Aug. 23, 1930, 1.

[Obituary.] "Burns Fatal to Aged Writer." *The Afro-American,* Aug. 23, 1930, 18.

Otten, Thomas J. "Pauline Hopkins and the Hidden Self of Race." *ELH* 59 (1992): 227–56.

"Pauline E. Hopkins." *CAM,* Jan. 1901, 218–19; May 1901, 47.

"Pauline E. Hopkins." In *Twentieth-Century Literary Criticism.* Vol. 28. Ed. Dennis Poupard. Detroit, Mich.: Gale Research, 1988. 168–71.

[Photographs.] *CAM,* Jan. 1901, 201; May 1901, 52; Mar. 1904. N.p.

Porter, Dorothy B. "Hopkins, Pauline Elizabeth." In *Dictionary of American Negro Biography.* Ed. Rayford W. Logan and Michael R. Winston. New York: Norton, 1982. 325–26.

Robinson, William, H. *Black New England Letters: The Uses and Writings in Black New England.* Boston, Mass.: Boston Public Library, 1977.

Roses, Lorraine Elena, and Ruth Elizabeth Randolph. "Pauline Elizabeth Hopkins (1859–1930)." In *Harlem Renaissance and Beyond: Literary Biographies of 100 Black Women Writers, 1900–1945.* Boston: G. K. Hall, 1990. 167–72.

Rush, Theressa Gunnels, Carol Fairbanks Myers, and Esther Spring Arata. "Pauline Elizabeth Hopkins." In *Black American Writers Past and Present: A Biographical and Bibliographical Dictionary.* Vol. 1. Metuchen, N.J.: Scarecrow, 1975. 389–90.

Shockley, Ann Allen. "Pauline Elizabeth Hopkins." In *Afro-American Women Writers, 1746–1933.* Boston, Mass.: G. K. Hall, 1988. 289–95.

———. "Pauline Elizabeth Hopkins: A Biographical Excursion into Obscurity." *Phylon* 33 (Spring 1972): 22–26.

Simmons, Simmona E. "Pauline Hopkins, 1859–1930: Writer, Editor, Playwright, Singer, Actress." In *Notable Black American Women.* Ed. Jessie Carney Smith. Detroit, Mich.: Gale Research, 1992. 515–18.

Smith, Albreta Moore. "Comment." *CAM,* Oct. 1901, 479.

Southern, Eileen. "Peculiar Sam; or, The Underground Railroad." In *African American Theater: Out of Bondage (1876) and Peculiar Sam; or, The Underground Railroad (1879).* Ed. Eileen Southern. New York: Garland, 1994. xxiii–xxvi.

Sundquist, Eric J. *To Wake the Nations: Race in the Making of American Literature.* Cambridge, Mass.: Harvard University Press, 1993. Esp. 569–74.

Tate, Claudia. "Allegories of Black Female Desire; or, Rereading Nineteenth-Century Sentimental Narratives of Black Female Authority."

In *Changing Our Own Words: Essays on Criticism, Theory, and Writing by Black Women.* Ed. Cheryl A. Wall. New Brunswick, N.J.: Rutgers University Press, 1989. 98–126.

———. *Domestic Allegories of Political Desire: The Black Heroine's Text at the Turn of the Century.* New York: Oxford University Press, 1992. Esp. 144–52, 160–65, 174–76, 193–208.

———. "Pauline Hopkins: Our Literary Foremother." In *Conjuring: Black Women, Fiction, and Literary Tradition.* Ed. Marjorie Pryse and Hortense J. Spillers. Bloomington: Indiana University Press, 1985. 53–66.

Toppin, Edgar A. *A Biographical History of Blacks in America since 1528.* New York: David McKay, 1971.

"The Voice of the Negro for March." *Voice of the Negro,* Feb. 1905, 139.

"The Voice of the Negro for 1905." *Voice of the Negro,* Dec. 1904, 580.

Washington, Mary Helen. *Invented Lives: Narratives of Black Women, 1860–1960.* Garden City, N.Y.: Anchor, 1987. Esp. 73–86.

Watson, Carole McAlpine. *Prologue: The Novels of Black American Women, 1891–1965.* Westport, Conn.: Greenwood, 1985. Esp. 9–31.

Yarborough, Richard. Introduction. *Contending Forces: A Romance Illustrative of Negro Life North and South.* By Pauline Hopkins. 1900. New York: Oxford University Press, 1988. xxvii–xlviii.

HOPKINS AND THE *Colored American Magazine (CAM)*

Analytical Guide and Indexes to the Colored American Magazine, *1900–1909.* 2 vols. Westport, Conn.: Greenwood, 1974.

Benson, Brian Joseph. "Colored American." In *Black Journals of the United States.* Ed. Walter C. Daniel. Westport, Conn.: Greenwood, 1982. 123–30.

"Biographies of the New Officers of Our Magazine." *CAM,* May/June 1903, 443–49.

Bond, Horace M. "Negro Leadership since Washington." *South Atlantic Quarterly,* Apr. 1925, 115–30.

Braithwaite, William Stanley. "Negro America's First Magazine." *Negro Digest* 6.2 (1947): 21–26.

Bullock, Penelope L. *The Afro-American Periodical Press, 1838–1909.*

Baton Rouge: Louisiana State University Press, 1981. Esp. 107–10.

Condict, Cornelia A. Letter to the Editor. *CAM,* Mar. 1903, 398–99.

Du Bois, W. E. B. "The Colored Magazine in America." *Crisis,* Nov. 1912, 33–35.

Elliot, R. S. "The Story of Our Magazine." *CAM,* May 1901, 43–77.

"In the Editor's Sanctum." *CAM,* May 1904, 382–83.

Johnson, Abby Arthur, and Ronald Maberry Johnson. "Away from Accommodation: Radical Editors and Protest Journalism, 1900–1910." *Journal of Negro History* 62 (1977): 325–38.

———. *Propaganda and Aesthetics: The Literary Politics of Afro-American Magazines in the Twentieth Century.* Amherst: University of Massachusetts Press, 1979. Esp. 4–14 (on *CAM*) and 65–68 (on the *New Era Magazine*).

Johnson, Charles S. "The Rise of the Negro Magazine." *Journal of Negro History* 13 (1928): 7–21.

Meier, August. "Booker T. Washington and the Negro Press, with Special Reference to the *Colored American Magazine.*" *Journal of Negro History* 38 (1953): 67–90.

Thornbrough, Emma L. "More Light on Booker T. Washington and the New York Age." *Journal of Negro History* 43 (1958): 34–49.

REVIEWS OF *Contending Forces*

Choice, Jan. 1979, 1518.

Colored American Magazine, Sept. 1900, 1.

Overton, Betty J. "At Best Lukewarm." *Callaloo* 2.7 (1979): 119–20.

Rosenblum, Joseph. Review of *Contending Forces,* by Pauline Hopkins. *Reprint Bulletin Book Reviews* 24.1 (1979): 35.

Setnick, Susan E. Review of *Contending Forces,* by Pauline Hopkins. *Kliatt* 14 (1980): 7.

BIBLIOGRAPHIES

Werner, Craig. "Pauline E. Hopkins." In *Black American Women Novelists: An Annotated Bibliography.* Pasadena, Calif.: Salem, 1989. 110–14.

Yellin, Jean Fagan, and Cynthia D. Bond. "Pauline Hopkins." In *The Pen Is Ours: A Listing of Writings by and about African-American Women before 1910.* New York: Oxford University Press, 1991. 104–10.

NOTES

I would like to express my appreciation to BethAnn Arundell, my research assistant, and to my fellow Hopkins scholars who generously contributed their own Hopkins bibliographies: Lois Brown, Carole Doreski, and especially John Gruesser. This work was supported, in part, by a research grant from the University of North Carolina–Charlotte.

1. In 1969, Negro Universities Press issued a reprint of the *Colored American Magazine;* thus, all of Hopkins's work originally published in *CAM* is available in the reprint. This listing of Hopkins's periodical publications does not include the many articles she wrote for *CAM* without a byline, nor the many unsigned articles and editorials that appeared in the two issues of the *New Era Magazine* (Feb. and March 1916), most of which, if not all, Hopkins wrote.

CONTRIBUTORS

ELIZABETH AMMONS, Harriet H. Fay Professor of English and dean of humanities and arts at Tufts University, is the author of *Edith Wharton's Argument with America* (1980) and *Conflicting Stories: American Women Writers at the Turn into the Twentieth Century* (1991). She is the editor of several books, including *Short Fiction by Black Woman, 1900–1920* (1991) and, with Annette White-Parks, *Tricksterism in Turn-of-the-Century American Literature* (1994).

KRISTINA BROOKS teaches English and women's studies at Agnes Scott College in Decatur, Georgia. In 1995 she completed a doctoral dissertation entitled "Transgressing the Boundaries of Identity: Racial Pornography, Fallen Women, and Ethnic Others in the Works of Pauline Hopkins, Alice Dunbar-Nelson, and Edith Wharton" at the University of California–Berkeley.

LOIS LAMPHERE BROWN is an assistant professor of English at Cornell University. In 1993 she completed a doctoral dissertation entitled "Essential Histories/Determined Identities: Images of Race and Origin in the Works of Pauline Hopkins" at Boston College. She is working on a critical biography of Pauline Hopkins entitled *Black Daughter of the Revolution*.

C. K. DORESKI is an assistant professor of rhetoric and humanities at Boston University. Her publications include *Elizabeth Bishop: The Restraints of Language* (1993) and essays on Gwendolyn Brooks, Sam Cornish, and the 1919 Chicago race riot. She is at work on a book concerning the African American periodical press and its literary impact, entitled *Writing America Black: Race, Rhetoric, and the Public Sphere,* which will include a chapter on Hopkins's tenure at the *Colored American Magazine.*

JOHN CULLEN GRUESSER is an assistant professor of English at Kean College of New Jersey and the author of *White on Black: Contempo-*

rary Literature about Africa (1992). He is working on a companion volume concerning twentieth-century African American literature about Africa, entitled *Black on Black*.

JENNIE A. KASSANOFF is an assistant professor of English at Barnard College. She is at work on a book concerning the modernism of Edith Wharton and is editing a collection of documents on nineteenth-century American women.

KATE MCCULLOUGH is an assistant professor of English and women's studies at Miami University, Ohio. She is working on a book concerning turn-of-the-century American women's fiction, genre construction, and the politics of literary history, tentatively entitled *Fictions of Identity: Constructing Gender, Genre, and the Nation in American Fiction, 1885–1914*.

NELLIE Y. MCKAY is a professor in both the Afro-American studies and English departments at the University of Wisconsin–Madison. Her many publications include *Jean Toomer, Artist* (1984) and *Critical Essays on Toni Morrison* (1988). She is at work editing the *Norton Anthology of African American Literature* and a new collection of essays on Toni Morrison.

CYNTHIA D. SCHRAGER, who teaches American literature at the University of California–Santa Cruz, completed a doctoral dissertation entitled "Both Sides of the Veil: Psychology, the Occult, and American Realism" at the University of California–Berkeley in 1995. Her essays have been published in *Feminist Studies* and *Women's Review of Books*.

MALIN LAVON WALTHER is an assistant professor of English at the University of North Carolina–Charlotte. The author of essays on Alice Walker, Toni Morrison, and Gwendolyn Brooks, Walther is working on a book concerning female aesthetics that will include a discussion of Hopkins's *Contending Forces*.

INDEX